THE INTIMACY PARADOX

THE GUILFORD FAMILY THERAPY SERIES
Alan S. Gurman, *Editor*

THE INTIMACY PARADOX

Personal Authority in the Family System

DONALD S. WILLIAMSON

Foreword by Carl A. Whitaker

THE GUILFORD PRESS
New York   London

© 1991 The Guilford Press
A Division of Guilford Publications, Inc.
72 Spring Street, New York, NY 10012

Printed in the United States of America

This book is printed on acid-free paper.

Last digit is print number   9 8 7 6 5 4 3 2

Library of Congress Cataloging-in-Publication Data

Williamson, Donald S.
  The intimacy paradox: personal authority in the family system /
Donald S. Williamson
    p.   cm. — (The Guilford family therapy series)
    Includes bibliographical references and index.
    ISBN 0-89862-106-2
    1. Family psychotherapy.   2. Authority—Psychological aspects.
  3. Intimacy (Psychology) I. Title.   II. Series
    [DNLM: 1. Family—psychology.   2. Family therapy—methods.
  3. Parent–Child Relations.   WM 430.5.F2 W729i]
  RC488.5.W575   1991
  616.89′ 156—dc20
  DNLM/DLC
  for Library of Congress   91-34484
                                                                  CIP

To Stella, a fountain of spontaneous love

To Stephen, an example of extraordinary courage

To Tracy, a pearl, a pearl of a girl

Acknowledgments

The first draft of this book was conceived in a fisherman's cottage at water's edge near the village of Crail, East Neuk, Kingdom of Fife, Scotland. What more can I say, except to thank Captain Humphrey Drummond, whose generosity made this magical place available.

The first draft was typed there by my wife, Stella Rabaut, JD, working on a laptop computer and transcribing from a small hand-held dictaphone. This worked well as long as I made lots of cups of tea and otherwise stayed out of sight. To call it a labor of love would scarcely do it justice.

Beyond the typing of the early draft, all the other considerable hard work has been performed by my secretary, Ms. Carol Clemens. Her speed, accuracy, and efficiency have been exceeded only by her patience, which has been tested to the utmost. Without her extraordinary abilities, this book would simply not have materialized, and I am most grateful.

I thank Carl A. Whitaker, MD, in general, for the liberating example of his professional life and, in particular, for the generosity of his foreword to this book. When Carl talks the listener becomes more engaged with his or her own possibilities than with the speaker. This is a rare gift.

I thank my colleague Linda M. Walsh, PhD, for contributing a very fine chapter on gender (Chapter 16) and my colleague James H. Bray, PhD, for his excellent chapter summarizing Personal Authority in the Family System related research (Chapter 18).

I would also like to thank Robert E. Rakel, MD, chairman, and the members of the faculty of the Department of Family Medicine at Baylor College of Medicine in Houston. This department strongly encourages and applauds any scholarly inquiry in a way that makes it easier to succeed and unthinkable to fail. It has been a particular pleasure to come upon a group of physicians who, without exception, express the highest level of personal caring for their patients and share a commitment to the loftiest standards of patient care. It has been both enlightening and stimulating to work among them.

I left Ireland in 1961 as an alternative to leaving home since I did not know how to, probably not even that I needed to. In subsequent years I made many trips back for family conversations, exploring the possibilities for leaving. These are life events that give one something to think about. The theory and method of family of origin work presented in this book grew out of these experiences.

So, finally, I would like to acknowledge William and Mary, my father and mother, and Norah, Eileen, and Willa, my three sisters. Each one responded with a consistently open mind and warm heart to what must have seemed like an insatiable series of interrogations and depositions. Having now traveled far enough to have a basis for comparison, my abiding impression of my family of origin is of its good heartedness.

DONALD S. WILLIAMSON

Foreword

When a dedicated clinician with a multifaceted teaching and research career shares his professional autobiography it's like a National Geographic Special. The Irish lilt and the American career make the tender therapist and the research clinician visible in every chapter.

The evolution of psychotherapy proceeded from research analysis of the individual to psychotherapy of the individual. Now research on the family has led to psychotherapy of the family as a unit. Donald Williamson has evolved a system for advancing the individual's request for help to an outcome of reconciliation with the family of origin. Furthermore, the client learns to expand the authority for his or her own life. The therapist opens with a few interviews to help the individual focus on an interest in change. Then, using a small group of peers as model foster parents, each group member expands the readiness to struggle with the remnants of past pain. This foster parent group becomes an exciting practical experience. Each client learns to play with these substitute parents in a deliberate rehearsal for the big family event he or she will have with his or her own parents.

This method has many advantages. It expands the courage to develop individual rights and also renegotiates a sense of belonging to the family of origin. In the play experience of learning adult to ex-parent peership the client is also becoming adept in living in the outside world. The role of therapist is quite modified from the usually massive transference project or from the family therapist who utilizes his or her own power to change the family as a unit. The peer group members share their growing-up pain and experiences. They even coach each other. The supervision by the therapist is almost casual. The client, meantime, is rehearsing the past and re-entering the family by imaginary conversations and real visits home. The result is further understanding and expanded competence to deal with the major confrontation each is organizing for the denouement with his or her own family. This experience is peership training and helps the client learn the use of playful and paradoxical language. It's as though each client was training to be a therapist. Each person evolves a kind of benevolent triangulation pattern for the final family therapy experience. He or she even becomes the person in charge of the family therapy agenda. The therapist is merely a monitor and protector of the parents' anxiety during this precipitous growth spurt in the family dynamics. Those final 6 hours that the client has structured so carefully for reasserting his or her status as an adult in the family scene are couched in mediation style, thereby evolving an added independence and much resolution of the three-way life scene when the client was a child.

Don Williamson describes many adaptations if one of the parents is dead or when there are other modifications in the family structure. Threading through all this careful description of a therapeutic methodology is the wisdom of an experienced therapist and a dedicated teacher. When a native of Northern Ireland elects to integrate with our melting pot and joins the psychotherapy of our culture with the maturing of his own family wisdom, he unites the intimacy of Ireland with the process of adaptation to the United States. Our psychotherapy has been increasingly polarized between individual therapy and family therapy. Many therapists in practice use a mixture that often weakens the usefulness of either. This therapist has evolved a solid and carefully structured process that begins where the client presents him- or herself as a person in pain and haunted by impotence. Using the small group and a deliberate conscious plan for family reactivation, he builds to a client-centered family interview that results in the client becoming a person of authority in his or her family of origin and thereby is self-activated to live his or her own personhood in full open interaction with the family of origin. The individual has structured an emerging love for his or her own future. What a place to be!

Don Williamson has spent an unusual amount of effort in recording references for all of his conceptional thinking and an extensive presentation of research work done with a small group over many years. He records many fascinating components of client response to his methodology and an extensive evaluation of the method (testing for both differentiation from and integration with the family). The report pictures a slowly developing, carefully studied methodology by a real professional student and practitioner of both family psychotherapy and individual psychotherapy. I read every page with relish and resonance. I commend them to you.

CARL A. WHITAKER

Contents

II. PERSONAL AUTHORITY METHOD: THE PLAY'S
    THE THING

PART ONE

Personal Authority Theory

CHAPTER 1

Personal Authority in the Family System: An Overview

> My goal is the expression of the essential in an increasingly
> simple way.
>
> — Paul-Élime Borduas,
> French-Canadian painter (1905–1960)

The Intimacy Paradox

Following the good example of painter Paul-Élime Borduas, quoted above, it is my goal to state the essential in an increasingly simple way. Such an attempt is made in this book as it addresses the core question posed. That question in its simplest form is, *How does one leave home emotionally and yet somehow still remain lovingly connected within the family of origin?* It is my thesis that this is both the fundamental psychological issue and the essential relational challenge of adulthood.

Any love relationship worthy of the name will compromise the freedom and spontaneity of the self of each party involved. Some relationships will obviously do this much more than others. And the character of a given relationship will change over time. Yet to some degree this threat to self is an issue for all emotionally significant relationships. Nonetheless, most people prefer the life shared to the life lived alone. We want to be emotionally free and self-determined, but simultaneously we want to share our ideas and feelings, beliefs and values, hopes and fears, monies and homes, with significant others in intimate relationships. So there is an inherent contradiction here and often conflict. This then is *the intimacy paradox*.

It is the argument of this book that how one finally resolves this issue of relationship to the members of the family of origin, especially father and mother, will largely determine how one handles this matter in all intimate relationships to follow in life, most especially in marriage. So the resolution of the question posed by the intimacy paradox will be considered here in the context of the intergenerational relationships within the family of origin.

The personal challenge for each individual, whether this challenge is to be met with or without professional help, is to discover how to "remember a different future." Remembering a different future means that one learns how to reconstruct the story of the personal past in the present moment, so that new possibilities for healthier future behaviors show up now in the mind. Although not acquired simply, these reconstructed memories are themselves simply different perspectives on the past. As a consequence, the opportunity to choose a different future is now immediately at hand.

The bad news about the personal past for many people is that it was like it was. The good news is that how it was is a constantly evolving story, with no one other than oneself writing the upcoming scenes. I do not, of course, by any means choose or control all the facts or circumstances of my life. But I am the author of all *meanings* to me of my experiences. It is out of these meanings that I construct my reality. It is in this sense, then, that personal history can be rewritten. Not so incidentally, since I make up the story in the first place anyway, why not make it up in a way most conducive to personal well-being?

For the adult (in his or her 30s or 40s) the leverage to make up the past differently comes initially from the novel experience of making up the parents in a different way. Re-mythologizing rather than pathologizing parents opens up new vistas and freedoms for one's personal future. For this reason, re-mythologizing parents (which implies resolving intergenerational intimidation and coming to relate to them as peers) represents at the very least an enlightened self-interest.

Achieving *personal authority in the family system* is jargon for acquiring the goodwill and energy necessary to imaginatively rewrite one's personal narrative in life. This book explores this possibility for resolving the intimacy paradox at length, acknowledging at the outset that personal authority, like any other awareness of self, is itself a moving target. The therapeutic and methodological question is, of course, How does one get from here to there?

The Question

The question addressed in this book, then, is this: How does the adult leave the parental home psychologically in a very complete sense and still belong emotionally with the family of origin? Is it possible at all? Or is there an inherent and irresolvable logical and psychological conflict between these two goals? Must one settle either for one or the other in order not to be torn apart by the contradiction? This foundational question will be posed repeatedly and variously from different perspectives until the underlying dilemma becomes crystal clear.

The Dilemma

The underlying dilemma is this: How does one embrace and cherish family heritage and simultaneously transcend family emotionality? How does one create a unique self in a new generation and simultaneously belong with the old? How does one decide to make no further mortgage payments to the past and simultaneously continue to show gratitude for what has been given? How does one enjoy a strong sense of identification with one's own flesh and blood and simultaneously acquire a clear and unencumbered title to one's own life and destiny? How does one differentiate a self out of the morass of the "undifferentiated family ego mass" (Bowen, 1966) and then subsequently reconnect voluntarily with love and intimacy with the members of one's own family?

How does one embrace and assimilate a family's corporate identity and values and at the same time not be driven by covert intergenerational loyalties and mandates (Boszormenyi-Nagy & Spark, 1973)? How does one validate a parental love relationship that is the very source of one's existence and simultaneously not be triangulated into the ongoing drama of the parental marriage? How does one develop a sense of personal celebration in life and simultaneously feel empathic with aging parents, increasingly constricted in their lives owing to lessening strength, failing health, and, often, diminishing hope? How does one manage the omnipresent issue of relational justice (Boszormenyi-Nagy & Krasner, 1986) so that one does right by each parent and simultaneously gives a higher priority to one's spouse? How, ultimately, does one do right by oneself with regard to everyone else? How does one sustain compassion for the most poignant losses in the history of the family and simultaneously cleanse oneself of any residual guilt or feelings of remorse with regard to those losses, both the mourned and the unmourned (Paul, 1967)? There can be not only addiction in the family but addiction *to* the family. Psychotherapy itself in this addictive society can become a "psychological fix." How then does one, in full acknowledgment of the conflicted patterns of family history, still link arms with parents and other family members and go "dancing in the streets"?

It has been suggested that families are in some ways cults or have similarities with cults. For example, in some families compliance may be required, there may be great dependence on the leader(s), dissent may not be tolerated, and there is a tendency to devalue the outsider (Deikman, 1989). Because we begin in total dependency, we always long for powerful parents to protect us. This is a yearning that persists throughout life. Security is that warm feeling that comes from being able to sleep peacefully in the back seat of the car, knowing that Mommy and Daddy are in charge of everything up in front and that one need not worry. This is a difficult feeling to give up, and the longing to recreate it never fully disappears. Gradually giving up the parent as parent means assuming more and more responsibility for oneself in the world.

This developmental task, which is much more than simply the differentiation of self, captures the dogged dilemmas of the adult emotional life. Neither is it just a question about intergenerational intimacy; it is rather, simultaneously a question about both differentiation and intimacy. How does one achieve a healthy balance between these two poles, without undue violation of either one? How does one reconcile the demands of both the inner and the outer self, both the private and the social self? It is suggested here that this is the primary psychosocial challenge of both individual and family life. This is the intimacy paradox.

Differentiation of Self

The notion of the differentiation of self within the emotionality of the family system has perhaps been the single most useful response to the question to date (Anonymous, 1972). It is demonstrably an essential developmental step in life, and a compelling argument can be made that it is a *sine qua non* of individual well-being. Nevertheless, it is the argument of this book that while differentiation of self is a critical step, it is not a satisfactory *end point* in the pursuit of human well-being and personal happiness. For if differentiation of self is held and pursued as an independent and commanding goal in and of itself, then undoubtedly a few people will end up alienated from family. Many people will end up enjoying greater personal freedom but feeling distant from family. Some will be much less emotionally burdened but lonely and unsure of whom they belong with. Regrettably, many will miss the opportunity to develop relationships of intimacy with one's own flesh and blood.

Personal Authority in the Family System Introduced

Personal Authority in the Family System (PAFS) is therefore offered as a synthesizing construct, connecting differentiation and intimacy (Williamson, 1982a). It allows for both the differentiation of self and, simultaneously or subsequently, the conscious development of intimate connections with members of the family of origin, in particular with each of the parents. These relational connections are experienced as voluntary, which is to say, chosen. However, in order to experience this voluntariness, it is usually first necessary for the adult to create a significant (r)evolution in family politics (Williamson, 1983). The essence of this revolution is the renegotiation and termination of the hierarchical power boundary between the parent and the child. Psychological power and control are redistributed across the generational boundary in the direction of psychosocial equality and relational peerhood. Son or daughter gives up, once and for all, the need to be parented. Simultaneously, the parents are accepted and embraced as A-OK Perfect As-Is. The parents are taken "off the hook" as parents. Their work is finished. It is complete. This is a very powerful message with far-reaching implications for both generations. It is a step not taken lightly or unadvisedly. It cannot be done unilaterally. Yet the initiative is always with son or daughter.

Grown sons and daughters give up the parent as one who protects and provides for, guides and nurtures, and carries ultimate responsibility for their general well-being. If the parent is still held as "parent" psychologically, then son or daughter will remain and behave as a "child," living within the emotional and relational dynamics of the intergenerational patterns of interaction. By giving up the parent as parent, and thereby establishing psychological peerhood, son or daughter gains emotional freedom, relational poise, and the language and behavioral skills necessary in order not to be often swept away by the tireless waves of family emotionality.

This addresses the underlying issue in family of origin therapy, indeed, in psychotherapy in general. How does one achieve and sustain the experience of personal freedom of thought and action in life, no longer controlled or even unduly influenced by the persuasive power of the memories of personal history or of current family dynamics? It will be argued here that achieving this break with family emotionality requires an emotional break with the parents "as parents." There is a kind of emotional, if not legal termination of parental rights. Legal termination occurs when the standard of parenting is gravely unacceptable. Psychological termination occurs when the work is complete, when parenting is no longer needed or age-appropriate (or available). This is a frightening prospect for most people and a discomfiting possibility for many parents. The upset cuts both ways, although the younger generation has the considerable advantage of being more in control of the timing, and when in therapy is working with focused guidance and emotional support. Clearly there is a need for sensitivity to the well-being of aging parents also.

Intergenerational Intimidation

The threat for many parents is emotional abandonment, with the resulting loss of role and an important part of the self, namely, self-as-parent, as well as the loss of a potential return on a major life investment. Second, there is the fear of a failing grade in the performance as parent. The most difficult problem for son or daughter is *intergenerational intimidation*. Intergenerational intimidation in its myriad forms is unquestionably the major obstacle in the way of the renegotiation of family politics and the establishment of personal authority in the family and therefore in life.

The dynamic at the heart of intergenerational intimidation is the primitive fear either of personal death or the death of a parent. At an unconscious level it is feared that calling into question the established social and political order, including the uses of power within family politics, may have very bad effects. This could mean the death of one or more of the involved parties, through suicide or homicide.

(These primitive fears and their management will be addressed at length in Chapter 7.)

I once asked Ivan Boszormenyi-Nagy if he had ever felt intimidated by his parents. He responded by chatting about his father. He said he had not felt intimidated by his father, whom he had experienced as "a very good man." He said they had often had long walks together and very enjoyable conversations. He repeated that he had a good relationship with his father. The follow-up question was whether he might have been intimidated by his father's goodness. He allowed that he would need some time to think about that. There are a myriad of ways a son or daughter can feel intimidated, including feeling intimidated by the genuine goodness of a parent.

It should be further noted that even after some successful work has been completed, whether in structured therapy or through maturation, the newly differentiated self still has to decide how relationships should continue to evolve with the members of the family of origin. And the differentiated self still has to make value decisions in life with this newly differentiated self. The suggestion presented here, is that the most fulfilling and satisfying possibility is to go on to relationships of intimacy and love with other human beings. But of necessity this begins with and is modeled on the new relationships evolving in adulthood with the members of one's own family. What follows in this book is the development of a theory and a description of a therapeutic method related to it whereby one can, once and for all, leave the parental home emotionally and subsequently reconnect with intimacy, love, and a strong sense of identification within the family of origin. (There are, of course, some qualifications and exceptions; these are noted at length in Chapter 12.)

Healthy Family Structure: A Matter of Timing

The political premise underlying this therapy, can be explained further by making a contrast and distinction between different developmental stages. In a family with small children it is essential that there be a clear and strong leadership structure in the family. It is essential that the parental relationship be the power relationship. A parent–child power coalition is a very destructive pattern. There must be a clear and firm hierarchical boundary between parents and children; otherwise there will be chaos in the family. The healthy political pattern in the family with young children is one in which the parental relationship is the source of authority and decision making, with a clear hierarchical boundary between the two generations. If this is not the case there will be a dysfunctional organization within the family (Haley, 1980; Minuchin, 1974). The corollary is just as true! That is, once a man or woman has achieved chronological adulthood—defined here as being "30-something"—this hierarchical boundary and power differential need to be renegotiated and respectively and respectfully terminated and rebalanced. If this is not the case, there will again be a dysfunctional organization within the family, with destructive consequences. Laing (1979) once commented to the effect that "a man will see every woman as his mother until he sees his mother as a woman." (Obviously, the same could be said about women and their fathers.)

This is why clients engaged in personal authority work are often encouraged to address parents by their given names. First of all, it is a clear message about the clients' political intentions. There are few parents who cannot decode the message. But there is a second and more important reason, and this is what often makes it an effective intervention. It is simply that things become more real when given a name. The central goal of personal authority work is to discover the "otherness" of the parent. Directly *naming* the parent is an important step on the way to dissolving the multiple layers of meaning associated with the words *Mom* and *Dad*. Parents sometimes respond with mild shock, sensing that they may be losing something of their special position; they are right! A few parents will be offended by this "disrespectful" attitude. While this response is a reconfirmation of the power of the underlying political issues, it also identifies a situation where the client should behave with considerable tact and flexibility. There is nothing good to be gained from alienating or wounding a parent. For just as there is no satisfactory unilateral divorce, so the act of giving up the child role interacts with and is reciprocal to the act of giving up the parent role.

A highly functional family with adult sons and daughters is one in which there are "former parents" and "former children," that is, family members who have established a relationship of psychological equality. As a result of this, they have psychological freedom of action and interaction between them. The "former parent" no longer has any special position of power or control or privilege, as was previously inherent in the role of parent. Neither has this "former parent" any continuing obligation to parent in the traditional sense. He or she is now freed, once and for all, from parenting responsibilities or burdens. Whatever else is given, is freely given out of affection, not obligation. The "former child" no longer has any *obligation* to attentiveness, obedience, or loyalty, behaviors previously inherent in the role of child. While there may be a deep love in the evolving relationship, son or daughter will experience his or her behavior as voluntary and therefore as more spontaneous. The therapeutic question is, How do the players get from here to there?

Humanization of the Parent

Personal authority is achieved by a kind of surgical reconstruction of family structure, resulting in a new dynamic pattern in family politics. Through hearing the personal narrative of the life of each parent firsthand and the private meanings of the various events and sequences of the life process of each, son or daughter demystifies and humanizes the parent. Despite all those fears this is only another human being who is there after all, just a bit older. It is this humanization that ultimately resolves intergenerational intimidation. Son or daughter is then free to terminate the intergenerational hierarchical power boundary and assume sovereignty over the self.

The de-mythologizing of each parent through hearing the personal stories leads first to a humanizing and then later to the "re-mythologizing" of the person of each parent (see Chapter 10, Act Three, Scene III). But the second time around this is done in a playful or "as if" way. This is the heart of the therapeutic work.

The result is a new sense of freedom for *both* generations. When son or daughter gives up the need to be parented, there is no further demand or expectation that the aging parent be or become something different or more than he or she is, or be anything or do anything to make up for what was or was not in the past. The parent is now accepted as A-OK Perfect As-Is. This brings enormous relief to older parents. The declaration is not, of course, an objective statement about the quality of previous parenting over the years. It is, rather, a subjective and compassionate statement about the *relational stance* now being assumed by the second generation. Nothing more is needed from the parent as parent. In the act of accepting the parent "as is," son or daughter is accepting in a new way the parent within the self, with a resulting diminishing of harsh self-criticism. It is therefore a healing of the self. Forgiving a parent therefore expresses an enlightened self-interest. It is also a model for the next generation. This healing dynamic spirals across and around the generations in fine circular fashion.

The Focus Is on the Primary Triangle

Personal authority work focuses most particularly upon the intergenerational experiences of the individual adult and the parents, previously labeled the "primary triangle" (Williamson, 1982b). This is not to ignore the fact that many people know their grandparents. For some people the relationships with grandparents are of considerable emotional importance, and the meanings of these relationships are always taken into account. The client will be encouraged to talk to grandparents and to debrief them with regard to the important stories of transgenerational family experience in general and the lives of the parents in particular. But except for those few instances where a grandparent has functioned psychologically as parent, the relationship with the grandparent does not especially intrude into the work with the primary triangle. Likewise, siblings are not included in the therapy, although they are frequently important sources of information and alternative perceptions and judgments about family dynamics and the role of the client in the family of origin. Sometimes siblings are a source of encouragement and support to the client in the work.

Occasionally, they represent an obstacle or threat. Frequently, they are simply neutral. How this all unfolds in a given family will be taken into account at the appropriate time in the course of the therapy.

Uncles and aunts can also be useful reference points and sources of validation (or otherwise) for the veracity and credibility of family stories, especially those relevant to the lives of the client's parents. But again, unless one of these persons has actually functioned psychologically as parent, in substitute or support for a biological parent, they usually will not be included in the work with the primary triangle. The same holds true for older personal friends, neighbors, and work colleagues of either parent, although these persons can be repositories of rich information because of their favored position in the life of a parent. A trusted older parental friend may have both factual information and valuable contextual interpretations of that information. This material may be sensitive and normally "classified," as far as blood family members are concerned, yet it may be highly explanatory of the mind and behavior of the parent. Again, such persons are to be sought out and recruited into the service of the client's work. Nonetheless, the work is sharply focused throughout upon the dynamic patterns within the intergenerational relationship, that is, the primary triangle.

There are two reasons for this steadfastness of purpose. The first is that, with rare exceptions, the client's significant power, control, and intimacy issues take place within the dynamics between the self and the parents. Since this is where the story was first written, this is where the script is to be changed. It is acknowledged that at multiple levels of consciousness, an adult life may express loyalties, mandates, burdens, and guilts transmitted from persons in the preceding generations. Nevertheless, whatever has been transmitted that is of continuing psychological significance in the life of the client is most likely to have been transmitted through the biology as well as the teaching and the modeling of the parents. There is no compelling evidence that actively pursuing information about multiple previous generations will *significantly* further reduce anxiety. It is therefore assumed that the most effective context for renegotiation and resolution is within the emotionality of the relationships between the self and the parents.

The Therapeutic Style in Personal Authority Work

In a nutshell, personal authority therapy prepares people to talk directly to their parents about everything that is important and to do so as adults and without fear. In psychoanalysis, as in psychoanalytically oriented psychotherapy, the therapist may move from information provided through free associations directly to emotionalized attitudes toward the parents. While this may facilitate insight, it is less likely to effect therapeutic change. The work will be more effective if the initial focus is on the client's relationship with the therapist and only subsequently on the parents (May, 1958; Menninger, 1938). The emotional power of the transference process provides the leverage for changing the underlying emotionality in which the parental introjects are embedded.

What will be described in personal authority work is, of course, very different from this. The client is encouraged to go directly and repeatedly, initially in his or her mind only, to the persons of the parents as they are perceived today and to the deeper feelings that characterize these relationships. A conscious effort is made by the consultant to minimize and certainly not to elicit the occurrence of transference phenomena in family of origin consultation. The client is explicitly encouraged to locate and relocate the original source of feelings, as well as to find nurturance and meet personal needs, within the family. The consultant is present as a real self.

The important feature in this method is that the client is being prepared to renegotiate *directly with the parents.* In this way both the ongoing relationships with the actual parents, who get a face-to-face opportunity to declare and reveal their own current psychological and social reality, and the inner relationships with the parental introjects change more or less simultaneously as they interact with each other. Change in the latter are initially triggered by change in the former. Then change in either one subsequently elicits change in the other in recursive fashion. In time, the old introjects and new perceptions of present-day parents fuse into one "real" current picture. This de-emphasis on the consultant as an important object proves effective, since the foremost therapeutic goal is not insight or understanding. It is, rather, the development of strategies and methods for renegotiation and change within contemporary family politics.

Relief comes to a client consumed by grief or anger at perceived neglects or abusive intrusions into his or her life throughout personal history by developing and practicing a different language to use to construct or reconstruct this personal reality. This leads to new sequences of intergenerational behaviors for use with the parents today. As a result, the client will soon have a much greater subjective sense of control over his or her own life and destiny. Simply learning to be nonreactive will reduce conflict, but it will also reduce both intimacy and romance. Perhaps it is a matter of "no guts, no glory."

As will be described in detail later (see Chapter 4), therapeutic practice in personal authority work is fused with humor and with the acknowledgment of the boundless natural absurdity in human experience, especially in intimacy. It builds upon that foundational human dilemma and natural paradox whereby human beings look at others who are very important to them and say, "I hate you because of the power you have over me, because I love (and need) you so much." Sometimes we take a further step and add the following:

"So then let us hurry up and get married and see if we can use the marriage to get strong enough not to need to hang around with the kind of person each of us is. Since neither of us can leave home just yet, let's get married and then see if we can heal each other, by leaving each other as practice for leaving home."

As a corollary to this, clients often offer the following comment about parents: "Until they change, I've got to stay the same. Show me how to change them so that I can be different." This plea is sometimes made with regard to a deceased parent, a therapeutic situation that is even trickier. There are many marvelous possibilities for playfulness when the natural paradoxes in intimacy show up, however disowned or disguised they may be (Laing, 1970; Selvini-Palazzoli, Boscolo, Cecchin, & Prata, 1978).

Transgenerational Family Therapy: Some Distinctions in the Interest of Differentiation

The point of view being presented may stand out in sharper relief if defined by virtue of certain distinctions with transgenerational family therapy in general. The latter has fallen somewhat out of favor in recent years, and for understandable reasons. Transgenerational family therapy methods and psychoanalysis share a similar problem. Many people who might benefit from family of origin consultation are reluctant to invest what may seem like endless time, energy, and money in seeking this redress. There is also often a problem with sustaining motivation. At times it seems as though only family therapists can (or should) develop this kind of detailed fascination with ourselves and our families. There is also a cost–benefit problem involving the law of diminishing returns. The point of view espoused here is that the greatest gains are likely to be realized through work directly focused on the primary triangle. Except where there is an unusually complicated story, proportionately less will be gained therapeutically from increasing time spent working with multiple prior generations.

Like psychoanalysis, transgenerational therapy can inadvertently give the impression that it is a process that never ends. It may be fair to say that this is in part because transgenerational family theory is somewhat pessimistic about significant change being possible in any circumstances. It certainly is hesitant about lasting change coming in a relatively short time (Boszormenyi-Nagy & Ulrich, 1981; Bowen, 1978). In perhaps the most seminal theoretical work of all, it is suggested that one must work a lifetime to make even a very small gain in the amount of "real self" achieved, as opposed to "functional" or "pseudo self" (Kerr & Bowen, 1988). "Basic level [of differentiation] is fairly well established by the time a child reaches adolescence and usually remains fixed for life, although unusual life experiences or a structured effort to increase basic level at a point later in life can lead to some change in it" (Kerr & Bowen, 1988, p. 98). Given what we know about the power of suggestion, this use of language is a mistaken way to construct a therapeutic reality and will not create positive expectations.

Ultimately, we are "making it all up" anyway, certainly as far as personal psychological "reality" or "truth" is concerned. So why not make it up as cheerfully as possible and in ways most likely to encourage positive expectations and therefore positive outcomes? It is true that Bowen made a valiant effort to construct and present a "scientific" theory of the family as an emotional system. According to Kerr and Bowen (1988), "an effort was made to couch new theory in biological terms, to make it easier for research minded people in the future" (p. 345). However, despite borrowing concepts from biology, the theory remains metaphorical and poetic, although it does contain a number of important propositions that are probably accessible to empirical inquiry. Furthermore, there is great power in poetry.

Achieving Peerhood

A perusal of the literature suggests that the ambience of transgenerational family theory and therapy tends to be emotionally heavy, even depressing, as well as slow-moving. This is understandable given the negative emotion-laden character of the transgenerational family matters to which this theory and method attend. However, I propose that an additional reason for the mood of general pessimism about outcomes is the fact that transgenerational family therapy has been reluctant to deal with intergenerational power politics, head-on and at the source. That source is within the primary triangle and at the point of the power position inherent in the role of parent. If this is indeed the case, then one might explain the reluctance to deal with this core political issue itself as due to the omnipresent influence of intergenerational emotional and therefore political intimidation. It is this specific focus on *the equalization of power between the generations* that constitutes the novelty of the point of view described in this book.

Achieving Peerhood with Intimacy

Another characteristic of the method described here is one that makes such a radical political step possible. This is the advocacy of a continuing commitment to, identification with, and intimacy within the family of origin. By contrast with the style displayed in the landmark anonymous article (see Framo, 1972), in this therapeutic style the parents are never fully objectified or fully excluded from an insider role in the therapeutic plan. Although many sorts of playful strategies and interventions are crafted, as will be illustrated later, the parent is consistently invited to come "on the inside" of these various moves. This usually happens just as soon as he or she gets the point and is willing to respond in a non- or at least less hierarchical fashion.

It is a deliberate intention that the various exercises to be described should take place in frank conversations directly with the parents rather than be, so to speak, "done to them." An ambience of playfulness, reciprocity and compassion is fostered. Playfulness is an antidote to anxiety. It also softens and mediates the impact of the political moves and of those other related strategic initiatives often necessary for redress. These might otherwise seem less than neighborly. Furthermore, the ultimate goal is not simply to achieve a differentiated self. It is rather to achieve a differentiated position but within the context of warm and intimate relationships with the members of the family of origin. If differentiation of self at the psychological level implies a reconnection with a colony as differentiation does at the biological level, Bowen theory does not speak of it. Personal authority is therefore defined as a synthesis between these two competing ideas of differentiation and intimacy.

Carl Whitaker told me the following poignant story (personal communication, October 1978). He was present on the speakers' platform during the famous 1967 conference between family therapists and family researchers. He heard Murray Bowen present his gripping personal story in the now-famous Anonymous presentation. As is noted in the book by Framo (1972), in the conversation that followed the presentation Whitaker said to Bowen, "I wish you were my brother!" Bowen replied, "Ackerman is." I asked Whitaker

whether he thought that Bowen's response indicated a strong identification with the psychoanalytic tradition. Whitaker replied that he
had not considered that possibility, adding, "I simply felt sorry for the
guy, isolated in his own family." This story points out the dilemma
facing all of us as human beings, not simply these two pioneers in the
family therapy movement. How does one differentiate a self and yet
stay connected to the family? This is the issue this book has been
written to address.

It should be noted in passing that some of the people who
worked closely with Bowen believe that his theory and method have
often been misunderstood, for example, if viewed as being "cold and
cerebral" (Gillis-Donovan, 1991). This reaction points up the fact that
different social contexts encourage not only different behaviors but
also alternative perceptions of behaviors, which is to say, different
constructions of reality. It does not necessarily follow that one point
of view is true and the other one false. There are rather different
perspectives (held as sincere beliefs), which have been influenced by
many different variables. Consequently, there can be different and
sometimes logically contradictory coexisting "realities" in the perception of the "same" events or persons. However, when it comes to
theoretical analysis, a theory is most appropriately understood and
evaluated on the basis of the way in which it has been committed to
writing by its author.

Valuing Both Reason and Emotion

Third, personal authority method does not place a higher value on
reason than emotion. Emotional reactivity and the problems it creates
are central and valuable concepts in Bowen theory. Bowen writes,
"Find the dividing line between feelings and intellect. Perhaps the
human can control his own evolution through controlling his own
emotions" (Kerr & Bowen, 1988, p. 386). However, both reason and
emotion are wired into the immune system, so both are necessary for
personal well-being. Therefore, the goal should not be to separate but
to distinguish the thinking process from the feeling process. If most
evil is generated at an emotional level, so also is most good. Clearly,
it is important for reason to control or influence emotion at critical
times. Ideally, behavior is informed and guided by a benevolent
emotionality, characterized by generosity, compassion, and good
will. The goal of personal authority, then, is for the client to transform
the emotionality of the intergenerational relationships so that such a
benevolent intent is in control of the behavior of family members
most of the time. The ultimate goal is to transform the emotionality of

the relational system. This will require some imaginative strategic *thinking* by the client. In that sense, every successful client is an intellectual, defined as "one who leads with his or her head." This allows for second thoughts and the fantasy of alternative choices.

Eisler (1987) argues that the basic struggle in human organization is between a dominance structure and partnership. She suggests that while a dominator socialization describes male identity, patriarchy and matriarchy in family structure are opposite sides of the same dominance coin. Since the general goal of social connection should be partnership and not dominance, the goal of psychotherapy should be growth (or transformation) and not adaptation. At the heart of this is a spontaneous and versatile interaction between thought and feeling.

The Theory of Therapy

I do not subscribe to the notion that if you get the theory right, the therapy will somehow naturally follow (Kerr & Bowen, 1988). The available evidence suggests, rather, that there is no necessary or predictable connection between the psychotherapist's theory and his or her actual clinical behavior. It is therefore useful to develop an explicit theory of a therapy method in order to evolve and master these skills over time. An earlier book of family therapy essays included chapters by the same two influential family therapists mentioned above, one arguing for the use of theory in clinical practice (Bowen, 1976) and the other arguing that theory is a hindrance in clinical practice (Whitaker, 1976). While an extreme position is at times essential in order to make an idea stand out in sharp relief, this matter may be an example of where attention to both sides of an issue is rather more useful than an either–or stance. It is probably true that a given theoretical construct crystallizes after, rather than before, the behavior it is used to explain or rationalize. Yet that understanding becomes the platform for another piece of spontaneous clinical behavior on the part of the therapist, again more likely to be understood later.

It would be most unusual to come upon a highly effective family therapist, who was not also frequently pensive about his or her work, or who was consistently confused about the theoretical underpinnings to his or her repertoire of clinical behaviors. At the same time, if one's therapeutic interventions are axiomatic and predetermined or restricted to exclusively rational inferences, then much will be lost. Such a doctrinaire approach is likely to retard the appreciation of key process information about the client that is transmitted at more relational and less rational levels of consciousness. Here again the dynamic is circular. Thus, it may not matter so much at what point one steps onto the carousel as long as the gate stays open and there are transition opportunities. It is the intention of this book to assume an open-ended stance toward the value of theory in therapy. The emphasis overall is on the therapeutic method, which flows from the core theoretical premise about personal authority and intergenerational intimidation. But whether or not the theoretical egg comes before the process chicken is another story.

The Role of Theory in Practice

The favorite point of view chosen by a psychotherapist for everyday reference is probably a matter of personal style and whim, regardless of the sophistication of the theoretical arguments used to justify it. There are disagreements about the importance of theory-guiding interventions versus spontaneity of clinical behavior. There are differences in attitude toward the use of the self, ranging from the self as the primary tool of intervention (Rogers, 1951) all the way to the self as an irrelevant variable, provided one is clear about one's intentions and methods (Haley, 1963). There are differences in the value and, therefore, emphasis placed on insight or understanding versus a "corrective emotional experience." There are certainly differences of opinion about the relevance of information about personal and family history in family therapy treatment (Barker, 1981). Obviously, if the psychotherapist is going to be both useful and comfortable (and probably one needs to be comfortable in order to be useful), then the psychotherapeutic practices espoused must have some affinity with the way in which the psychotherapist makes up his or her own world and manages his or her own life. This calls for large doses of "both–and" and small doses of "either–or" in the making of theoretical judgments and the construction of comparative theoretical values. To hold a constantly evolving theory is one way to stay professionally alive, although it calls for sturdy sealegs.

It does not follow that everything and anything one can think of to do is therefore somehow equal to everything else that might happen in the world of psychotherapy. Some ideas probably are more true than others, if only in the sense that certain practices undoubtedly are more effective than others. However, who is there among us who can call the right shots all the time, and how could we identify (or tolerate) such a person? There are great variations in therapeutic style, even within family of origin family therapy. Bowen declined to see clients along with their parents on the grounds that this would undercut the differentiation process of the client. So he coached the client alone and sent him or her off on excursions to the parental home (Bowen, 1978). Boszormenyi-Nagy and Krasner (1980) have made an attitude of "multidirectional partiality" central, which means to take sides sequentially and provide support wherever redress is most called for. This is done with a view to achieving and maintaining fairness and balance throughout the family system over time, regardless of who is or is not present in the interview. This focus can be exercised with individuals, couples, or whole families.

By contrast with both of these, Framo (1981) much prefers to include not only the parents but also the siblings in his interviews and to do so right from the beginning, if possible. In this way, all the important emotional issues in the family can come to light spontaneously, with a view to clearing the air all around. Paul and Paul (1975) work extensively with individuals and couples as well as families and bring in family members selectively, both in person and through photographs, videotapes, and other artifacts. The emphasis is on an existential and emotional acknowledgment of any significant loss experience in the patient's life. Whitaker, who defies any kind of categorization, prefers to work with all three generations present in the room. He then plays on the keyboard of the family's collective unconscious (Neill & Kniskern, 1982). So there are lots of ways to skin a cat, and we have not even left the transgenerational segment of the field yet. To each his or her own! Find your models where you can and, in due course, create your own. That itself would be an exercise in personal authority.

A How-To Book

The point of view developed in this book builds upon the work of those noted earlier, from whom I have learned, with appreciation and admiration. Then it takes its own course. Although they disagreed about the uses of theory in therapy, neither Whitaker nor Bowen chose to develop a systematic theory of a therapeutic method, although they declined for different reasons. Whitaker distrusts theory in general, and Bowen distrust theorizing about therapy, while emphasizing the value of theorizing about theory. Bowen has written, "I proposed a method of therapy in which every move was determined by theory" (Kerr & Bowen, 1988, p. 371). In a similar vein he wrote, "A basic thesis would say that if one knows theory, then family therapy comes automatically" (Kerr & Bowen, 1988, p. 339).

This book, by contrast, is an unashamedly how-to book. Few

therapists appear to have mastered clinical practice by mastering abstract theory. If there is no theory about therapy, then therapy becomes atheoretical. The therapeutic method to be described in this book is more highly ritualized and stylized than any of those referred to earlier. Clearly, this has both advantages and disadvantages. Personal authority theory and method have evolved through trial-and-error practice with about 400 families over the last 20 years. Like every other method, it has its restrictions and limitations (see Chapter 12), and it is mandatory to be sensitive to these.

Personal authority method is one that has proved teachable—but under two conditions. First, it needs to be consistent or at least compatible, with the ways in which the student makes up reality and has decided to manage his or her own life. Second, it is best learned in a setting where the student has freedom to innovate in ways that make the method his or her own. There is no strict party line to follow. It is essential that the learner not be unduly intimidated by any other human being, including teachers and supervisors. This is experiential on-the-job training, where the apprenticeship model of education is working at its best. Pursuing conversations with parents, of the sort found later in this book, is excellent remedial training for family therapists. As in any psychotherapy training, family therapists are taught to discipline themselves so as to be able to take more of an observer and less of an active or reactive participant role in the emotional process with clients. This is almost a universal characteristic in psychotherapy practice. Frequently, however, one undesirable consequence is that therapists lose their spontaneity and become increasingly incongruent in everyday behavior. Wondering who is up to what and who else is up to what else can be so internalized that it becomes a reflex response to almost every human situation. Family therapists (like other therapists) can become addicted to metacommunication as an alternative to spontaneous self-expression. Talking openly and freely with one's own parents can be a powerful antidote.

Personal authority within the family system is not presented as the only way to practice intergenerational family therapy. Instead, it is offered as one coherent way to think and pratice and as a way that has worked pleasingly well for those, not surprisingly, for whom it has worked well. Fortunately, this has been an encouragingly large proportion of those who have chosen to show up in my office.

CHAPTER 2

Background Theoretical Assumptions

A constant war of opposing tendencies is the dynamic heart
of the universe.

—Karl A. Menninger et al.
The Vital Balance (Chap. VI)

Six Basic Assumptions

There are six basic theoretical assumptions about human behavior
underlying the stance taken in this book:

1. Well-being is indivisible; at the heart of human well-being is
   psychological integrity.
2. Psychological integrity is the result of the integration of
   various aspects of the self.
3. Most of life is managed most of the time by most people at an
   unconscious level.
4. The integration of self implies a harmony between the conscious and the unconscious aspects of mind. It also requires an
   integration not only within the larger social context in general
   but within the family of origin in particular.
5. Healthy family organization requires a renegotiation of family
   politics in the fourth decade of the lives of sons and daughters. By the time most adults are in their thirties they are ready
   to deal with and therefore to permit much more material to
   become conscious.

6. The essence of this psychological and political change is that the healthy adult gives up, once and for all, the "parent as parent" and consequently relinquishes the need to be parented.

We can describe each of these basic assumptions in greater detail.

Well-Being Is Indivisible

Well-being is indivisible because it is an integrated pattern of experiences in body, mind, and spirit. Some people are uncomfortable with the term *spirit*. They would prefer not to use such a construct at all or to speak of "mind-spirit" rather than regard spirit as a distinct aspect of the human being. However, there comes a time when one moves from a dispassionate, objective description of behavior as a way of conceptualizing personality and begins to speak of character. Then one is making a moral or ethical evaluation of personality and behavior. It can be argued that one has now moved from the purely psychological into a different domain. Certainly, in everyday language we speak of a person's spirit as being good or bad, assess the spirit of a marriage or a family, and refer to the spirit of a team or a group or a company, even of a nation. While this notion obviously includes psychological and social aspects, it perhaps cannot be fully reduced to this.

To say that well-being is indivisible is not to imply that the state or degree of well-being is necessarily equal within one's body, mind, and spirit. There are obvious examples where the mind is creative and brilliant even though the body is seriously dysfunctional. Recent examples of this include the influential and innovative Milton Erickson, who drew hundreds of psychotherapists to his teaching and to his creative mind, although he was physically handicapped most of his life as a result of two bouts with poliomyelitis. In his later years, he was extremely weakened physically and confined to a wheelchair. A second example is the contemporary physicist Stephen Hawking (1988), who has captured both the professional and the lay imagination with his theories of the cosmos and time, although confined to a wheelchair as a result of Lou Gehrig's disease. Likewise, the body can reach unusual levels of achievement even while the mind or spirit is functioning (or dysfunctioning) at a much lower level. A recent example of this is the record-breaking performance by certain competitors in the Seoul Olympics while at the very same moment they were cheating by using illegal drugs to enhance that performance.

What is being affirmed is that a spirit of well-being, or something less than that, is likely to fuse and infuse the self system of an individual in all of its various expressions of self. This includes the body, mind, and spirit in ways that are holistic and indivisible. To take such a view is to adopt a rich systems perspective on individual health and well-being. This perspective can enhance a systemic understanding of the self in the family and of the impact of family on the life of the individual. But to restrict systems thinking to the emotional life alone, whether of individuals or families, is to adopt an unduly narrow view of human health. Just as physicians are trained routinely to do a "review of systems," thereby thinking systemically but restricting their inquiry to the biological, so are family therapists encouraged to think in terms of systems, but usually at an exclusively emotional level. One consequence of this is the tendency to underestimate the enormous impact of family dynamics on the physical, psychological, and spiritual health of family members, and vice versa. When an attitude of wellness and an expectation of and commitment to wellness permeate a family, they will cross body–mind boundaries and will have enormous influence on the health of family members. Likewise, negative attitudes and expectations will adversely affect the physical health of family members.

The Integration of Self

The spirit of an individual self expresses itself in psychological integrity. Psychological integrity is a result of the integration at an emotional level of divided and rejected aspects of the self. Rogers (1951) has described the psychotherapy process as learning to create language to symbolize rejected thoughts and feelings, so that these can be made explicit and therefore acknowledged and integrated into the self system. Evidence is now increasing that much of life's experience is recorded not simply in the mind but also in the body. Perhaps the emotional aftermath of experience is somehow recorded physically (Chopra, 1989). Consequently, integration of the self implies an open interaction and information flow between the subsystems of body and mind within the self system.

Management of Life at Unconscious Level

The third assumption is a simple acknowledgment of the Freudian discovery that human experience occurs simultaneously at multiple levels of consciousness or awareness. Key decisions emanate from deeper psychological levels. This means that an innovative therapist who does not use interpretations to produce insight may yet assume the posture of "playing with meanings." This is an alternative to searching for and presenting "true" interpretations, including interpretations of the client's "resistance" to interpretations. Therapeutic interventions, including interpretations, will then be more fun for all concerned. In this way, those who are neither trained in nor theoretically committed to the psychoanalytical model can nonetheless, if they care to, take note of and respond to unconscious phenomena. It is assumed that most of what has happened in personal history has been recorded in the cortex and, although forgotten, is not lost forever. Yet most of what has not been lost is nonetheless not easily remembered.

The implication of all this, which for many fits nicely with observation of self and others, is that much of what is most important in life is handled at a level not immediately, and sometimes not at all, available to consciousness. It has been adequately demonstrated that much can be made conscious through the technique of free association. However, at least for patients, this information usually begins as someone else's discovery. By contrast, in intergenerational work the client has an opportunity to captain his or her own ship in searching for the hidden treasure. This distinction has enormous implications for the speed and efficacy of the change process in talking therapy. Not the least of these is the immediately compelling power of "truth" that has been self-discovered. One crucial beneficial characteristic of self-discovery is that the discovery is likely to occur in accordance with the client's personal emotional timetable of readiness to see, accept, and use the new information. Consequently, "resistance" is rarely the same pervasive problem that it has been in psychoanalysis.

The major treatment implication, if one cares to make the assumption that most of life is managed at an unconscious level, is that interventions can address multiple levels of awareness simultaneously. In Erickson's terms (Erickson & Rossi, 1979), it is constantly useful to "seed the unconscious." In order for this to occur comfortably, the therapist will need to have the personal freedom to perceive and respond from different levels of personal consciousness. This implies for example that there are no further greatly disquieting surprises left in the therapist's own repertoire of unconscious responses. This in turn means that he or she is on fairly comfortable speaking terms with the crazier aspects of his or her own self (Keith & Whitaker, 1980). (It would be interesting but not now relevant to speculate about the implications of this educational goal for the clinical training of psychotherapists.)

Conscious and Unconscious Aspects of Mind

The third assumption about human nature underlying the position taken in this book is that there is harmony between the conscious and unconscious aspects of mind. The unconscious mind is in large part a product of social, including family, experience; hence the importance of the connection between the integrating self system and the larger social context of the community in general, including, in particular, the biopsychosocial context of the family of origin. Realizing this harmony includes the challenge of resolving the conflict that sometimes occurs between the values of the family of origin and the values of the social and cultural context that surrounds the individual member of the second generation, values with which he or she has chosen to identify. The particular interest and focus of this book is on one aspect of these experiences of integration: the challenge to reintegrate the self with and within the family of origin in ways that are appropriate to that developmental stage in life known as middle adulthood.

Renegotiation of relational politics—or differentiation of self—within the family of origin implies a contemporaneous integration within the self of rejected aspects of self. These include previously rejected memories and the emotionality and impulses associated with them. The initiative for renegotiation or change can begin at any given point within the individual's inner dialogue of self with self. Or it can grow out of a dialogue with a person within the family of origin. The particular starting point is often determined by whether the person who assumes the role of psychotherapy client chooses to engage in individual therapy or in family therapy. The important distinction is that family therapy will promote both inner reflection and active relational changes at the same time. It is possible, of course, that an ideologically rigid family therapist may discourage or minimize the personal reflection aspect of family therapy. On the other hand, while the therapist practicing individual psychotherapy may at times acknowledge or even embrace family, he or she will also frequently wittingly or unwittingly, exclude it or side against it; how the issue of family is handled depends on the knowledge, flexibility, range of competence, and belief system of the individually oriented psychotherapist.

At its best, family of origin work continues simultaneously within the individual as well as between the individual and the members of the family of origin, in circular and mutually reinforcing fashion. However, from one perspective the family, whether two generations or more, exists only as a construct in the mind and within the intrapsychic processes of the individual observer. This reminds us yet again that of all the dialogues that occur in a person's life the most influential is the ongoing dialogue of the self with the self. However, the fundamental point being made here is that personal health at all levels of being is directly and powerfully related to family experience. The majority of persons are raised within the environs of a biological family, however well or poorly it may function, however integrated or fragmented that biological family may be. Much of the key information about these experiences is stored at an unconscious level and needs to become more available. The therapeutic method described in this book is geared toward making the deeper levels of emotional life more available to the client.

With few exceptions, persons are engaged in creating a new biological family in a new generation, or are struggling with the obstacles to this achievement. Also with few exceptions, persons of adult age are dealing with the emotionality of creating a third generation, that is, struggling with their feelings about the children they have or want to have or don't want to have, or have and wish they didn't have. Apart from the influence of family genetics, family emotionality in the most general sense provides, as it moves backward and forward in time, the fabric out of which personal well-being is first cut and then woven.

Renegotiation of Family Politics

The fifth assumption underlying this book is that there comes a time when sustaining a healthy family organization and experience requires the freedom to renegotiate family politics. This act of renegotiation implies the presence of emotional strength, independence, and effective political and moral sanctions on the part of the second generation. The renegotiation of relational politics usually comes after first having established enough physical and emotional distance from the parental home to be able to return and reconnect in a different way. The adult must first gain enough emotional distance from the family of origin to be able to begin to observe it, in order to be able both to appreciate it differently and to see his or her role in it. Seeing one's role in it is, of course, a condition of changing one's role in it. And changing one's role requires the power of those sanctions that become available in mature adulthood.

The primary sanction of the second generation is the power to give or withhold validation and acknowledgment of the person and achievements, especially the parenting achievements, of father and mother. Few adults find it easy to use this power consciously.

Because infancy is a period of total and lengthy dependency, dependency becomes a learned response that is very difficult to extinguish. Add to this both the power of the emotionality of family values and expectations at a conscious level, and family loyalties and mandates transmitted unconsciously. It is evident why the renegotiation of family politics is perceived as a formidable challenge and why the hesitation is usually considerable. Intergenerational intimidation is resilient and yields slowly. But yield it can.

Giving Up the Parent as Parent

The final assumption is that the essence of the therapeutic work to be described is the giving up of the parent as parent, once and for all, thereby giving up the need to be parented. This break in dependency is the central developmental task in adult life. In adulthood we continue the admittedly never fully complete task of identity resolution begun in adolescence (Erikson, 1968). Identity resolution may be viewed simultaneously as an individual and a family life-cycle task and life-cycle stage. Observation suggests that it does not complete before the individual's 30s (Williamson, 1982a) and that it requires careful psychological preparation of both generations. The resolution of identity goes well when there is a thoughtful and detailed preparation of an intergenerational agenda by the client. At its most intense, the preparation can be experienced simultaneously as a disorganization within the self and a destabilization of intergenerational (and often spousal) relationships. The future is less and less scripted. This uncertainty can be unnerving, but it means that the moment of activity—and therefore change—is at hand.

Some years ago Menninger et al. (1963) suggested that a disorganization of personality is a necessary step in order to reorganize at a higher level. Obviously, the subjective experience of disorganization can be quite difficult to live through. For this is indeed the ultimate and most painful moment of de-illusionment in life. The young child goes to sleep happily each night, drifting off on stories that conclude with the expression "and they all lived happily ever after." This benevolent "lie" is the effort of caring parents to create peace of mind, thereby encouraging restful sleep. Gradually, the child finds out that neither he or she, nor Mom or Dad, nor anyone else lives happily ever after. Growing up is, from one perspective, to experience a sequence of de-illusionments whereby one comes to terms with the frailty and the hypocrisy of the adult world that one is about to join. *The ultimate de-illusionment is giving up or losing the parent as parent.* This means having to come to terms with the fact that in the last resort, and when the chips are down, there is no one and nowhere to turn to except the self. As Bowen (1978) has repeatedly insisted, one cannot achieve more of the self from outside the self. Paradoxically, invariably one first hears that very idea from someone else, that is, from outside the self.

Some adults experience themselves as having grown up in their families of origin emotionally distant and feeling very unconnected to their parents. They are puzzled to think that they must "leave" the family, since they do not feel that they ever really belonged. The challenge here is the same, namely, to deal with the intense feelings in relationship to father and mother, which in this case may have to do with disappointment at what did not occur rather than grief at losing the sense of being strongly parented and protected.

From the point of view of the first generation the essential change in family politics is that the parent gives up his or her historic position of authority as parent to the second generation. The parent will, of course, forever be a unique person, occupying a unique place, for better or for worse, in the life of son or daughter. The power of the biological connectedness is not negotiable and the psychological imprinting leaves its trace. Notwithstanding this, a parent can resign from the role of parent in the sense that he or she no longer offers protection and nurturance and a willingness to take responsibility for the health, happiness, and success in life of the former child. In return, the parent gives up position, power, privilege, and an expectation of continuing first priority. The old contract has run out and becomes null and void; a new one is to be negotiated to take its place.

Four Assumptions about Parents Underlying Personal Authority Work

Reflecting on my work over time, I have made a number of observations that are summed up in four useful working assumptions about parents. A comment may be made as to the meaning of the term *assumption* as used here. This is not a way of denoting a proposition known to be true. What it does denote is an idea that has proved consistently effective in constructing a context of meaning within which clients find both encouragement and the courage to complete the work.

Parents Are Already Prepared and Waiting

The first assumption is that, with rare exceptions, parents are already prepared and waiting to renegotiate the hierarchical boundary with former children. They are but awaiting the signal that the latter are now ready to get on with it. Sometimes they are not fully aware that they are ready and are given help in recognizing this.

Parents Are Initially Suspicious

The second assumption is that parents are routinely initially somewhat suspicious or hesitant when the second generation first initiates conversations about the parents' lives—understandably so. Children begin life in a condition of total physical and psychological dependency, which is to say, politically powerless. Therefore, one primary skill to be acquired during the growing-up years is to learn to identify points of weakness and vulnerability in the parent, which can then be used to gain at least a temporary advantage. A major available sanction arises in the area of calling the parent into question as parent and provider of all things necessary and good for the child. The parent learns ways to protect self-esteem in general and sense of self as parent in particular from the ever-present possibility of attack or criticism.

Consequently, when son or daughter first signals an interest in moving inside the inner life of the parent, the latter may respond with some initial degree of alarm or at least caution. Is the purpose of this inquiry to discover more facts in order to make an evaluation and assess blame, pass judgment, and issue a grade? Once a parent feels reassured that son or daughter is not still approaching in the mode of a critical child but more in the stance of an accepting and compassionate friend, then he or she can relax and breathe deeply enough to be able to talk. Then key information will begin to emerge. Needless to say, clients frequently need to learn and practice in a small therapy group the kinds of behavior, including the crafting of language, that can provide such reassurance.

Parents Are Hungry to Talk

The third assumption is that once their anxieties have been allayed, parents are invariably hungry to talk and share the inner experiences of their lives. There is no one with whom aging parents would rather share the inner experience of life than their own flesh and blood, most especially their own former children. There is no one with whom they would rather share memories, current fears, and remaining hopes. Certainly, there is no one for whom they, from their own perspective, would rather set the record straight. There is no one from whom they are more eager to receive acknowledgment and validation. A young child is often observed in the backyard swinging as hard and as high as he or she can go on the garden swing and then calling out passionately, "See me, Mommy; see me, Daddy." In most families the time comes when this poignant moment reverses itself. The aging parent carries around a similar, if muted or coded, appeal for acknowledgment and validation from the next generation. The older parent wants to be seen.

Discovering "Otherness" Is the Road to Intimacy

The final assumption is that this political, relational renegotiation is the "right royal road" to intimacy between the generations. It begins with the discovery of the parent not as an object but as an other, a human being with a personal story to tell. The heart of intimacy is the spontaneous and unlabored sharing with the other of the inner private meanings of the most important experiences in one's life. First of all, this intimacy presumes a relationship that is experienced as being safe—that is, accepting and nonjudgmental and, therefore, trustworthy. Secondly, it assumes that the two parties have overlapping interests and values in life, that are of some considerable meaning and importance to each and well worth talking about. Thirdly, intimacy presumes an easy mutual identification with one another. This requires a sense of psychological equality or peerhood between the parties. Superiors may drop occasional crumbs of self-revelation to inferiors, but this scarcely deserves the term *intimacy*. Inferiors may bare the soul to superiors, but this is usually done in a context of evaluation or in a plea for help. The aftermath is likely to be embarrassing, or at least somewhat uncomfortable, for both parties; frequently, the inferior one will be inclined to cross to the other side of the street upon casual encounter.

Individual spontaneity, relational trust, and contextual freedom are necessary for peerhood and, therefore, for intimacy in human relationships. Clearly, this is not the character of the transactions occurring between two persons who remain with each other in the traditional roles of parent and child. Children and their parents will appropriately enjoy the warmth of closeness and fusion. But adult intimacy awaits the termination of the intergenerational hierarchical power boundary and the assumption of equal standing on the part of the second generation.

CHAPTER 3

Personal Authority: The Construct in Theoretical Context

> . . . it is the counselor's function to assume, in so far as he is
> able, the internal frame of reference of the client, to perceive
> the world as the client sees it. . . .
>
> —Carl R. Rogers
> *Client-Centered Therapy* (p. 29)

Language, Consciousness, and the Authority of Personal Authority Work

From one perspective human living as we know it began with the arrival of symbolic interaction, and especially with the development of language. We now speak of humans having consciousness, which is to say, language. Capra (1989) suggests that "we live in language. Consciousness arises and is communicated and shifts direction through language. Consciousness or mind is the dynamic of life itself." Language arises through social interaction and, therefore, creates a socially and culturally determined construction of reality. Consciousness is a construction of self-awareness, as language expresses ideas and beliefs. Meanings result from social experience. Hare-Mustin and Marecek (1988), referring to Watzlawick (1984), point out that constructivism takes the position that we do not discover reality, but create it. In this view, we do not directly experience reality but, rather, live with a representation of it that has been constructed in language (Rorty, 1979). It follows that there are no objective (which is to say, uninterpreted) "facts." Using metaphors from biology such as differentiation and fusion does not make a theory scientific or objective. Facts cannot be separated from values, since values strongly influence what are perceived as the facts. The theory determines what can be seen (Kuhn, 1962). Or in everyday parlance, "If I hadn't believed it, I wouldn't have seen it." So the constructivist is less interested in the facts themselves and more interested in the assumptions behind the facts.

This attitude toward "the facts" is a matter of great importance for family of origin work. For it means that personal history and the attempt to make peace with it is not simply a matter of discovering and then accepting the objective facts or truth. Personal history is, instead, itself seen as a constructed or made-up story. It is a piece of "true fiction." All the meanings that compose it are highly subjective and are therefore, by definition, partial and subject to distortion. Capra (1989) writes that "the peak experience is a deepening sense of mystery which accompanies the letting go of certitude." One can, of course, become less emotionally reactive within the family and in that sense become a little more objective. But when it comes to the perception (or construction) of "reality," neither the client nor the therapist nor any other observer can achieve a position that is outside the system.

This perspective avoids the subject–object split of traditional epistemology. Cognition and perception become functions of inter-actional life processes, especially relational experiences. From this position, statements about "reality" are first understood to be state-ments about the observer. Thus, so living systems can be seen as cognitive systems, and life itself as an experience of cognition. To observe the system is to join the system (Maturana, 1978). Can one become less reactive? Yes. Become objective? No.

Winnicott (1986) has eloquently illustrated the concept of the individual family member's construction of the family:

> If a mother has eight children, there are eight mothers. This is not simply because of the fact that the mother was different in her attitude to each of the eight. If she could have been exactly the same with each (and I know this is absurd, for she is not a machine), each child would have had his and her own mother seen through individual eyes. (p. 40)

> For the five children in a family there are five families. It does not require a psychoanalyst to see that these five families need not resemble each other, and are certainly not identical. (p. 132)

If that is the bad news, then the good news is the surprising implication that personal history can indeed change. If history is a made-up story, the story can be rewritten. This, then, is the crucial point: personal authority work is all about rewriting the story of personal history. *Personal history is rewritten in light of new understandings generated by sustained and intimate conversations with the former parents.* Yet the impetus to change the story does not come primarily from the new facts or interpretation of facts offered by parents, although these are both copious and influential. Rather, the story changes in response to an adult son's or daughter's new and dramatically different experience with and perception of the person of and the personal narrative (or construction) of each parent. This new experience and new perception are happening in this immediate moment in time through face-to-face contact and conversation.

The dynamic that changes the client's personal story is, therefore, not the new information, although the new information is the vehicle for it. The dynamic for change in the personal narrative of the client is the changing perception of the character of the personal narrative of the parent. The client cannot continue to make up the self in the same old way if he or she now begins to see (that is, make up) the person of the parent differently. Change in one brings change in the other regardless of which change begins the process. In personal authority work this interaction becomes indistinguishably circular. In its most interesting moments, it is like a tennis game in which the players are constantly jumping across the net with the intention of playing on both sides simultaneously. The political and emotional nature of the relationships between the generations is being reconstructed under our very eyes. The foreground figure of the client exists in its presenting form only against an unchanging family background. As the parental stories unfold and the family background changes, so does the client's story, since it exists only as one aspect of the context. As the client looks at and begins to see this older man and woman, who used to be "Mommy" and "Daddy," and begins to discover them as they are today, then the client also begins to change the pictures of who each parent was in the past and, in particular, who each parent was to him or her.

The notion that the personal story or "reality" is made up creates a dilemma for traditional psychotherapy theory, for the traditional goal of psychotherapy has been to help the client get in touch with "reality" and learn to accept it. But what now can this mean? Does it mean acceptance of the therapist's reality, that is, the therapist's construction of the patient's reality? Is it some kind of consensual reality, but, if so, according to whose version of that? A few years ago in her Broadway show that well-known philosopher and "high school graduate" Lily Tomlin suggested that "reality is a collective hunch." Is this the best that can be done? So the question remains: In the psychotherapy venture, toward what are we in motion? The argument of this book will proceed by taking an "as if it were true" and "because it is useful" stance as the source of confidence in what is proposed.

Personal Authority Work in the Context of Psychotherapy Theory in General

How does one achieve psychological integrity and personal well-being in life? That is the central question about autonomy and intimacy in therapeutic psychology and is the question underlying the question addressed in this book. How does one achieve a meaning and purpose in life that is not determined or overdetermined by family history, family dynamics, or family expectations and values on the one hand, and is not simply a reflex oppositional response to or alienation from or rebellion against family on the other hand? How does one let go of or cleanse oneself of those aspects of family emotionality that are personally destructive or clearly not useful in creating one's own life? That is the central clinical question in family therapy, although it permeates psychotherapy in general (Nichols & Everett, 1986). Different emphases have appeared in the psychotherapy literature, and all of these have some relevance to the point of view and the method described in this book. Five such foci of interest are noted in the following paragraphs in the interest of theoretical continuity and in an attempt to relate this therapy procedure to traditional psychotherapy procedure in general.

Catharsis

Family of origin clients have cathartic experiences, beginning with the small group preparation for the conversations with parents that are to follow. Catharsis also occurs during the direct feedback to parents, as clients share inner experiences and feelings continuing from their own earlier years.

Corrective Emotional Experience

A corrective emotional experience occurs as the small group creates a surrogate primary family for each client, with the other members becoming surrogate brothers and sisters. At its very best, the small group provides a kind of family experience that is validating and supporting, nurturing and healing to the client. It is as though everyone had the same set of parents who are showing both similar and different sides of themselves to each group member.

Insight

In direct conversations with parents, siblings, and members of the extended family, as well as with other informed figures in the lives of parents, the client receives much new information about the details of family history and new perspectives on his or her place within it. New information generates new levels of both intellectual and emotional insight.

Reframing

Reframing and positive connotation are used in family therapy to create a more benevolent meaning and therefore a more conducive emotionality around a particular event or sequence of behaviors. In the method described in this book, reframing is applied in sustained fashion to personal history so that early events take on different meanings in light of a more informed and more compassionate understanding of parental motives, intentions, and limitations.

Reality Testing

Reality testing acquires a rich meaning in this kind of family of origin work. In conversations with parents and other key figures in the family's history, the client is able to check patterns of perceptions and clarify specific mysteries. The client can go directly to the parents and explore thoughts, fantasies, and memories in order to validate or correct existing constructions of reality. This offers a very powerful and immediate possibility for resolution, by contrast with the recreation of early experience through inferences from transference phenomena in the controlled environment of psychotherapy. The advantage of the latter method is that therapists' responses are intended to be consistently therapeutic. But with careful preparation the client can usually have a good response from the direct conversation with parents. At least, difficult responses can be neutralized by the support and nurturance of the ongoing surrogate family small group.

A plus to the personal authority method is that the client can review directly with the interested parties his or her own place and role in the social system that is the family. He or she can then proceed to reposition or "de-scapegoat" the self or go on to further define a new self in the immediate context of the contemporary family. He or she can actively give up or return intergenerational burdens or mandates or renegotiate previously covert loyalties. The client can directly pursue the truth behind family secrets and explore un-mourned or unresolved family losses. A different "reality" inevitably emerges around the person of each parent. In a reciprocal interaction, through all of this the client defines and tests out a sharper and more clearly bounded reality to the self.

Personal Authority: The Theoretical Construct

Personal Authority in the Family System (PAFS) is presented as a new stage of both individual adult and family life-cycle development. ("New" simply means hitherto unidentified and unnamed; William-son, 1981; Williamson, 1982a; Williamson & Bray, 1988.) Briefly stated, PAFS is the ability to claim authorship and responsibility for all of one's thoughts, feelings, and actions and to do so voluntarily. This ability exists in concert with the ability to choose consciously and spontaneously to be connected to and in relationship with other persons—especially those in the family of origin—to whatever degree of intimacy one desires, including choosing to forgo intimacy at any given moment in time.

This stage of mature development is achieved contemporane-ously by both the individual and the family. It comes about through an interdependent termination of the intergenerational hierarchical power boundary between the first and the second generations. It is assumed that this political renegotiation occurs both formally and informally within individuals and families and on both conscious and unconscious levels. In other words, the renegotiation is often as a result of, but frequently happens without, therapeutic consultation or intervention.

The theoretical construct of personal authority is the source of an evolving methodology of clinical practice, which is used with indi-viduals and families who frequently present themselves as being "stuck" in their current life circumstances and relationships. This "stuckness" is usually represented by difficulties within primary love relationships or intergenerational relationships or at work. It is as though there is a loose piece of wiring or a loose connection as a result of which there is either overheating and dangerous sparking within the relational system or a failure to generate the juice necessary to produce energy and vitality. Frequently, these various problems, wherever they present themselves, can be seen to be reminiscent of and therefore, it is hypothesized, the products of the less than

successful behavioral transactions characterizing relationships between the client and members of the family of origin.

Personal Authority: A New Stage in Both the Individual and the Family Life-Cycle

Vaillant (1977) has concluded that the psychological life-cycle stages
within adulthood have not been well defined. He notes, "Between
the decade of the 20s and the 40s, Erikson left an uncharted period of
development" (p. 202). However, there is broad agreement on the
fundamental developmental principle. According to Levinson (1978),
"even the most disparate lives are governed by the same underlying
order—a sequence of eras and developmental periods" (p. 64).
Erikson (1978), himself addresses the issue in a family-oriented way:
"In contributing to an inclusive human psychology, psychoanalysis
cannot shirk the task of accounting not only for the way the
individual ego holds the life-cycle together, but also for the laws
which connect generational cycles with individual ones—and the
social process with both" (p. 23).

Much has been written previously about the life cycle and the
tasks constituting a healthy and successful passage from one phase of
development into the next (Combrinck-Graham, 1985; Erikson, 1982).
Many writers and researchers have recognized the act of leaving
home *physically* as an important stage in the family cycle (Cohler &
Geyer, 1982; Erikson, 1982; Levinson, Darrow, Klein, Levinson, &
McKee, 1978; Haley, 1980). However, that is neither the same thing as
nor necessarily a guarantee of the completion of the subsequent
critical developmental step of renegotiating relationships with parents in order to leave home *emotionally* as well.

Although they do not specify this particular stage as such, Carter
and McGoldrick (1989) provide a useful lens for viewing individual
and family development within the framework of the life cycle. They
begin the life cycle with the single adult leaving home (physically),
then getting married, then parenting children at different stages
(families with young children, families with adolescents, then
launching children from the home), and conclude with the family in
later life. Personal authority is a unifying principle between individual and family theory. It can be seen as the continuation in mature
adulthood of the personal identity issue carried over from the teenage
years. There is considerable evidence that this "stage" takes place
during the fourth decade of life and the years following (Levinson et
al., 1978, pp. 59–60; Sheehy, 1974, p. 35; Vaillant, 1977, pp. 202, 344).
A contextual individual–family developmental task in the human life

cycle (such as PAFS) makes it easier to make sense of individual problems within the parameters of family systems thinking. This, in turn, suggests a more versatile range of therapeutic interventions.

Personal Authority: A Definition

Personal Authority in the Family System (PAFS) has been summarized previously as a matrix of certain relational abilities and behavioral skills. These abilities are defined in the following paragraphs.

1. PAFS includes the ability to know and direct one's own thoughts and opinions as well as the emotional freedom to choose whether or not to express these at any given moment or occasion, regardless of intense social pressures or expectations from family members or others.

2. PAFS includes the ability to value one's personal judgment consistently and to be able to make decisions and act on one's own good judgment. This skill assumes the ability to be able at times to be an observer and critic of one's own processes and responses.

3. PAFS includes the ability to take responsibility for all of one's experiences, decisions, and actions in life and for the consequences that flow directly from these. The underlying assumption is that one creates all of one's experiences in life. One does not, of course, originate or hand-tailor the detail of every circumstance or every outcome. However, it is assumed that one does "decide" in which ways to give meaning to events. One is, therefore, constantly and continuously in the business of constructing a "personal reality" in life: one "chooses" an associated emotional response to every circumstance, "chooses" how to assimilate or internalize it, and "chooses" how to behave in light of these.

4. PAFS includes the ability, coexisting and interacting with the aforementioned abilities, to connect emotionally with other people in as self-expressive and intimate, or in as reserved, a fashion as seems appropriate, and as one freely chooses at any given time. This ability includes the skill to fuse with another in an intense love relationship, but at the very same time to retain some degree of voluntariness and self-control within the decision and the fusion. This indeed is the case whether it is a decision to initiate intimacy or to respond to an initiative, or a decision to decline or to move away from such moments and acts of emotional fusion.

5. Finally, personal authority includes the ability to relate to all other human beings as *peers*—including, indeed beginning with, the parents—in the psychosocial meanings of the term *parent* as one who disciplines, nurtures, and assures responsibility for. The acknowledg-

ment shared between the generations that they, faced with life and death and all the other expressions of human vulnerability, are both in the same "leaky boat" is a precondition for first embracing and then transcending, beginning with human intimacy, the absurdity of the human experience (Williamson, 1982b). The physical and psychological well-being of adults interacts with a continuing sense of emotional connection to and belonging with one's own flesh and blood. Claiming title to one's life and destiny and yet staying connected to family in intimate ways is the most influential and difficult developmental challenge in adult life. Success in this challenge paves the way for a good final resolution of identity and intimacy issues, which first rise in adolescence and young adulthood and then arise again and again through the entire life span. This success ensures an outcome more of integrity than despair in old age.

In summary, the essential distinction of this theory is the declaration that intimacy interacts with differentiation of self in such a way that there is a resulting synergy known here as "personal authority" (Williamson, 1982b). Personal authority then expresses itself in the continuing emotional freedom and energy to initiate, sustain, review and renegotiate, or terminate the experience of emotional intimacy at any given time in any relationship. In partnership with this freedom and energy is the ability to acknowledge and tolerate the same freedom in the other. There may be a strong emotional identification or fusion with the other whereby the clear psychological boundary to the self is *temporarily* obliterated. This clear emotional boundary of the self can be voluntarily and fairly readily regained, and within a relatively short period of time.

A pattern of the aforementioned abilities is the compelling evidence of the presence of a higher level of personal authority within an individual's construction of self in the world. On the other hand, an individual incapable of even momentary psychological fusion is probably incapable of "falling in love." A person who has become incapable of a relatively intense "transference" response, who therefore is unable to find the parents in another in a fairly profound way, is probably incapable of romantic love to any compelling degree. The ideal is to fall in love with the healthier aspects of that parent the first time around; if possible.

Personal authority enables the individual to establish an intimate primary love relationship and still maintain recourse to an independent identity to the self. An intimate love relationship will often reflect the unresolved issues within the previous generation, both personal and marital. It may also recreate the unsettled issues continuing *between* the first and second generations. It is useful to settle conflict and indebtedness with parents in order to avoid encumbering present love relationships—including one's children as well as one's spouse. An effective way to establish personal authority is to address the often powerful parental coalition directly and in this way deal with power politics in the family at the source. This is one way to resolve the intimacy paradox.

In the Interest of Further Definition

It is obvious by now that personal authority builds upon previously presented related themes. These include detriangulation, the differentiation of self, and the establishment of a strong "I" position (Anonymous, 1972); the achievement of "a balance of fairness" and "relational justice" in the family and the resolution of covert family loyalties (Boszormenyi-Nagy & Ulrich, 1981); the resolution of unmourned loss experiences in the family (Paul, 1967); the settling of intrapsychic conflict generated by negative aspects of transgenerational introjects and the subsequent experience of mutual forgiveness (Framo, 1981); the realignment of the family's basic functional structure (Minuchin, 1974); and the open acknowledgment of powerful family dynamics moving backward and forward across the three-generational cycle (Whitaker & Keith, 1981).

It can be argued that although the language and the concepts seem different, there is in fact an underlying similar theoretical continuum in the work of Bowen and Boszormenyi-Nagy, the two major theorists in the transgenerational field. On this continuum, differentiation of self and relational justice are at one end, with the latter and more comprehensive concept implying, indeed requiring, the former. At the other end of the continuum are the concepts of fusion–triangulation and covert loyalties–split loyalties. These terms present differing perspectives on the same underlying phenomena.

At one end of another apparent continuum is the "nonreactive" stance of Bowen with clients, which at first sight seems a fully neutral attitude by contrast with Boszormenyi-Nagy. However, it does achieve the same impartial outcome, which is the intent of the more proactive multidirectional partiality stance of Boszormenyi-Nagy. His notions of "relational justice" and "balance of fairness" do point to a multifaceted social and ethical outcome within the family. Personal authority work is intended to achieve such an integrated outcome.

PAFS is therefore offered as a synthesizing construct on yet another continuum. This is the Hegelian dialogue between autonomy or differentiation of self on the one hand and intimacy or community on the other. PAFS is presented as a model of relatively brief, symbolic–experiential, strategic intergenerational family therapy (see Chapter 4). It goes to the very heart of the family's political structure. Paradoxically, one becomes more political in order to create a context that is less political. This means no one is up to anything.

As noted earlier, the termination of the intergenerational hierarchical power boundary is quite different from the physical "leaving home" that the young adult accomplishes in the late teens or early twenties. It is a subsequent and separate developmental task, which occurs ten or more years later. It is possible only after other life achievements have been accomplished. It does spell an end to the intimidation often the mutual intimidation characterizing the interactions between the generations. Intimidation on both sides of the intergenerational equation is based ultimately on the primitive but well-grounded fear of the death of the self. For the second generation there is the fear either of parental rejection or the equally threatening fear of being invaded and thereby controlled by the parental mind and spirit. Both of these scenarios represent some form of death of the self. On the other hand, if the parent is no longer to be perceived as nurturing, protecting, and providing, then son or daughter must face the loss of the comforting fantasy of perfect and unending care.

On the other side there is frequently parental guilt over not having been a better, or at least a more "successful" parent. Often there is an accompanying dread of the evaluation of a parenting performance that has had inevitable, far-reaching negative consequences. Additionally, there is the fear of the loss of that very special position of "parent" and of the feeling of social contribution that comes with it. For both generations the most difficult challenges are the acknowledgment of aging and the changes in authority and status in life that aging inevitably brings. Underlying these challenges is the fear of approaching death and the recognition that when the parents die, they do so just a little bit ahead of their children.

Intergenerational intimidation and denial frequently hold adults in the second generation in a protective and fused relationship with parents while simultaneously creating an increasingly intense need for social distance and separation (Williamson, 1983). This dynamic can be characterized as simultaneously systemic–family and intrapsychic–individual in nature. Clinical experience suggests that involuntary fusion, perhaps a kind of pseudo-intimacy or pseudo-mutuality (Wynne, Ryckoff, Day, & Hirsch, 1958), is more likely to occur in the life of female clients while separation or cutoff (Bowen, 1978) is more likely to characterize the dysfunctional behavior of male clients. This hypothesis deserves controlled observation.

It has already been acknowledged that some people undoubtedly move naturally and successfully through this developmental stage in life without recourse to professional help. In healthy families clinical observation suggests that differentiation of self occurs in the context of a loving and accepting parental relationship. In these families children do not become chronically involved in parental conflicts, and multiple loyalties are allowed to develop freely. Children are encouraged to develop a sense of self, separate from either parent and from each other. They are also adequately protected from external threat. They are encouraged to feel safe and secure in themselves and in their home environment. In the ideal picture, as these children move up through adulthood, the renegotiation process with parents is woven spontaneously and seamlessly into the fabric of the interactional patterns of family life over time. Both the evolving young adult and the parent are aware of the diminishing need for attention and guidance. This allows each one to move gradually toward a peer relationship that facilitates personal freedom of expression and a shared intimacy. This would have been both impossible and psychologically inappropriate at any earlier stage of individual and family development. This is then the best-case scenario for the development of personal authority and healthy adults in healthy families. This book, however, is about the development of a therapeutic method for helping the considerable number of people who are not quite so fortunate.

Personal Authority Work as Power Politics

The realization of personal authority within the family is essentially a political goal and a political experience. The evidence for that allegation is as follows:

1. The goal of personal authority work is the achievement of fully egalitarian relationships between the adults in the extended family. This begins with the relationships between the generations and then, by both logical and psychological implication, includes relationships between male and female. By contrast, transgenerational theory in general validates the parent as parent and thereby affirms the political status quo.

2. It is both intended and assumed, and repeated observation confirms, that changes in intergenerational politics result in changes in important contemporary relationships, especially love relationships. Any movement toward more egalitarian intergenerational relationships is prone to destabilize the current marriage and will

encourage movement toward a more fully egalitarian marital relationship, wherever the present imbalance may be. For this reason, personal authority work is sometimes the most effective form of marital therapy and may be recommended for that reason (see end of Chapter 5).

3. Third, there is the matter of politics of gender, as this frequently expresses itself in the life of the family. Freud wrote that the most valued asset of humankind is the intellect. He noted that when ideas are dominant, a high level of civilization exists (Freud, 1930). However, humankind has been through a lot since Freud wrote this, including the aftermath of some very powerful but destructive ideas. Some of those who worked around Hitler were asked how they knew when he was giving an order. The consensus response was this: When he was in a rage they knew to ignore him, but when he was cold and controlled and quiet and thoughtful, they knew this was an order (Speer, 1970).

In principle PAFS values thoughts and feelings equally. In particular client situations one or the other may be favored in order to counter the client's prevailing discrimination. The uses of humor to be described later (see Chapter 4), certainly mock rationality and, by implication, honor feelings. A father's political control over children is likely to be more physically coercive and therefore more overtly political than the mother's control, which is more likely to be expressed through emotion. Father's incestuous behavior is therefore more apt to be expressed physically and mother's is more likely to show up through the emotional bond, but deep and powerful emotions are common to both. The political control in the one may be more overt and in the other more covert; the one is perhaps more related to fear while the other is more related to love.

4. In personal authority work in general, men are encouraged to deal more courageously with the emotional life and women are encouraged to deal more directly with the political process inherent in relationships. For example, notice that the concluding event in the client's conversations with parents is the statement of admiration (see Act Three, Scene III, of Chapter 10). This particular aspect of the intergenerational conversation is laced with profound feelings. There is no one by whom older parents can or want to be validated more than by their own sons and daughters. The process has now come full circle. At the same time, this statement of admiration occurs in a general context of debriefing of both parents on the personal narratives that constitute their lives. This inquiry is not only an unmistakable and formidable *political initiative*, it also elicits and encourages

gender empathy. (The matter of personal authority and gender is addressed at length by my colleague Linda Walsh, PhD, in Chapter 16.)

Admittedly, exercising personal authority in the family does from one perspective refer to the degree to which an individual's behavior can be based on reflection rather than be determined or overdetermined by some mix of the genetic code and family emotionality. However, this "reflection" is by no means an exclusively rational process. Just as intense feelings are modulated by rational thought, so the thinking process in this "reflection" has access to and is informed by profound feelings as well as emotion-laden values. While the reasoning mind with its binoculars and its radar may be on the bridge of the ship, the emotional life of the engine room represents the heart and the soul of the vessel.

PART TWO

Personal Authority Method:
The Play's the Thing

CHAPTER 4

Setting the Scene: Playful Interventions as a Method of Therapy

But things that fall hopelessly apart in theory lie close together without contradiction in the paradoxical soul of man . . .

—Carl Gustav Jung
Freud and Psychoanalysis
(Collected Works No. 4, p. 756)

Personal Authority Family of Origin Work: A Script Note

The omnipresent and the core psychotherapeutic question is; How does one leave home emotionally (presuming one has already left physically) and at the same time stay connected with the family of origin in a free, voluntary and intimate way? This question may be seen as an immediate derivative expression of a larger question: By virtue of what choices can one achieve meaning, value, and purpose in life? The larger question takes us into the domains of philosophy, ethics, and religion, and these are not within the scope of this book. However, embedded in intergenerational family theory in general is the assumption that a successful management of the core family of origin question is an enormous step toward solving the larger question of finding personal satisfaction and happiness in life.

Obviously, there are alternative ways to approach this question, including the option adopted by many people of simply deciding not to deal with it directly and consciously at all. Everyday observation

49

suggests that this option works quite well for some people, although probably not for the majority. For that reason this book is a description of an explicit and direct therapeutic approach to the resolution of the question: How does one leave emotionally from the home into which one was born and, while maintaining personal freedom, remain intimately connected with the members of the family of origin?

The proposal presented here in response is this: a successful negotiation (or, more accurately, renegotiation) in adult life of the politics of the intergenerational relational patterns between the self and the parents is a most valuable preparation for a successful management of life's overall opportunities and problems. Successful renegotiation with the family of origin does not guarantee any particular good outcome in life in specific detail. On the other hand, what it does do is create a subjective mood of much greater voluntariness and personal freedom. This mood spreads to the choices to be made in all the important decisions in life. This sense of emotional voluntariness is a result of the debriefing of parents about both the actual events and the personal meanings of these various sequences within their personal histories. This debriefing reveals the hopes and fears, the successes and failures, and the values and judgments of each parent over the storied course of his or her lifetime. These stories include each parent's personal evaluation of and response to his or her life experiences and achievements. As will be described in detail in the chapters to follow, this conversation creates an opportunity for the new generation to make freer and more differentiated choices and to have a greater sense of control over individual destiny.

Personal Authority Psychotherapy Practice in Context

Doherty and Colangelo (1984), followed up by Doherty and associates (1985), completed a conceptual analysis of the thirteen schools of family therapy identified by Gurman and Kniskern (1981). They divided theories into three groups, depending on the primary emphasis of each theory. The three distinguishing dimensions used to categorize each theory were inclusion, control, and intimacy. The relative emphasis of a theory with regard to these dimensions yields the differential judgment. The *theoretical constructs* that inform the point of view in this book build on Bowen theory and contextual therapy theory (Boszormenyi-Nagy). Both of these are classified by Doherty and Colangelo as emphasizing inclusion. The therapeutic *style* in personal authority work has been derived primarily from symbolic–experiential (Whitaker) and, to a lesser extent, from family of origin (Framo) family therapy. Both of these are classified as focused on intimacy. The therapeutic *methodology* to be described here borrows heavily from the practices developed in strategic therapy (Erickson, Haley, MRI group, Milan group; see Simon, Stierlin, & Wynne, 1985).

Consequently, the personal authority model (my secretary first typed in "muddle"; her unconscious has been trained also) can be seen as crossing various traditional boundaries and drawing from many quarters. The relationship of personal authority theory to transgenerational theory has been addressed already. What follows is a brief comment about the relationship of the psychotherapy style and method in personal authority work to both symbolic–experiential family therapy and to strategic family therapy.

Personal Authority Work as Symbolic–Experiential and as Strategic Family Therapy

Personal Authority Work and Symbolic–Experiential Family Therapy

Personal authority work is reminiscent of symbolic–experiential family therapy in the sense that it is growth-oriented and uses directive methods. In particular, it accepts Whitaker's proposition that "personal craziness" can be seen and experienced as a positive resource for creativity in therapy and in life. The second core shared goal is to seek to create connectedness between family members while simultaneously encouraging personal freedom. Both therapies focus on how the family's relationships with members of previous genera-tions influence the family's behaviors today. Both encourage the boundary demarcation between the generations, working to clarify and restructure the boundaries as may be necessary. It was from symbolic–experiential therapy that I learned to teach family members how to play together. These therapies demonstrate on a symbolic level that the myth of individuality is an inadequate guide to life if it is held in isolation. This "truth", like every other truth, is simply a perspective, though an important one.

By way of contrast, it may be noted that personal authority work does put an emphasis on the value of judicious reflection and insight. It assumes that change can come in this way as well as through playful symbolic interactions with the family. In both methods, the therapist's stance is one of multidirectional partiality. I endorse Whitaker's belief that trust on the part of the therapist in his or her own creative unconscious, derived from experience, is probably a more useful and certainly a more interesting source of interventions than adherence to formal and learned therapeutic techniques. There is in personal authority therapy clearly a great appreciation for the ingenuity of the unconscious mind. In this way, new experiences are transmitted through symbolic primary process.

Personal Authority Work and Strategic Family Therapy

Personal authority work can be seen as strategic therapy in the sense that it begins by negotiating the goals of therapy and then develops very explicit strategies for achieving these goals. In that sense, it is also a directive therapy. Furthermore, by comparison with transgenerational family therapy in general it can be considered to be brief. With so much focus being placed on the dialogue between the generations, it is, like strategic therapy, derivative of communication theory. It is also assumed in personal authority work that family problems are the result of a dysfunctional hierarchy or organization within the family, often expressing itself in pathological triangles. However, by contrast with strategic (or structural) family therapy, which focuses on the blurring of boundaries between the generations when children are young, personal authority work focuses on the importance of terminating hierarchical boundaries when former children have become adults. But both personal authority therapy and strategic family therapy focus on achieving an age-appropriate character to the generational boundary. They are opposite sides of the coin.

Both personal authority and strategic therapy focus on the family's interactional rules while trying to avoid power struggles between the therapist and the family. Likewise, both presume that a change in any one element will change the system. Both assume that it is possible to do family therapy with one person, that is, without having the whole family present physically in the room. Finally, both put a sustained focus on ongoing client behaviors and on giving assignments. Favored interventions include symptom prescription, reframing and positive connotation, and the reclassification of behaviors. All of this takes place in a mildly hypnotic atmosphere.

The Uses of Absurdity

Some years ago the Clown Prince of family therapy wrote that "craziness is the only real solution to boredom" (Whitaker, 1975).

That comment sounded absurd enough at the time. Whitaker went on to explain that in psychotherapy of the absurd, paradox takes on absurd overtones. The client spontaneously presents something that strikes the therapist as absurd. The therapist accepts this offering and then builds on it, escalating the absurdity, until the whole cognitive tower comes tumbling down. The point then is to exaggerate the overly rational until even the client recognizes the absurdity. Whitaker (1975) writes, "Success with this maneuver demands that it be lovingly done, and this caring is the anesthesia for the amputation of pride that takes place" (p. 6). In this view of things, absurdity as a style in psychotherapy is simply an escalation of the natural absurdity that characterizes all of human life, especially intimacy. In a beautiful statement Whitaker (1975) continues his concept of absurdity:

> Paradoxically, we attain power at the sacrifice of reason. When we try to act reasonably, we deny our personhood. Furthermore, as we struggle to "be" who we are, it is impossible to stop acting. These are the self-defeating paradoxes of our lives. They portray our power and our impotence but also our knowledge and our ignorance, our attunement and alienation. In essence, we are both tragic and farcical. This Janus mask is thus our absurdity. . . . by this microcosmic experience, the patient evolves a kind of immunity to the strange assault of the absurdity in our living process and some experience in how to zig and zag with the absurdity of his life. (pp. 10–11)

In a somewhat related comment, Watzlawick and associates (1974) and Watzlawick (1978) suggest that a psychological symptom is simply a piece of behavior that is so spontaneous that even the client himself experiences it as uncontrollable. So when the symptom is prescribed, the oscillation backward and forward between what is experienced as spontaneous and what is experienced as coercive makes the symptom paradoxical even in the patient's own experience of it. If the client performs the symptom as an assignment from the therapist the symptom loses its spontaneity and, consequently, much of its psychological power. The therapist is not outside the system generally, but is outside the boundary drawn around the client's symptomatic behavior. As a result, the "outsider" can provide a change in the rules, something that the system cannot provide for itself (Watzlawick, Beavin, & Jackson, 1967). In commenting on Madanes's work with play, Haley (in Madanes, 1981, p. xiv) notes that because play and pretending can be used to reclassify human behavior, they are very powerful means of change. It can be seen that all of this takes place within an ambience of absurdity.

From a darker perspective life can be seen as an experience of loss, whether predictable but nonetheless formidable developmental loss or the unexpected insults from trauma. There are constant multiple threats, experienced both from within and outside the self and as both real and imagined. Life is a continuing de-illusionment about life. The child growing up gradually learns that no one lives "happily ever after," not even the parents. Life itself is life-threatening. Everyone lives with existential anxiety or fear of non-being (Tillich, 1952), or lives with the symptoms born of denial (Becker, 1973), since "the paths of glory lead but to the grave" (Gray, 1751). Growing old with integrity is therefore some kind of a challenge. Embracing the absurdity of the human experience, which means finding oneself fully alive within it, can bring some relief. Just as personal authority is a synthesis of differentiation and intimacy, absurdity, in this context, is a synthesis of comedy and tragedy, transcending both. If "the world is a comedy to those that think, a tragedy to those that feel" (Walpole, 1769), then perhaps life is compassionately absurd to someone who has integrated thought and feeling. Discovery and acceptance of inner or natural absurdity prepares the way for forgiveness of the self and others. Playfulness in life is a compromise between either polarity. It creates the pun while not ignoring the pain.

Absurdity allows the individual to transcend the personal past, thereby making something unpredictable possible in the future. The moment when the client does not know his or her next line is a moment of creativity. The ambience allows reconciliation between the "they-all-lived-happily-ever-after" pretense and a relentless and disheartening assessment of the "real world." For some it offers an alternative to being psychologically vulnerable and without defenses, a situation that many believe can promote that condition known as schizophrenia. Whitaker (1980) has characterized this as "the disease of too much integrity." For others absurdity offers a resolution to the dilemma caused by the attempt at a simultaneous embrace of contradictory ideas like personal responsibility and circular causality. This way of working obviously comes more easily to the therapist who has embraced his or her own absurdity, irrationality, and "personal craziness" (Whitaker & Malone, 1953). As an eventual outcome, the therapist can learn to trust his or her own basic biological and unconscious self. That therapist is confident that he or she is no more likely to seduce or murder the client than to destroy the self. These are good things to be confident about. Absurdity has its uses.

Building the Set: The Ambience of the Therapeutic Process—Trembling on the Edge

The following chapters in this section will describe a strategic, symbolic–experiential approach to intergenerational family therapy. The ambience of the psychotherapy drama is constructed out of several propositions. These propositions, introduced in the following paragraphs, are both playful and suggestive. All of them are conveyed to the client gradually over time, although with different degrees of explicitness.

Change Has Already Begun

The first proposition alleges that change has already begun, as signaled by the fact that the client is now sitting in the room, discussing his or her life situation; the very decision to come in the first place is itself an expression of change already begun. It is explained that only people who have been "selected" for significant psychotherapeutically induced change in this lifetime ever show up in the therapist's office. Even if the client feels very stuck in his or her life situation or relationships, that awareness of "stuckness" and the energy within the frustration behind it, is the evidence that the change process has not only begun but is picking up momentum. Indeed, "stuckness" is just a colloquial way of acknowledging that energy is being dammed up and saved with a view to generating the powerful dynamic thrust needed to bring change in chronic situations. The more "stuckness," the higher the dam is rising and the greater the risk for breakthrough. All the more reason for caution and an attitude of "easy as you go." The client is then to be congratulated for being one of those persons selected and destined for change by forces, both inner and outer, that none of us probably will ever fully understand.

Change Is Involuntary

Now that change has begun, a continuing process of change and changing is inevitable—indeed, one might almost say involuntary. This communication of involuntariness is in contrast to traditional psychotherapy, which is usually focused at a more rational level of connection and communication. Traditional psychotherapy will routinely represent to the client that no promises or predictions can be made. His or her problems cannot be solved without his or her active involvement and commitment to the work, and it is too soon to know about that. By contrast, this position need not be taken with a client like this one, coming to do personal authority work, which means that he or she has obviously been selected and destined for change.

The evidence that change has already begun includes the changes the client thinks he or she has made, even inadvertently made, the changes the therapist thinks the client has probably made or wants to make, or "wants to want" to make. Also included occasionally are the changes the client "would like to want to want" to make and changes a client wishes he or she could think of in order to have a chance to want to want to make, or want to want to want to make. Finally, just about anything else that the client can think of to say at this moment can be seen by an imaginative therapist as further evidence of change, near change, or "pre-change change." The feeling of stuckness is a most powerful evidence of pre-change change, exceeded as a predictor of change only by feelings of hopelessness. This client is on his or her way. The possibilities are well-nigh limitless. Everything, spoken or unspoken, is grist for the mill. By now the client should be adequately mesmerized, so the consultant can continue with the induction.

Since the course of change is more or less involuntary, as has probably now been accepted, it cannot, therefore, be stopped except by some extraordinary event of a sort seldom seen. Because of this very "involuntariness," there is present in the room a feeling, to be encouraged, on the part of both therapist and client, that each is but an observer of an experience that neither one of them has really all that much to do with creating. They, especially the consultant, will, of course, nonetheless have many thoughts and comments about it as it goes along. By putting this suggestion into words, the consultant can often accentuate this incipient awareness in the client's mind.

The Client Comes to Structure Involuntary Change

It may be suggested to the client that he or she has come for consultation at this time in order to get help in slowing down and structuring this involuntary change process so that it will not get recklessly out of hand. This is known as voluntary control of involuntary change. Everyone, of course, knows that precipitous and headlong change that has not been adequately prepared for and that is out of sync with one or more of the parties involved can destabilize both persons and relationships and have an unfortunate and destructive outcome. So runaway change is to be avoided at all costs; clearly, the client does not want that to happen! Having already intuitively sensed that he or she has been chosen for change, the client is now being wise enough to seek help in the structuring and management of this experience of change, so that it can be used to the maximum benefit of all parties concerned. The therapist, therefore, is delighted to be attentive to the cues being sent out by the client, whether wittingly or unwittingly.

The therapist is happy to validate and reinforce the client's own instinctive wisdom that he or she should be going slowly and warily at this time. The therapist will reassure the client that it is impossible to go too slowly in this kind of high-voltage intergenerational work. The only significant threat or danger that exists rests in the possibility of going too quickly, given the complexity of family dynamics. When a client first arrives feeling unusually "stuck," he or she may be given an initial assignment to note all the occasions when premature change threatened or came closest to threatening to happen. In the intervals between therapy sessions it may be useful practice for the client simply to note down what defensive measures he or she could have taken if impulsive change had threatened. An additional benefit of this kind of early exercise is that it loosens up the muscles of the client's mind and imagination in preparation for the playful assignments to come.

Change Takes Place on the Client's Personal Timetable

The fourth proposition is the acknowledgment that change takes place on the client's personal timetable, in concert with his or her individual rhythm. The determining reference point at all times is the client's timing and no one else's, certainly not the group's timing or the consultant's. (The consultant may check the clock from time to time, and even ask if he or she is reading it right, but will not try to move the hands, except maybe occasionally to correct his or her own watch.) Notice, incidentally, that the client's timetable may well have been predetermined from the foundation of the world—and who can fight that? This means that there may well be delays or wasted time that the client will simply have to suffer through. Clients, of course, cannot slow down the process any more than they can speed it up in any particular way. At best, the client can simply let change happen as it is going to happen and perhaps try to cooperate with it. Consequently, there are certain maneuvers, routines, and assignments that the client will simply go through willy-nilly, if only to kill time. (The fact that not all of these six propositions are consistent with one another logically is of little consequence, since they do hang together very nicely psychologically for most clients. Anyone who has difficulty with the apparent inconsistency can be congratulated for a perceptiveness that predicts exceptional change. Anyway, inconsistency simply underscores the complexity.)

Understandably, there are clients who will get nervous at this point. They will remind the therapist that they have previously spent considerable energy and money in getting pretty much nowhere in their attempt to resolve their problems. The therapist can respond that this is exactly the point being made. "You simply cannot do much to influence your predestined timetable. However," the therapist may add, "for some reason I have a strong feeling as I listen to you that your time of waiting is almost over and that you are right on the edge of a breakthrough. Indeed, you are *trembling on the edge*, one might almost say."

Clients who respond in the opposite way, that is, the few for whom therapy is a way of life or a pleasant regular "date," can be reassured that they can indeed continue this process on into their next incarnation. If change should begin to feel irresistible, there can always be a referral. Moreover, even if these clients should make no significant change in relationships with parents in this lifetime, they can at least die happy in the knowledge that they will have remained consistently loyal to the family code to the very end. Of course, if the parents should happen to die first, then the client can always look forward to the remaining 5, 10, or 15 good years left, which he or she can devote to personal purposes. That isn't so bad! The occasional client for whom being in therapy is life's vocation should be reminded to manage the change process in as hesitant and modest a way as will make it possible to continue in therapy for the foreseeable future without undue embarrassment. The consultant should be alert to the possibility that a few clients cannot accept this much empathy and may insist on making some token changes in behavior. C'est la vie!

Multiple Assignments as the Dynamic of Change

The therapist will explain that during this work he or she will offer many assignments to be practiced inside and completed outside the office. This is the primary dynamic of the therapy. These assignments usually transpire in relationships with parents, spouse (or lover), boss, or colleagues. The therapist may explain—indeed, do so in all honesty—that he or she will probably not initially understand the full purpose of every assignment any more than the client does. So they will simply both have to take it on trust. The really good assignment, when it comes along, will have an emotional hook in it that engages the client. It will usually have something absurd about it that tickles the funny bone and is also in this way engaging. In anticipation of these assignments, which will evolve in the small group, the therapist will explain to the client as follows:

"These are assignments that surprisingly, you will tell me to tell you. They will initially come probably from your unconscious to my unconscious, then to my conscious, and finally back to your unconscious from me. This means that they may only make sense to both of us in retrospect. I'll probably know *what* they are to be but not *why*. However, you'll know *why* even though initially you will not know *what*. So the construction of these assignments is a team effort between us. As soon as I know *what*, I'll tell you.

"Now it may take you some time to discover what it is that you alone know about the *why* of the assignment, and then you can tell me. I shall then have thoughts about all of this to pass on back to you. Sometimes these are like time capsules that you swallow whole now even though they do not begin to work until later, as they release the good stuff gradually over time."

Parents Are Already Ready and Waiting

The therapist may further explain that many of these assignments now being anticipated will have to do with the client's parents. The therapist will explain that, as a rule, parents are already prepared and waiting for these assignments. They are often asking themselves about son or daughter, "I wonder what is keeping him or her?" At the same time, parents being the good parents that most parents are, are also very concerned, as the therapist is, that son or daughter not proceed so fast that he or she is no longer reasonably comfortable with the self. As a consequence, the parent will frequently and sometimes rigorously test the client's emotional readiness for change.

If a parent appears to be unduly slow in responding to an invitation or a suggestion or question, even appears unwilling to participate, then the client needs to do one or both of two things. First, he or she should thank the parents for their sensitivity and generosity of attitude. Whether this thank-you is actually spoken to the parent or simply noted inwardly in the client's mind will be left to the discretion of the client. Second, in the event of persistent parental hesitation to participate, the client should ask himself or herself, "Why am I still continuing to require them to behave in this way?" Now, of course, good parenting is a skill and an attribute that becomes deeply internalized with time. It follows, therefore, that parents will naturally continue to protect their offspring in these ways, most often without even knowing that they are doing it and usually declining any recognition for it. The client will simply have to put up with this. For such is the commitment and sacrifice of parents!

The good news is, I tell my clients, that this is a drama that all parties can survive and exit from while still on their feet. But, at the same time, the client can keep in mind that even if they don't—well, everyone has got to go sometime. Incidentally, hasn't the client noticed ambulances with active sirens and lights, running frantically throughout every big city ever visited, and wondered who was inside? Well, these are parents responding in shock to the behavior of sons and daughters carrying out assignments of the sort soon to be recommended to the client. Still, everything will probably be okay.

As these ideas work together to create an ambience for the psychotherapy, the client hears these various comments not as literal facts but, rather, as an alternatively amusing and alarming litany of encouragement and reassurance about what will be a demanding but nevertheless safe process with, in all probability, a good outcome. The central dynamic of the stance taken is that every client until found otherwise by a jury (or small group) of his or her peers is *trembling on the edge* of change, an edge from which it is probably already too late to draw back. This is a ready atmosphere for those autohypnotic experiences from which changes in emotion, attitude, and behavior more easily flow.

Staging Notes: Four Assumptions about the Therapeutic Interaction

The ambience of this style of psychotherapy activity is influenced by four assumptions, which are described in the following paragraphs.

Bypass the Rational Level in Self and Client

The first of these assumptions is that it is important both for client and therapist to be often willing to bypass the rational process. Whitaker (1975) has noted that a therapist who stays rational cannot help clients who are stuck in their own rationality. This approach is reminiscent of the story-telling style of the Muslim mystics known as Sufis. Sufi teacher Idries Shah (1980) describes it as the practice of "nonsequential thinking." (There are, obviously, a variety of ways to encourage second-order change, and they began a long time ago.) While the therapist stays at a rational level, the client can always respond by pointing out that he or she has already thought of the behavior suggested—indeed, may well have already tried it, to no avail—or perhaps has already thought about why it would not or should not work in the future.

In standing ready to bypass the rational process at the drop of a hat (or a Kleenex), the therapist makes two further and related assumptions. The first is that the personal narrative in life belonging to the client is but a "constructed reality" and, moreover, a story that exists nowhere other than in the client's mind. Even there it may be unclear, unformed, and inconsistent. The therapist will of course take the client very seriously, in the sense of being sensitive to and empathic with his or her innermost feelings and deeply emotionalized attitudes. Carl Rogers continues to be right. The internal frame of reference is indeed "the supreme vantage point from which to understand the client" (Rogers, 1951). Milton Erickson is rarely thought of as a professional bedfellow with Rogers. But he resonated to this comment when he wrote (letter to the author, December 1978), saying, "The most important question facing family therapy today is the same as the most important question facing all of psychotherapy. That is, how can we know and be sure that we know just what the client means by the words which he or she uses." The consultant will listen carefully to the nuances of the client's language but will usually not take the story itself either literally or unduly seriously.

These are glad tidings that can bring great joy, not to mention relief. If the client does, in fact, make up his or her own story (that is to say, personal history), then the story (that is to say, history) can be changed. History can be rewritten. This is startlingly good news. Psychotherapy now becomes a matter of training individuals to be more open-minded and skeptical historians. The client becomes increasingly agnostic about personal history even as he or she, paradoxically enough, becomes increasingly confident about the future. This is a client *trembling on the edge of falling in love with the future*. The second related assumption is that since we make up the story, it follows that we do therefore construct for ourselves most of our own dilemmas and paradoxes in life. The psychotherapy process can, as a result, often usefully be seen (or made up) to be a sustained counterparadoxical response (Selvini-Palazzoli et al., 1978).

It is now a cliché to say that much of human thinking and perceiving goes on outside of awareness. It is less obvious that honesty is frightening because of the fragility of the ego. Moreover, the almost universal presence of intrapsychic power and control issues compels people to reject or at least dull the impact of outside suggestions. This is why playful and "absurd" interventions, which bypass the rational process, are regularly called for. These are sometimes perceived by the observer as "devious." However, in the therapeutic milieu being described here the therapist is always on the lookout for and instantly ready to let the client come right on the inside of things. In other words, it is not the case that a paradoxical intervention is being crafted by the therapist, whether alone or in consultaiton with colleagues, quite apart from the client. This is, rather, a process that evolves spontaneously out of the bonding relationship between therapist and client. The therapist is deliberately allowing himself or herself to free-associate and thus generate surprises that cannot be predicted by the client. Therefore, the client cannot as easily parry these or make a scripted response. This creates a moment of uncertainty and confusion, the precondition of creativity and change. There is immediately at hand the possibility for something completely different. The client is trembling on the edge.

Interventions Go from the Unconscious of the Client to the Unconscious of the Therapist, to the Conscious of the Therapist, and Finally Transformed Back to the Unconscious of the Client

These nonrational responses or interventions by the therapist do not go from the conscious mind of the therapist to the unconscious of the client. Rather, they move through free association mostly from the unconscious to the conscious mind of the therapist and then directly back to the unconscious of the client via unexplained assignments. It is assumed that the therapist, of course, has previously picked up this information unconsciously from the unconscious of the client. This usually happens in response to a direct question from the therapist. The transaction is, therefore, most accurately described as beginning with a direct and rational question from the conscious mind of the therapist that is addressed to the conscious mind of the client. The client responds very often on both conscious and unconscious levels. Ideally, the therapist keeps the mind in neutral and does not start thinking too hard about the manifest content of what the client is saying. The unconscious part of the response is then picked up by the "idling" unconscious of the therapist and is expressed through his or her own free associations. These associations come through initially without much conscious understanding of these sequences by the therapist. Frequently, they are first experienced as ideas for assignments to give the client. These assignments give useful feedback to both the conscious and the unconscious mind of the client and are frequently antidotes for "natural" paradox.

When these interventions are comments rather than assignments, the comments are not addressed from the conscious mind of the therapist to the conscious mind of the client, so they are not experienced as interpretations of the sort that would characterize traditional psychoanalysis or psychoanalytically oriented psychotherapy. For this reason, this kind of intervention is not vulnerable to the usual forms of "resistance" or "denial." That is to say, since no "truth" (or, indeed, proposition of any sort) is being alleged, there is nothing to be rejected or defended against. This can make life a little easier for both parties.

Assignments Are Symbolic Acts That Sabotage the Cognitive Status Quo in the Client's Life

The personal authority therapeutic style consistently produces interventions that take the form of assignments to perform metaphoric or symbolic acts. These acts tend to make the status quo in the client's life untenable, including both the way in which the client talks to the self and the way in which he or she holds the self in relationship to a parent, spouse, employer, or other emotionally charged transference figure. These assignments are conveyed in offbeat ideas that play with the thoughts and language that the client spontaneously uses to create and sustain meanings in his or her mind. This approach frequently sabotages the cognitive structures that hold these meanings in place, thereby pulling the rug out from under the crazy behaviors that flow from them. (These kinds of assignments and their sequelae will be illustrated in Chapter 6.)

This kind of therapy behavior is always an expression of a therapist–client relationship that the client finds safe, empathic, and trustworthy, odd as that may at first seem. Otherwise, it is not likely to work. Erickson (letter to a student, December 1978) insisted that paradox not be learned and used as a technique but that it grow out of the relationship. Whitaker (1980) has suggested that paradox can represent "a failure in caring." These interventions work when the relationship is experienced as safe by the client, perhaps safe because the therapist communicates nonverbally that he or she sees himself or herself in every behavior that the client has tried (it takes one to know one). When it becomes clear that this identification is just not possible, therapist and client are probably out of business together and a referral is in order.

The Use of Humor as the Ultimate Weapon

One final comment should be made about the general ambience of personal authority work and about the assignments in particular. This refers to the use of humor. For many people, and undoubtedly for most people who find their way into psychotherapy, family history is heavily emotion-laden. These emotions include rage and its variations, grief and its various expressions, fear and its derivatives, and despair. Most likely there will be some mixture of these. This is emotionally very toxic and is hard on both client and therapist. The therapist who can consistently show the classical Rogerian "unconditional positive regard" (Rogers, 1951) has not yet been born. And what a way to make a living! Yet, these deeply held feelings cannot be short-circuited; nor can the pain be avoided or forever ignored. But in due course there does come a time when humor is the most appropriate and powerful (and sometimes the only) antidote adequate to the challenge. So a vulnerability to levity, a readiness to laugh, and an absurd quirkiness to the assignments may be just what the doctor orders. Some things are altogether too deadly to stay serious about. There is hope for the client who can see the funny side as well as the poignant and the painful. To be able to laugh about it is to be able, however briefly, to take an observer stance. To be able to take an observer stance is to be halfway home—or, to be more accurate, away from home.

If you, the reader, have found yourself at times a little confused as you have come through this chapter then you got the point about "the paradoxical soul of man."

CHAPTER 5

Auditioning and Casting: Background Preparations for the Conversations with Parents

> Two principles we should always have ready, that there is nothing good or evil save in the will; and that we are not to lead events, but to follow them.
> —Epictetus
> *Discourses* (Book III, Chap. 10)

Production Notes

The argument of this book is that one quite effective way to leave home emotionally is to engage in a radical face-to-face and psychologically surgical conversation with parents. This conversation builds upon itself and is sustained over time. The purpose of this talking is to identify and review the basic relational and political patterns that constitute the dynamics of the relationship between the generations. The five elements of this ongoing conversation are described in the following paragraphs.

Debriefing Parents

The first step of the experience is a detailed debriefing of the parents, much of it conducted individually, about the historic events and sequences of their lives. This will include a delineation of the private inner meanings of these events to each one of them and their subsequent assimilation and resolution of these feelings, or lack thereof.

This proves to be much more than a matter of simple remembering, since to some extent the parent discovers and rediscovers personal meanings of events in a very immediate and moving way.

Assuming an Observer Role

Asking for this information implies the assumption of a more objective posture and more of an observer stance by son or daughter. This in turn begins to increase the sense of differentness or differentiation between the two parties. Simultaneously, it encourages a more compassionate understanding and acceptance of the older by the younger generation. All of this leads to a gradual demystification or de-mythologizing and a humanizing of the person of each parent and of the family of origin as a whole.

Redistribution of Power

This demystification and humanizing results in a redistribution of psychological power across the generational boundary in the direction of an equalization. There is a rebalancing and a redressing with a view to the establishment of a more egalitarian relationship. There is a growing impetus toward the termination of rigid and fixed power boundaries. Overall, the movement is in the direction of psychological equality between the generations.

Dissolving Projective Identification

This new status of peer to one's parents generalizes from the relationships with parents to the world at large. This is particularly so in relationships representing authority and/or nurturance, the traditional responsibilities and characteristics of parents, and nowhere is this more obvious than in the marital relationship. The development of personal authority reduces and minimizes the scope of projective identification and the degree of transference in the relationship with a spouse. This is why in some situations intergenerational family therapy is a more effective intervention into a conflicted marriage than marital therapy itself. When an adult engages in these conversations with parents, he or she first noticeably reduces the amount of projection onto the parents. This then generalizes toward every other significant person in the individual's life.

It may be noted in passing that this way of resolving projection has potential implications for the termination process at the completion of a successful (or, for that matter, unsuccessful) psychoanalytic treatment. Suppose an analyst was willing to be debriefed about the reality of his or her own life by a terminating patient. Not only might it be validating of the treatment gains made by the patient but it could also be an effective way of terminating the transference, often otherwise thought of as interminable or at least incomplete. Debriefing is one way to terminate the hierarchical boundary in the treatment relationship. However, just as most parents respond with apprehension when son or daughter presents the idea of such a conversation, so most psychotherapists practicing intensive psychotherapy are likely to be apprehensive at such a prospect.

Just as a third party consultant can mediate between the generations, a consultant who helps humanize the doctor could help to bring about a good termination in the closing phase of treatment. The psychotherapeutic relationship is invariably somewhat asymmetrical. Most of the time neither party will have the psychological freedom to initiate a transformation of the relationship toward "peerhood". Each may also resent any outside intrusion into the privacy and intimacy of the relationship. But that may be just what the consultant recommends. A brief, skilled, and tactful consultation to the psychotherapeutic relationship, with a view to achieving psychological equality between the parties, may be well worth considering. But this assumes the therapist is on for it!

"Re-mythologizing" Parents

Finally, there is a playful "re-mythologizing" of the person of each parent. As will be described in more detail in the following paragraph, the essence of the change process is the giving up of the need to be parented and the giving up of the "parent as parent." After having completed that task, son or daughter adopts a new stance of acceptance and compassion toward the parent. He or she begins a new venture of rehabilitation and re-mythologizing of this older man and older woman. Everything that has been or now is perceived as admirable about the life or person of either one can be identified and acknowledged and celebrated. Aspects of the hero and the heroine reemerge. Son or daughter falls in love with father and mother again but in a more mature, nonerotic, and less possessive way.

Screening, Selecting, and Assigning the New Client to a Small Family-of-Origin Group

There are several aspects to screening and selecting a new client for a small family-of-origin group.

Assessing the Marriage

The first task is to assess the client's marriage or other significant love relationship. The intention is to evaluate the degree of support and stability or conflict and stress in the relationship. If there does not seem to be adequate support coming from the primary love relationship, the obvious question arises as to whether or not the client can complete the work of therapy effectively without it. It is difficult to fight a war (or transform relationships) simultaneously on two fronts. The question is, How well has the client come to terms with an absence of support in the primary relationship? Some people can do the work well without much spousal support, provided that the partner is at least neutral and not in active opposition to it. If the love relationship is highly volatile or unstable, it is most unlikely that the client can sustain good work with the family of origin. In this circumstance much of the client's energy will be diverted to dealing with the primary relationship. The level of threat to the latter will frequently make any significant risk taking impossible with the former. It is a rare client who can cope well with concurrently destabilizing situations on two of the most crucial emotional boundaries in life.

With a view toward stabilizing the marriage, the consultant may recommend a preparatory conjoint therapy for the couple. Alternatively, he or she may simply recommend letting some time go by and holding things "steady as you go" in the family of origin until it becomes clearer how the client's love relationship is going to evolve. What the consultant categorically will not do, acting out of loyalty as a family therapist, is offer a family-of-origin experience that will support the client in moving unilaterally away from the marriage. In assessing the current love relationship, the key information is, of course, the client's own view of the relationship. The one exception to this is where the client is obviously struggling unrealistically to put the best possible face on things while his or her heart is clearly not quite in what is being said. This situation will require some further exploration before assignment to a group.

Briefing and Debriefing the Spouse

The spouse or "significant other" of the potential client is an excellent, indeed essential, source of information and should be included at some appropriate point in the screening and selection exercise. There are several reasons to debrief (and brief) the spouse:

1. The spouse is likely to be the most informed person with regard to the client's current life situation in general and specific problems in particular.
2. The spouse will have an important perspective to offer on the character of the love relationship between the two.
3. The spouse will provide an interesting and not infrequently provocative perspective on the client's family of origin and the client's relationship to it.
4. The question to be pursued is, Does the spouse agree with the idea of therapy and think that this will help and does he or she therefore, support it? Furthermore, what questions or particular fears does the spouse have about the prospect of the client entering therapy? This is an opportunity for the consultant not simply to provide reassurance but to actively recruit the spouse on the side of the treatment program.

The Ground Rules for the Therapy

The next task is to describe the therapy procedures to the potential client. First, it is explained that the therapy will not focus on the client's marriage. Not only is such a focus an inappropriate way to seek to bring redress to the marriage, but such an attempt is unacceptable out of loyalty on the therapist's part to the absent spouse. This does not mean that comments about the marriage are forbidden or will not be acknowledged. It is simply that such comments will not become the sustained focus for the work; nor will the consultant or the group take sides in the matter. Furthermore, it is explained that if any of the three parties involved—that is, the client, the client's spouse, or the consultant—should become concerned about the marriage, any one of them can initiate a conjoint consultation.

The consultant commits to being unabashedly attentive to the undertones of communication about the ongoing marital process. If the marriage should enter any crisis, attention to that takes priority over anything else that is going on for this client. There is little else that can encourage a general sense of trust in the consultant quite as much as this opportunity to observe directly the consultant's loyalty to the client's spouse, the marriage, and the family around it. It is a general rule of this work that whatever matter is of most pressing concern to a client on any given day has first priority for attention. It matters not whether it is personal, relational, or work-related, or whether it relates to the past, present, or future.

It is further explained to both client and spouse that this work will probably destabilize the marriage relationship—if not sooner, then later. If the client significantly renegotiates the political patterns between the self and the parents, there will inevitably be repercussions for the political structures of the marriage. As a rule, neither party can really grasp the implications of this in advance. However, when things do become stormy, the memory of this prediction and benevolent warning and of their own "informed consent" is of considerable value to both partners. This awareness can generate some additional resources for riding out the storm.

Finally, during this preliminary screening, the spouse is informed that he or she can attend any meeting of the small group at any time and without advance notice. The group, of course, has been informed that this is a standing ground rule. The spouse obviously cannot attend regularly except by joining a group. But he or she can attend occasionally if alarmed or puzzled by what is happening. This author has routinely offered this recourse over many years. As of this date not one person has taken up the invitation. However, because it is clearly an offer made in good faith, there is something powerfully reassuring about it to the spouse. It underscores an important intention of the screening procedure: to make it explicit to both parties that there is nothing secretive about the treatment program. There is no aspect of it from which the spouse will be necessarily excluded. This does not mean that the client must share every thought and feeling with the spouse. Sometimes he or she will be specifically advised not to talk about something and, if need be, to make an issue of this with the partner. The point is, rather, that nothing that is demonstrably of importance to the life and future of the spouse will be hidden from him or her.

With this in mind, the client is advised at the beginning not to reveal to the consultant or the group any information that he or she feels must of necessity be concealed from the spouse; again, it is not that everything must be told. It is, rather, that neither the consultant nor the group should be immobilized by having some compelling information that must not be known by the spouse. One is reminded here that John Warkentin is reputed to have said to a client on some such occasion, "Why do you want to be more intimate with me than with your spouse?" It will also be pointed out to the client that carrying a secret into a new group is not a very smart way to begin. If a spouse becomes sufficiently distressed or motivated to do so, he or she may join another group or together go to a couples group, or be referred to a close colleague for consultation. (The term *close colleague* refers to a professional who is informed about and sympathetic to one's way of working and so can collaborate effectively.)

Assessing the Parents

Another focus for the screening conversation is an inquiry about the ongoing lives of the client's parents. The debriefing goes like this:

"Are both your parents alive? Still living together? Working or retired? How is their marriage as you see it? Anyone else in the house? How are their finances? How is the physical and mental health of each parent presently? What is the character, content, and frequency of the ongoing contact between you and your parents? How are siblings involved in these patterns? Is your spouse involved with your family with an unusual amount of energy or unusually strong attitudes? Are grandparents still alive?"

Assessing the Client's Motivation

Next, the consultant pursues the client's spontaneous understanding of, anticipation about, motivation for, and emotional readiness to engage in this work. This is valuable even when the therapist is the one to have first suggested this work as a possible response to a presenting problem that was framed in some other fashion. The idea may come first from the consultant, but the commitment and the change can only come from the client. Occasionally, a potential client shows strongly ambivalent feelings about entering family of origin work. The strong positive feelings augur well, but the strong hesitation incites the therapist to second thoughts. A useful response to this quandary may be to tell the client that in the therapist's opinion, he or she is a long shot as a potential beneficiary from this kind of work. In fact, the therapist would rate it as about a 1 in 100 chance. However, on the other side and for what it is worth, this client does clearly have four of the five characteristics that tend to identify that rare 100th person. The client's response will be a useful guide.

Explaining the Therapy Procedure to the Client

There now follows a brief but explicit description of the program and the routines upon which the client is considering embarking.

"The work will take place in a very small group of four or five people. You begin by writing out an autobiography, and you will be asked at some point to present it to the group. This autobiography begins with earliest memories and should outline the history of your relationships with your parents, right up to the present day.

"Next comes your evaluation of the current status of these intergenerational relationships and the related reasons for engaging in this work.

"Once you are actively involved with the small group, you will receive many suggested assignments. These include writing letters, making audio taped letters to parents to be presented in the group, making and taping telephone conversations with parents, observational and exploratory visits to the parents' home, and chats with siblings and other persons who might prove to be important sources of family information.

"All of this is by way of preparation for the construction of a detailed agenda. This will be used to organize the direct conversations with parents, which will eventually be held here in this office if both you and they are agreeable to it.

"If you do come here for these conversations, it won't be until you feel very comfortable with the idea and feel ready for it."

To the extent it is possible to do so in anticipation, the listening client will now have some sense of what is involved in this family of origin therapy in a small group. Since aspects of the description can be a little chilling to some clients, the consultant again reassures the listener that each person is working on his or her own timetable and that no one will be asked to engage in any assignment until it feels reasonably comfortable to do so. For that matter, nothing that has just been described is absolutely mandatory, rather, these suggestions represent a myriad of opportunities, some of which will in due course be selected by the client.

Matching the Client to the Group

The next screening task is to match the new client to the most appropriate available group, occasionally waiting for an opening in a more compatible group. Some clients seek a same-sex group and some a mixed gender group. Other important variables are age, socioeconomic status, education and general sophistication, and degree of "psychological mindedness." There is also the measure of psychological strength or emotional dependency, in the potential member as well as in a given group. This factor will influence both the range of the work and the speed of the group.

All these matters are evaluated by the consultant. This is done in collaboration with both the client and the potential group. There is also a guidance that comes from an "intuitive," which is to say, not fully rational, level on the part of the therapist. This has to do with expectations about chemistry and shared, if as yet unrevealed, history. This more esoteric but invaluable skill is acquired by the consultant through experience. The good news is that this learning begins on day one in the professional life of the therapist. Despite this, misadventures and incongruities do sometimes occur. In such cases the beginning client will move from one potential new "family" to another. This may be traumatic, but the drama itself becomes more grist for the therapeutic mill. It generates a dynamic, whether welcome or not, that provides the new client with an emotional flying start on the work. Like most everything else, it can be seen as an asset as readily as a liability.

Client's First Meeting with the New Group

Upon first attending the group, a new member will be invited to be present merely as an observer, at least until the closing minutes of this first meeting. The other members will go on about business as usual, much as any family will make special allowances for the "new baby." The client is already being indoctrinated into an "observer" stance, an essential skill in the pursuit of the work to follow. Toward the end of the session, the newcomer will deliver driver's license information about the self, including current family structure and the work situation, if any. This is followed by a summary of the current politics of the family of origin as this person understands it. Then, the client will declare his or her motivations and goals for joining the group. The group members will respond by clarifying the information received and filling out the gaps, usually ending by saying, "Welcome to the club." There being no objection voiced from the group, the consultant will now inquire whether the client thinks that he or she has ended up more or less in the right place. If the client responds affirmatively and without undue hesitation, then he or she has now joined the group and is in business.

The expectations have been made crystal clear. The new client is now trembling on the edge and teetering on the brink, poised for change. The die has already been cast. The outcome is now inevitable, even involuntary. There is not too much that the client can do, either to speed things up or to slow them down. The work has a life of its own. This then is the ambience that is created as the new member joins his or her new "family." All of this encourages a high sense of mission on the part of the client and initiates a commitment to make this work central in his or her life. From this point on every contact, however casual, with any member of the family of origin represents an exciting opportunity for new information, clearer understanding, and changing relationships. From the moment the client joins the small group, I change my title and present myself as consultant rather than as therapist. This is done for two reasons. First, it affirms the personal authority of the client as someone in charge of his or her own life, including any changes to be made in it. Secondly, it acknowledges the role of the group itself as consultant to each member, with the paid professional just one part of it, even if the lead consultant. Now, as NASA likes to say, "we have lift-off."

Personal Authority Work in Small Groups

THE LOGISTICS OF THE GROUP PROCESS

The small group meets for a weekly session lasting 90 minutes. It is composed usually of four members, occasionally of five. The rationale is that four or five people can each do a useful piece of work every week in a session of 90 minutes. The format is therefore somewhat stylized in that each person has a certain range of minutes to speak, followed by group feedback; then the opportunity passes on to the next member. This procedure is modified when someone has an evolving crisis to present or an event that provokes intense emotion. In this case, that person will get some extra time borrowed from someone else. This indebtedness will be repaid in subsequent sessions.

This small group method can be contrasted with traditional group therapy in several ways (Williamson & Malone, 1983). (1) Little focus is placed on group interaction. Instead, members are encouraged to place interpersonal issues within the family of origin. (2) Transference reactions are discouraged and are likely to be reframed in ways that cause them to dissolve. (3) The group process is highly stylized rather than unstructured, and there is a ritualistic use of time. (4) The leader is quite directive and goal-oriented, and especially interested in current behavioral transactions with members of the family of origin of each group member.

When a group is newly formed, the likelihood is that all members will start attending on the same day. However, the group is open-ended, and each person is on his or her own personal timetable. This means that members terminate individually, and as someone terminates another person is added to the group. In time the group will completely reconstitute itself physically, even as it reconstructs itself psychologically. An average length of stay in the group is 9 to 12 months for those who get hooked on the process. If someone begins with noticeable hesitation, it is suggested that he or she commit for a trial period of four visits and then make a decision to continue or withdraw.

With regard to the different phases of the therapy, a typical progression would be as follows. The client spends 2–3 months handling the intense and negative emotionality presently felt toward parents; this is the experience of catharsis. Next the client might spend 2–3 months actively engaging the parents in the process through phone calls and letter writing and visits to the parental home. The next 2–3 months are spent on the preparation of a detailed agenda, leading up to the in-office visit with parents and the consultant. Finally, the client might spend a concluding 2–3 months assimilating all that has happened, generalizing it into all important relationships, and preparing to fire the consultant and the group.

The client will be asked not to be in any other ongoing therapy with another therapist during this period. The exception to this occurs when a client's work in the group appears to be destabilizing or bringing undue stress to the marriage. The client is then encouraged to seek a marital consultation, whether with the group leader or a colleague consultant.

If the client's personal timetable or financial timetable or work timetable will not permit this 8–12 months' commitment, there is an alternative available. A client may meet for a more limited number of sessions, either alone with the consultant or as a member of a small group that has limited itself from its inception to a shorter number of total sessions. Whether the work is done individually or in such a time-limited small group, the client will pick out a particular issue or issues to be worked on. Therapeutic attention will then be focused on these issues in a very directed and consistent fashion. If it is the therapist's judgment that the essential presenting problem(s) cannot be helped significantly in this way, the client will be so informed and advised of other options.

ASSIGNMENT TO A PERSONAL AUTHORITY GROUP VERSUS MARITAL THERAPY

Some clients come to their first appointment clearly asking, whether directly or indirectly, for some kind of family of origin consultation. Such a client is naturally likely to be prepared for and then assigned to a small personal authority group. On the other hand, one or both members of couples who come to the consultant's office seeking marital consultation for moderate to severe marital conflict will, from time to time, be referred to a family of origin group. The question immediately arises as to how this differential judgment will be made. When the following three conditions are met, referring a client to a personal authority group has usually proved to be a good decision: (1) when the marital problems are chronic and repeated attempts to achieve resolution, whether with or without outside help, have proved futile; (2) when it is clearly visible that the client has a continuing conflicted relationship with one or both parents and presents evidence, wittingly or unwittingly, that these issues are actively interacting with the marital problems (the connection is presented as not so much causal as contextual); (3) when clients appear to be looking not so much *at* as *through* and *beyond* each other, even as they repeat old war stories to which even they themselves do not appear to be fully attentive (in other words, there is circumstantial evidence present in the room that one client—or both—is looking right through the partner at a more distant figure); the final moment of validation comes when a client responds positively to the therapist's suggestion that marital issues may become more amenable to resolution if certain family of origin issues are addressed first.

It may be noted in passing that when the treatment of choice is straight marital therapy, the focus of the work is in sharp contrast to personal authority work. In this case, therapeutic attention is directed almost exclusively to the current ongoing interactions between the partners. Each is asked to keep a marital diary with yellow-markered highlights so as to be able to recreate the details and the mood of the week that has passed since the last visit. These reports generate playful assignments to be carried out during the next week. These assignments make it increasingly difficult for the couple to continue to perpetuate the same marital interactions and therefore the same old conflicts. The couple is under pressure to come up with some new ones. The scene is set for change.

Couples are sometimes recommended to couples groups to do personal authority work. This work is usually high voltage and exciting. There is a tendency for the immediacy and the power of the marital relationships to overwhelm everything else. Persons who are already reasonably well differentiated within their marriages can use this method extremely well. Very fused couples will do better working separately provided that the therapist embodies a strong loyalty to the marriage. This does not mean that the marriage should be maintained at all costs but simply that both spouses should be consulted at all times.

BRIEF PERSONAL AUTHORITY CONSULTATIONS AND INTERVENTIONS

It is possible to offer a brief ad hoc consultation to a client upon request, using the general theoretical background and method of personal authority work. For example, a client comes in presenting an ongoing conflict with parents focused on where he and his family will spend Thanksgiving Day and attend Thanksgiving dinner. This is the issue. The client can be seen for four to six sessions using the following interventions: First, the client will be given some help in becoming less emotionally reactive to parents. Second, he can be helped to reconstruct the problem itself as being blessed with parents whose caring simply will not quit. Third, behaviors will be suggested to him so that he can relate to his parents as a peer on this matter. (While this new stance of "peerhood" may or may not last, at least it can last long enough to resolve this particular problem.) Last, he can be helped to create new language for use with his parents as a way to bring a little playfulness to the situation. This defuses it somewhat and introduces more flexibility of attitude on both sides. For example, he might apologetically whisper that the reason he and his family are going to his wife's parents for this upcoming Thanksgiving is simply that they seem to be so emotionally dependent and insecure; it looks like they may not be able to survive this holiday without the supporting presence of their daughter and her husband. The son is glad that his parents are more mature than this. Alternatively, he might explain that he and his family are spending Thanksgiving at home this year. The article he has just read has recommended doing this when the marriage shows two or more of the five critical signs of being in a "pseudo-prestressful condition." Just a few visits may resolve such a presenting family-of-origin problem, provided that the experience can be kept from becoming so interesting that the client wants to do more.

CHAPTER 6

Black Out Sketches: The Group at Play

"When *I* use a word," Humpty Dumpty said, in a rather scornful tone, "it means just what I choose it to mean—neither more nor less."

"The question is," said Alice, "whether you *can* make words mean so many different things."

"The question is," said Humpty Dumpty, "which is to be master—that's all."

—Lewis Carroll (1871)
Through the Looking Glass (Chap. 6)

Playful Interventions, Assignments, and Perturbations

Autonomous or differentiated behavior is always so labeled in relationship to some given environment, which is itself always changing. Thus, achieving personal authority means making a change in relational patterns, even as the whole context of the changing relationship is itself simultaneously changing (Taggart, 1985). Since no initiative by son or daughter can force its way inside the parental system or bring change in the parent's behavior (Keeney, 1983), it has been suggested that behavioral interactions between two autonomous systems should not be called interventions or inputs but, rather, "perturbations" (Maturana & Varela, 1980). Some of the assignments to be described in this chapter, might in this sense be regarded as perturbations. In fact, a core intention of small group work is to create perturbations in families.

The internal map of the world carried in the individual mind determines how that person thinks, feels, acts in the world, and produces symptoms. As the character of this model becomes clear in the therapeutic consultation, the scene is ripe for reframing. As fluctuations occur in the intergenerational relational system, they can be amplified to produce confusion or chaos. This chaos will eventually give way to a new order as the family changes (Dell & Goolishian, 1981). The new organization in the family can be seen as an ongoing coevolution of the generations.

The most important goal of absurd interventions is to disrupt the cognitive structures that hold in place and sustain client behaviors that are not conducive to client well-being. As these cognitive structures and the contents that they hold begin to dissolve, clients may experience the feeling that they are beginning to lose their minds. Although uncomfortable and sometimes frightened, when feeling confused and uncertain in this way, the client is at the very edge of creativity and, therefore, transformation. However benevolent the intention, psychological interpretation that is too dissonant and too far removed emotionally from the client's sense of self can often be accurately labeled as psychological rape, at least as far as the client's subjective experience is concerned.

By contrast, playful and absurd interventions bring many possibilities into the client's conscious mind but do so in a way that gives the client total freedom to accept or reject any inferred or implied proposition. Or the client may be offered an idea for consideration at some later date, when he or she feels more comfortable in contemplating such a possibility. The challenge is to make these interventions in such a way that they not only pick up on the client's unconscious conflicts (rather than the consultant's) but also so that the conversation between therapist and client maintains an aura of credibility throughout. Escalating the absurdity while maintaining the credibility creates a refreshing challenge as a healing balm for the consultant's boredom.

The underlying presumption is, of course, that most of life is handled most of the time by most people at an unconscious level. And most of the time it may be better not to know this, or at least to pretend not to know it. This deliberate not knowing is a benevolent example of the extraordinary human skill we possess of not letting beliefs and values interfere unduly with the conveniences of everyday living. In this regard, it is crucial to make a distinction between being paradoxical in a formal sense and being playful. Being paradoxical is not a healthy way for the consultant to live—nor anyone else for that matter. Although human intimacy is laced with natural paradox, willful intentional paradox is antithetical to intimacy. The chronic and unrelieved use of paradox can express disillusionment with human relationships and can be an alternative to caring. For that matter, paradox is always the second choice even in the practice of psychotherapy. It is always preferable to deal with clients in a straightforward and direct manner. Unfortunately, this is not always possible or effective. By contrast with formal paradox, playfulness in which both parties are on the inside of the joke is almost always appropriate and productive. It is not only life-giving but is also romantic and is therefore an attractive characteristic of love relationships.

Practice Change

One general assignment with repetitive usefulness is to assign "practice change." The assignment of practice or "pretend" change enables the client to do certain things that he or she has been resisting doing because there is some apprehension and fearfulness associated with them. A calming assumption is that because this is practice change, the change will not stick or persist. Moreover, it is being openly acknowledged that the client has made no lasting commitment to this change and is taking no personal responsibility either for it or its consequences at this time. If there should be intense repercussions, it will be easy for the client to say, "Just kidding" or "Can't you take a joke?" A refinement or escalation of this intervention is to assign different *levels* of practice change. For example, there is beginning practice change, midrange practice, and, of course, advanced practice or pretend change. As an alternative, a client already clearly changing but feeling conflicted or guilty about it can be given an assignment to pretend *not* to be changing, while allowing only a very small, secret healthy inner core of the self to know that change is indeed taking place.

A particularly fruitful application of this assignment occurs in "practice relationships." They give a client the freedom to be spontaneous without having a sense that the stakes are too high. A marriage may be framed retrospectively as a practice marriage. An example of a practice marriage may occur when the parties are acting as though it will not ever be possible to bring any real change to the marriage. This practice marriage is clearly intended to enable them to get ready for the next marriage, which is, of course, more likely to work because of this practice. Whether or not that next marriage is to each other remains to be seen. At the very worst, a marriage that a couple cannot seem to redeem and yet cannot leave can be used as a practice

marriage for the next incarnation. At that time, a happy marriage will
be a more likely possibility, thanks to this practice. All is not lost!

Framing Dreams

A second useful general strategy is to encourage clients to bring in
dreams when these spontaneously occur. Since dreams are by
definition ambiguous stimuli and since they need to be decoded in
some fashion in order to be useful, they present an outstanding
opportunity for imaginative framing and reframing. The spontaneous
free associations of the client to the dream do, of course, give a
guiding clue. But provided that one stays within the bounds of
credibility, the consultant can create a meaning around the dream
that validates both the progress the client has made and any new
moves that he or she seems capable of making. In this regard, an
experienced small group learns to respond with free associations to
any client's presentation of aspects of his or her story. This response
is obviously useful to both the client and the respondent and can lead
to interesting discussions.

The Angel of the Lord

A third intervention of general usefulness happens when the consultant has an overnight visit from "the Angel of the Lord." This
benevolent figure only appears when there is something to be said to
a client that needs to be said or, more importantly, needs to be heard
with a little more authority and credibility than the consultant acting
alone can muster. The Angel of the Lord almost always brings good
news. For example: "The Angel of the Lord said to tell you that he
recently dropped in at your parents' home and was quite taken aback
to discover how proud they have become of their daughter. But that's
all he would say. I couldn't get another word out of him."

Leading the Witness

Typically a small group session begins with the consultant asking,
"Who's up?" or "Who's on first?" or simply "Open for business," or
"The floor is open." Members will speak in whatever order, and each
will be acknowledged for either the good work that has in fact been
done or for having given evidence of good work about to begin. The
third possibility is that the client will have given evidence of being in
the space that is right next door to the space in which good work is
about to be done. The client's timing is always the correct timing,

even though a client who appears to be loitering will be given many opportunities to review the personal timetable and consider upping the RPMs. A (playful) background assumption is that the course and conduct of the client's therapy has been predetermined from the beginning of time. (Wow! Am I that important?) Consequently, when a client simply does not do an assignment, at least he or she has successfully completed one of the preplanned weeks of not doing it. He or she has now moved effectively, if unwittingly, one week closer to doing it.

The client will receive feedback for the manifest content of his or her presentation and probably some additional response to the unspoken and usually unconscious communication. This is usually followed by an assignment that, more often that not, has been triggered by the unconscious communication. (These assignments will be illustrated presently.) The pervasive and persisting assumption throughout the group process is that every client is both already changing and *trembling on the edge and teetering on the brink* of even more significant and worthwhile change. This notion of "trembling on the edge" becomes the watch-word for the group.

Then there is a style of intervention used by the consultant that could be described as repeatedly offering a comment that is discontinuous with the ongoing conversation. Common examples follow:

"Is there anyone in the group who thinks that in the session after the next one you may say something that you will tend to regret later or perhaps want to change in some way after you have said it? You might all be thinking about that possibility this week."

"Let's make it easy on ourselves. What are the things we should not talk about today? Who in particular should not talk about which things? We will need to discuss whether we have agreement on the reasons why certain persons should not talk about particular things today."

"Is there anything that anybody thinks that I might be tempted to project onto the group or someone in the group today or perhaps next time?"

"There is a fascinating possibility that has not yet really properly occurred to me. But what I've come close to thinking is that I would not be surprised if part of this group has been thinking about it or at least something quite like it. What do you think?"

"Here's an idea that I don't really want to mention too strongly in front of [a given group member] just yet. But I'll go ahead and mention it to the rest of you so that you can all be thinking about it, and I'll bring it up again at a later time."

(*to a group member*): "Now here's an idea that has just occurred to me and that in a way would make an awful lot of sense, except I can't quite see how it fits in with you and your family."

"Who would like to talk about something inconsequential today and save all the good stuff for next week, when it will probably be raining?"

(*to a group member*): "Let me tell you something that I'm pretty sure you are not saying or feeling, and then you think about it and let me know if I'm missing something important."

"Let me explain that I'm only presenting this notion because I feel strong encouragement from the group to say something like this to you. So I feel very hesitant about this idea, since I don't really know for sure where it's coming from."

"You know when I think about it, what's really so wrong about devoting your first 50 or 60 years to pleasing your parents? I mean, the chances are you'll still have 15 or 20 good years to devote to yourself. That way everybody can be happy."

As long as he or she does not get caught in truly believing in any particular model, the consultant can respond to both conscious and unconscious material, respond to either intrapsychic process or systemic process, be hierarchical or totally democratic, have all the answers or no answers, be purely reflective in the Rogerian sense, or offer playful "interpretations." Ideally, what the consultant chooses to do or to be, is the thing that seems most likely to be useful in the moment and in the given situation. This is "situational therapy." However, this versatility is clearly a developmental skill acquired over time. The downside to such an approach is, of course, that the therapist forfeits the right to be right, in terms of his or her interpretations and interventions. So one has to be able to sustain such a narcissistic wound.

This style of playful intervention will go over well with most clients, and perhaps most therapists. But even among clients there are exceptions. It should not be used with the very naive, the openly paranoid, or those who walk in with their transference showing. It is not likely to be effective with the humorless, and it may backfire with the hostile client.

Scenes from a Group

The real-life interventions that follow, illustrate the group at play and fall into the categories of neutralizing intimidation, paradox, reframing, absurdity, small perturbations, and short takes. It should be remembered that all of these transactions occur in the context of the rapport established in the therapeutic relationship. Read in isolation they can seem insensitive or just plain silly.

Neutralizing Intimidation

MOTHERS'S BIRTHDAY

A female client was very intimidated by her mother; the role-played telephone conversation was intended to start to dissolve this intense intimidation. Since this very day happened to be mother's birthday, this was a birthday phone call:

> DAUGHTER (*played by consultant*): (*singing*) Happy birthday, dear Sara, happy birthday to you. Well, old girl, you must feel like hell. I mean, another whole year gone down the drain. Not so many more left! I was thinking about that today and thinking how awful it must be to be your age. By the way, did you get any presents?
>
> MOTHER (*played by daughter*): Daddy is taking me out to dinner.
>
> DAUGHTER: Daddy! I thought he was dead . . . oh, you mean your husband? Well, that's a relief. I thought for a moment, I might have to be my father's granddaughter.

The client, of course, will not make this call or even anything like it to her mother. But being able just to entertain the fantasy of such a call, and live to remember it, begins to neutralize the intimidation.

OVERWEIGHT

One day a fellow in the group said, "My overweight (268 pounds at 5 feet 8 inches) has been and continues to be a family secret. Just the thought of talking to my parents about it openly shakes me to my inner core and frightens me." The assignment was to tell each parent separately on the phone that he had just found out that he is overweight. He is to tell each parent that he wants to keep this a secret from the other, asking each parent not to tell the other one.

LOOKING FOR A NEW LINE

> DAUGHTER: I'm calling up on the same old line.
>
> MOTHER: I can hear you quite well, dear.

DAUGHTER: Okay, because I think I may change my lines.

MOTHER: Your Dad's on the line now.

DAUGHTER: I'm looking for a new line.

MOTHER: What do you mean?

DAUGHTER: The old lines aren't working anymore.

FATHER: What do you mean by the "old line"?

DAUGHTER: That's it. That's the old line. Right there.

FATHER: You're confusing me.

DAUGHTER: That's good. That's a new line. It's beginning to work.

MOTHER: Are you taking your antidepression pills?

DAUGHTER: I just put one in the mail for you.

THE ANSWERING MACHINE

A client complained that his brother only called him when he wanted something, never simply to talk or inquire about him. In this way he reminded him of his parents. But he couldn't tell him that, nor indeed anything. His assignment was to call his brother on the phone and say the following: "Oops! I thought I would get your answering machine. That's what I wanted, because I was going to leave a message saying, 'I've just realized that you don't know that I know how much you are missing me,' but now that you're home, I don't know what to say."

THE THREE-WAY CONFERENCE CALL

A woman got caught in a conflict between her mother and mother's sister. The two older women were no longer on speaking terms. Each would speak to the younger woman and send messages to each other through her. Her assignment was to set up a three-way conference call so that all three parties would be on the phone at one time. As soon as she had both of the others on the phone, she was to explain that she had just discovered this marvelous three-way calling system and wanted to try it out. Then she should find herself being called urgently to the front door. She would have to excuse herself, leaving the two women to talk on the phone.

SEEKING PERMISSION

A man came to his group one day saying that he had written to his parents asking their permission and support in this task of growing up and leaving home. After he had mailed the letter, he wondered,

Was this an okay thing to do? The consultant's response was that it probably was okay except that he had inadvertently skipped over a couple of prior critical preparatory steps. First, he should have written to his parents initially to get permission to write to them to ask for permission to grow up. But even before this he should have sought the group's permission to write to his parents to get their permission to write to them asking for permission to grow up. Perhaps he could now write his parents and quickly explain that he had gotten things out of order. Would they please hold the letter they had just received as the second letter and not think about it or act on it until they had received the upcoming real first letter. The group members, picking up the cue, unanimously decided that they were not quite ready to give the client permission to write the first letter to his parents. The client looked quite confused. The empathic group offered the client permission to look confused.

THE INSENSITIVE FATHER

Father explained to daughter on the phone that women who have had both ovaries removed become fat and unattractive. Later, daughter accepted the assignment to call father back to tell him about the recent article published in a British medical journal and summarized in the local newspaper. This article reported a study showing that 17% of women who have had both ovaries removed (as client had) become highly sexual and expressive as a result. This small 17% minority were described, and the client discovered, to her amazement, that she has four of the five essential characteristics. Is it okay if she continues to try to hide this part of herself from them?

FRIGHTENED BY DAD

This man has had a very strained and disappointing relationship with his father, by whom he felt very intimidated. He role-played the following conversation in his small group.

(*Phone rings at Dad's home.*)
SON (*played by consultant*): Hi, is Big E home?
DAD (*played by client*): Is that you, Joe?
SON: Yeah.
DAD: Is everything alright?
SON: Yes, great.
DAD: Good, I'll get your mother. (*Immediately puts phone down.*)

Mom: Hi, Joe.

Son: Hi, Mother. I have a favor to ask.

Mom: What's that, Joe?

Son: Lay down the phone and go get your husband, Big E, back to talk to me some more.

Mom: What's wrong? Is something wrong?

Son: I'm great. I just need to talk to Big E.

Dad: Hi . . . what did you want to talk to me about?

Son: That's my question. What did you want to talk to me about?

Dad: No, you said you wanted to talk to me. What do you want to talk to me about?

Son: Well, okay, I'd like to talk to you about you and me.

Dad: I don't know what you want.

Son: Well, as a matter of fact, I just found out something very interesting this week. It just came to me like a bolt from the blue. Suddenly I realized how much you miss me. In fact, so much so that you just can't find words to express it. You have to pretend it's not true.

Dad: Well, you've been in a big fog most of your life.

Son: In other words, I'm right. It's been hard to find me again. You do miss me a lot?

Dad: Of course I miss you a lot.

A few weeks later, this man called his father and asked him to watch the movie *Field of Dreams*. It took six phone calls to bring this about, and it only happened when the movie obligingly showed up on network TV. Then father and son talked by phone after the showing. The father said, "The worst movie I've ever seen in my life." But at the end of the conversation he said, "When you're up here in the spring, we'll throw the baseball." The younger man may now be left with no choice but to experience intimacy with his father.

EXORCISING MOTHER

A woman referred to her mother as a "poison" inside her and was dreading going to visit her at Christmastime. The assignment was to take with her a wooden cross that she had previously mentioned as one that she could wear around her neck. Anytime she felt mother speaking to her or looking at her in a "poisonous way," she was told to touch her mother's nose with the cross and simultaneously give her a kiss on the cheek. She returned to say that it had worked like a charm, even though she didn't get much chance to use it.

PARENTAL PERMISSION

A 42-year-old previously married male client had been courting again for 3 years and was considering engagement. He was very anxious that his parents would not approve. His assignment was to visit the parental home and ask each parent to vote secretly on whether or not he should go ahead with the engagement. If they both said yes there was no issue with the parents. This did not necessarily mean that he should get engaged. It just meant he didn't have to worry about parental feelings if he did. If one or both said no, then he should explain to the parents that he is past the point of no return, and will get engaged anyway but that he is willing to commit himself to a very short-term and unhappy marriage. This would serve two good purposes. In the long term, it would show that they were right from the beginning. In the short term, he would not have to deal with the disappointment of not getting married now. He could even let his fiancée know beforehand that this is what is likely to happen. For some reason the client refused to take the suggestion seriously and then even refused to continue to take the issue seriously. So no more could be done. Some days are like that.

CRACKING NUTS

A shy and reserved minority professional woman felt intimidated by the Caucasian males who dominated the faculty of a graduate institution of which she is a member. One day she announced herself ready to fight back, even though she did not yet know quite how. She agreed to bring a nutcracker to her office and then place it on her desk. Later, as a symbol of the change, she was to take home the little mouse that was already there.

Paradox

SETTING THE WEDDING DATE

A couple reported that right after they had sat on a beautiful beach and set the wedding date they had a horrendous fight from which they had not yet fully recovered. The consultant explained that they were simply testing out the worst that could happen in the marriage to come. Indeed, in exaggerating it to this degree, they had shown great moral courage. They had plunged to the depths together to test the resiliency of the relationship. Most people on a prewedding vacation like this become lethargic and irresponsible, simply lazing around on the beach soaking up the rays and dreaming of dinner. This precocious couple was already working diligently on the relationship, already developing skill at being together without being intimate. They were reminded that this usually takes years of marriage to achieve. Can they possibly keep this up? But for how long?

PORT-A-CANS

A client came from a family of therapists all of whom obsessed about the meaning of every detail of every interaction. At a parking lot near his home sat dozens of Port-A-Cans, in storage for an upcoming city event. The client accepted an assignment to count these dozens of cans, dividing them into their different colors. He did so well that, he accepted an advanced assignment to observe and analyze the uses of these cans by people of different sexes, different colors, and different ages. Was there any relationship to temperature or time of day? (Too often these questions are gathered into clusters and then forgotten.)

UNSATISFACTORY COURTSHIPS

A client complained that all his relationships with women turn out to be either too intense or not intense enough, either too long or not long enough. None were just right. He was advised to preplan an upcoming relationship, choosing in advance both the intensity level and the length of the relationship. He was advised to do this in order to gain a sense of mastery over the twin issues of intensity and length. He was also advised to review this matter in advance with the next woman in his life. That way he could elicit her early cooperation. If she expressed no interest in such an arrangement, at least he would have had another chance to practice a very intense and very short relationship. If she agreed, then he could show her a chart of different relationships of varying lengths and intensities and solicit her first three preferences. The client found this a bit funny and said he was already doing this in his relationships. The consultant pointed out that he was only doing it at an unconscious level and so was experiencing victimization rather than mastery. The purpose of this exercise was to experience mastery rather than mystery. Could he rise to the challenge?

BORN WITHOUT A STOPPER

A client cried throughout every session of her group week after week. No amount of empathic response could help. The client explained that her mother also wept all the time just as she did. Finally, an accurate diagnosis was made. She had an inherited genetic anomaly: she had been born without a stopper. She was advised to buy a stopper, a very special one for herself, and also to get a stopper for each member of her family as an upcoming Christmas gift. She was also asked to photograph all the members of the family, especially mother, opening their stoppers and to bring back the photographs to show the group. The client made a hobby out of this and acquired all kinds of stoppers, from the large sort for use in the bath to those used in tiny decorative perfume bottles. She even found some that could be worn like jewelry. She then refused to continue to take the assignment seriously. Before the group could come up with a better one, she ran out of tears.

Reframing

EPISODIC IMPOTENCE

It was explained to the client that episodic impotence of this sort on the part of the male frequently expresses a transcending biological integrity that will not permit a mindless sexual intimacy regardless of the quality of the commitment and the motivation in the relationship. This is an impressive example of the body calling the mind to accountability. At a deeper level yet, the unconscious is expressing itself through the body and is protecting both the client and his partner. The most immediate danger in a situation like this is a premature loss of impotency through psychological suggestion.

FAKING THE ORGASM

Faking an orgasm, it was explained, can be a potent sign of true love. If a woman has an orgasm spontaneously, she may or may not be spontaneously expressing love for her mate. There is no way for either one of them to know for sure. However, if she is willing to voluntarily fake an orgasm for the sake of her mate, this is probably a sign of love, provided that the faking is not spontaneous. The higher levels of willful faking cannot be involuntary.

THE BRIEF KISS

"Not only does he work all day but he works every evening out of his briefcase," the wife complained, "just like it is an office." Assignment from the therapist to the husband: "Work on a briefcase schedule, so that your wife will know how to work around it." The husband heard the therapist say "brief kiss schedule." So a brief kiss schedule was woven in with the briefcase schedule in a way that seemed acceptable to both.

GETTING GROUNDED

This fellow fell on the slopes several times while skiing, something that had rarely happened to him before. He showed up at his next group meeting on crutches and a little embarrassed. The consultant explained that given where he was in his therapy, this was a most appropriate time for this accident to have happened. The client had given evidence of his commitment to become "grounded." This was something he could now build on, more or less one step at a time.

THE LACE HANDKERCHIEF

A shy and reticent unmarried middle-aged woman announced one day to her group, "I also think I'm ready to begin dating again." Sometime later in the session, a member noticed that the woman was using a lace handkerchief not seen before. Said the consultant, "I know why you're carrying this lace handkerchief today. It is so that you can drop it at the right time." She smiled and said she had a dozen at home. She accepted an assignment to practice hanky dropping at home the following week and to be prepared to come and give the group a demonstration next time.

A SIGN

A client has complained on the phone to Dad: "I didn't ask to be born. You are responsible for that. So you should have taken better care of me." Assignment: Put up a sign, large enough to go from one corner of the room to the next, saying, "I choose to be alive."

RE-FRAMING

This chap had not spoken to either parent in 8 years. With encouragement he made contact, and after a couple of phone calls, a process was under way. There came a time when the client was offered the assignment to put up framed photographs of his parents at the desk where he worked. He felt absolutely unready to do this. It was then suggested that he could put up photographs of parents but turn the photos to the wall so that only the backs were exposed. He felt unable to do this for fear someone would turn them around. It was then suggested that he hang empty photograph frames on the wall beside his desk. If anyone asked what this was about, he could say, "This is the space reserved for photographs of my parents for sometime in the future." He accepted this assignment.

Absurdity

ON NOT WORKING AT IT

CLIENT: The more I work at it, it seems like the less I change.

THERAPIST. And do you think you could work at not working at it?

CLIENT: Well, wouldn't that still be working at it?

THERAPIST: I get your point. You would like to stop working at it without working at not working at it.

CLIENT: Yes, but I don't know how to do that.

Therapist: You mean you don't know how to do that without working at it?

CLIENT: Yes.

THERAPIST: It may be that you need to move back a stage to the NW3 level, the Not Working at it, level 3. That is, you could work at mastering the skill of not working at it while not working at that.

CLIENT: I'll have to think about that.

THERAPIST: Okay, think about it this week, but practice thinking about it without working at thinking about it.

WANT LEVELS

The presenting problem for this man was the fact that his wife didn't care that he didn't want sex. The problem was not that he didn't want to have sex, and the problem was not that his wife didn't want to have sex, because she did want to have sex with him. The presenting problem was, rather, that his wife didn't seem to want him to want to have sex with her. Clearly, he wanted her to want him to want to have sex. The consultant explained that this was working on the problem at the Want Three, or W3, level. It is often very difficult to get change at that level. Change is more likely to begin at the W6 level. For example, the client wants his wife to want him to want sex. But since that isn't immediately available, we can note that he wants his wife to want him to want to want sex. However, since she is apparently satisfied with the current state of affairs, clearly she does not want him to want her to want him to want to want sex. This then clarifies his problem, which now can finally be clearly stated. He wants her to stop not wanting him to want her to want him to begin to want to want sex. Finally, we are at the W6 level, the level at which the problem can not only be clearly understood and stated, but change can be expected to begin to begin.

The client had two afterthoughts. First, he thought that maybe his wife did to some extent want him to want but not as much as he wanted her to want him to want. That was a dilemma. Secondly, he thought that maybe there was a lack of honesty in the marriage and perhaps that was what had led to this very high level of complexity. The therapist thought that maybe he was making matters too complicated.

QUADRUPLE-TALK

A client accepted an assignment to set a new goal for herself. The goal was to move from quadruple-talk to doubletalk. Quadruple-talk, which she was alleged to have been using, means talk that absolutely no one can follow. Double-talk, by contrast, is talk that the listener readily understands but knows is probably not true to what the speaker is thinking or feeling. After reflecting a moment, the client responded that she was not sure that she understood this assignment. She was immediately complimented on having moved spontaneously from quadruple-talk to double-talk.

WHO CAN CHANGE?

A client explained that he did not think he could change until his father changed first, because he was so like him. However, he also realized, using the same logic, that his father could not change until *his* father, the client's grandfather, first changed. However, the grandfather was deceased and therefore could not change—except obviously he had changed dramatically! The problem was that he could not be seen to have changed. As a way out of this dilemma, the client accepted the proposition that if he could come to believe that his grandfather both could have and would have changed had his son (the client's father) asked him to do so, then by implication the client's father would have had the chance to change, and probably would have, had he wanted to avail himself of the opportunity. This, in turn, meant that the client's father would now have become the sort of person, who could have changed into the sort of person, who would now be the sort of person whose son, namely the client, now is the sort of person who can choose to change. So that is where things stand today. The client nodded knowingly.

THE NATURAL PARADOX

This woman said she wanted to be nicer to her mother but only if she could do it of her own free will. The problem was that her mother very much wanted her to be nicer to her and the client felt this pressure strongly. So it was hard to keep these voluntary and involuntary pressures apart. This meant the client could only be nicer to her mother if she could be sure that her mother knew that she, the daughter, knew that her mother knew that she was only doing it because she wanted to do it and not because her mother wanted her to be nicer, even though they both knew it was true that her mother did want her to do it. The dilemma was solved when the consultant reassured the client that the preponderance of the research evidence indicated that there is no way that her mother could not both know this and also know that she knows this. (Fortunately, it was not necessary to elaborate on what "this" referred to.)

ON NOT TAKING A JOB

A client expressed concern that he could not make a decision whether or not to take a job, a job he also simultaneously said he could not decide whether or not he wanted. His particular concern was that he was afraid that he might be or might seem to be saying no to this job without having an adequate reason to say no to this job.

> THERAPIST: Is not having an adequate reason to say no to the job an adequate reason for not saying no to the job?
> CLIENT: I don't understand. That's too abstract for me.
> THERAPIST: Well, that's a start. The resolution begins once you have moved to a level that is one level beyond the level of understanding.
> CLIENT: I understand that.
> THERAPIST: You're slipping.
> CLIENT: I was just pretending.
> THERAPIST: I don't understand.
> CLIENT: Thanks, I needed that.

THE OBSERVER

The major presenting complaint by this client was that he felt that most of the time he took an observer role in life. He didn't like that. The consultant gave the following suggestions:

"You cannot stop being an observer until you first master the skill. That is, sometimes you spontaneously observe, but at other times you forfeit the observer role spontaneously. In these latter times, you need to learn the art of observing voluntarily when you're not able to observe spontaneously. Then, as a second step, you will be able to go on to learn the art of voluntarily observing yourself in those moments when you are observing spontaneously. This is called the O^2 level. If you can learn to observe voluntarily at both levels, you will become capable of learning voluntarily not to be a spontaneous observer."

The client looked off into the distance and seemed disquieted by the challenge.

REALITY LEVELS

A fellow expressed difficulty in "feeling real" when he spoke about himself in the group. He said that he wanted "to be real." He went on to express a strong feeling that he didn't simply want to be real, he wanted to be "really real." He then went on further to say that, in fact, he would like to be really, really real. The consultant congratulated him on stumbling upon the awareness that there are, in fact, six different levels of "realness." It is important to clarify on what level one is or wants to be at any given time. These six levels are, of course:

1. Unreally real
2. Real
3. Unreally really real
4. Really real
5. Unreally really really real
6. Really really real

The assignment for the week was for the client to evaluate his inner self every hour on the hour and note down what level of realness he was operating on at that moment and to also note the level he would like to be on, whether the same or different. There were some dramatic changes in this man's life in the following weeks (although with no obvious really real connection to the assignment). Realness has its downside also.

WHAT TIME IS IT?

A client had completed the in-office visit with his parents. The following conversation occurred in a follow-up visit some months later:

CLIENT: I visited with my parents last weekend and I thought it went very well at the time, but today I'm not so sure.

THERAPIST: So the weekend visit was good at the weekend . . . but today the weekend visit is not so good.

CLIENT: Well, I thought it was good at the time, now I'm not so sure.

THERAPIST: Right now are you not sure that at the time it was good at the time or that it was good at the time today?

CLIENT: It was good at the time, but it was not so good at the time when I get to thinking about it afterward, like today.

THERAPIST: Well, if you could reverse these two, and I think you probably can, then you could feel better about it today.

CLIENT: What do you mean?

THERAPIST: Well, if you were to decide now today that at the time it wasn't so good at the time, then you could go on to decide that today it seems good at the time. And since this is today, then you could feel good about how it was at the time, today.

CLIENT: Well, I know how to do it the other way. I don't know if I know how to do it this way.

THERAPIST: Okay, except the very fact that you can think today about doing it this way and yet can also think today about doing it the other way, means that you probably can do it both ways with a bit of practice.

CLIENT: Well, at least I am feeling different about it now.

THERAPIST: Feeling different at this time about which time?

CLIENT (*grinning*): Now you stop that!

A FOLLOW-UP VISIT

This conversation occurred with the same client a few weeks later. Again, what was striking was the spontaneous way in which the client moved through time, mixing up the three tenses in his language.

CLIENT: My strong hope today is that sometime in the future things will be different between my parents in the way in which they have experienced their past life together.

THERAPIST: Can you accept the fact that here now in the present the fact is that their past lives will continue into the future to be the same as they seem today to have been in the past?

CLIENT: Oh, but they were so unhappy back then!

THERAPIST: Okay, so your job in the future will be to learn to accept that they were so unhappy in the past.

CLIENT: Oh, but they were!

THERAPIST: You know, it's possible that today and in the future for them they will have had exactly the same and even just the right amount of unhappiness in the past.

CLIENT: As I look back on my last visit to their home, I was doing much better the day before I left to visit them, thinking about their unhappiness in the past, than I'm doing now a few days later.

THERAPIST: Maybe then it would be better to go ahead and cancel that trip that you made last week.

CLIENT: That's absurd.

THERAPIST: In what sense?

CLIENT: I'm not going to talk about this anymore.

Small Perturbations

STANDING TALL

A client who happens to be 6 feet 4 inches tall felt that, generally speaking, he was selling himself short in life, including in his work and his important relationships. Assignment: Make a mark on the wall at 5 feet 11 inches, and stand with your head under the mark for 4 minutes at 7:00 P.M. each evening, using a timer. The client reported feeling "stooped and humiliated." He then claimed that he had learned to stand this way in life from his father. He accepted an assignment to invite his father over to his apartment, and father practiced standing in this way under the 5 feet 11 inches mark also. They took photographs of each other in this unusual position. Then they discussed who would change first.

BORN WITHOUT FEELINGS

A man came to therapy because he could not ever feel much about anything. Clearly, here was another genetic anomaly; he was suffering from a broken feeler. Rehabilitation treatment was in order. Assignment: Do three things—(1) keep a diary of all the feelings that it turns out that you do not have this week; (2) keep a separate diary of feelings you think that "normal people" would have felt this week in your place (if it helps you to do this, you can go through the motions of having "pretend feelings"); and (3) keep a note of all the feelings you would like to have had this week, had your feeler not been broken. A week later the client returned irritated and agitated at the absolute futility of such a stupid assignment.

THE DISCOUNTED RABBIT

A female client said, "I talked to my parents on the phone last night, and as I talked I began to feel again those old defective feelings about myself, feelings of being totally defective." Assignment: Go to a discount store and find something lying partially unwrapped on the floor. When you find something you like, take it to the counter and get it discounted, on the grounds that it is in some way defective. Then take it home and every day cherish it.

The following week the client reported that she had acquired a small ceramic rabbit with a very small crack in it and had negotiated for it and bought it at half price. She keeps it on a table by her bedside, talks to it each evening, strokes and cuddles it every night before sleeping.

SEPARATE BEDROOMS

A client declared her great sadness that her parents' marriage had not been happier over the years. Things had now come to the point where they slept in separate bedrooms. Assignment: On an upcoming parental wedding anniversary, just a week away, give a joint present to the parents of a large fluffy animal with the understanding that they have ownership rights night about. (This event occurred during the preparation for the in-office visit with the primary triangle.)

FREUDIAN STUFF

> CONSULTANT (*responding to unconscious communication from the client*): I might as well tell you, and I hope you don't mind, but I never did go for that old Freudian stuff about sons and their mothers. And I say that, no matter what the group—indeed, no matter what even you yourself—might be thinking.
> CLIENT (*hesitantly*): I don't know what you're getting at.
> CONSULTANT: Exactly, although it's really what I'm not getting at or trying not to get at about you and your mother. You see, I think some of the things you've been saying and not saying could easily lend themselves to certain misunderstandings with regard to you and your mother. Anyway, think about it this week. See if you can clarify what all is not there and then tell us about it next week.

FOUL UP YOUR BLISS

A couple came into a couples' family of origin group one week and reported that the previous two weeks had been "absolutely blissful." One spouse said she just couldn't stand so much bliss and so she created an ugly scene. "I think I'm addicted to intensity, and things were just too peaceful. How can I stop doing this?" Assignment: Make three audiotapes of scenes of disharmony at three different levels of upset from mild through moderate to all-out war. When the urge comes upon either one, do not resist it but as soon as it is possible sit down with the spouse and select and play an audiotape at the appropriate level of conflict intensity. One or both can mime to the tape. The tape can be replayed if necessary, or a higher level of intensity can be invoked if needed.

Short Takes (Untitled)

A client admitted, "I very much want to say something nice to my husband, but for some reason I just absolutely cannot let myself say it. I've been so mad with him for so long." Assignment: You could say to him, "Jack, you're getting to be more and more like the kind of guy I could get fond of and want to live with, if I wasn't already married to such a turkey." She showed a wicked grin and felt she could do this, even enjoy it.

> CLIENT: We do a lot of joking in this group. Someone told me recently that cracking jokes is a way of grabbing power. What do you think, Doc?
> THERAPIST: It sounds like a joke to me.

A couple, both therapists, report that they talk and think and feel and analyze and make things up about everything that's going on in the house every day. One of them is beginning to think that this might be a mistake. Assignment: This week practice doing more of less thinking.

A couple, working in a couples' family of origin group, got distracted and obsessed with a power struggle between them. Assignment: Twice a day, and apropos of nothing, the husband is to approach his wife either in person or by telephone and say, "You know, I have been thinking about it . . . and you are right." Her one and only response is to be "Thank you." There the conversation must end. The reciprocal aspect of this is that once a day she will approach him, and look in his eyes, and say, "My hero."

CLIENT: My parents don't think much of my wife. I think maybe that bothers me too much.

THERAPIST: Loyalty to your wife is halfway to a position of loyalty to yourself.

CLIENT: Why do they treat her this way?

THERAPIST: As Groucho once said, "I can't respect any daughter-in-law who would marry a son of mine." And, of course, the unspoken part of that is "Sometimes it's hard to respect a son who reminds me of myself."

THERAPIST (*to anxious client*): You are within the tiniest hairs breadth of handling this situation extremely well. At this point you may have no other alternative.

DIVORCED CLIENT: I haven't seen my daughter in 19 years. I have a new formal photograph of myself I'd like to send. But I'm afraid she wouldn't want it.

THERAPIST: Take an informal photo of your formal photograph and send it with the message, "Here's a photo of a photo I could send you, if you'd like it."

This kind of absurdity and playfulness in the group process serves a number of good purposes. Without doubt, the most important of the purposes served is the resolution and dissolution of *intergenerational intimidation*, which is to say, the various patterns of fearfulness in being around, sometimes in just thinking about, mother and father. A good management of intergenerational intimidation makes possible all the interesting events that are about to follow.

A second crucial effect of these experiences within the small group at play is the development of a strong sense of *reciprocity* within the group. In the hunter–gatherer stage of civilization belonging to, contributing to, and receiving from a small band in fully reciprocal ways was not only the essence of everyday life, but it was actually essential for survival. As Glantz and Pearce (1989) point out, this core feeling of reciprocity is not easily come by in modern society, and its absence has highly detrimental results.

CHAPTER 7

The Rehearsal: Preparing the Client for Political Renegotiations with Parents

I did not gladly hold her old hand. I could not find the words of comfort that I might have found in my heart for almost anyone else. I sat next to her bed with an icy and armored heart and waited . . . until I could flee in terror, lest her spirit would invade me and defeat my lifelong struggle to be separate and different. . . . I dreaded any intrusion on my boundaries from her, to the extent that I could not tolerate her asking me the most trivial question. I believe my exaggerated need for independence is still related to my dread of being invaded by my mother.

—Sophie Freud Lowenstein (1980)
"Mother and Daughter: An Epitaph"
Family Process (Vol. 20, No. 1)

Once the client has been assigned to a small group, the experiences that follow can be conceptualized under the themes described in the following pages.

Discovery

To begin with, there is the experience of discovery as the client both recovers some old information and acquires some new. This comes about through recall and reflection (including dreams) on the one hand, and sustained inquiry with family members and other important dramatis personae on the other. The climax of the initiative toward discovery is, of course, the presentation to parents of the detailed prepared agenda. This presentation takes place over several hours and in the course of two or three different days. It is not unlike the discovery phase in a legal proceeding, except that the intent is benevolent and collaborative, not adversarial. As this new knowledge is integrated, it is reminiscent of what has traditionally been called insight.

Release

There is also an experience of release as the client not only expresses the feelings associated with this varied information but beyond this makes expressive audiotaped letters that further delineate aspects of inner feelings. These tapes, although addressed to parents, are not sent to them but are intended only for the private listening pleasure of the client and the small group (any unlawful use will, of course, be investigated by the FBI). When instructed to make such an audiotape, the client is typically given the following instructions:

"Find a quiet moment when you know you have time to spare and will not be concerned about time passing. Find a place where you know you will be safe from intrusion, being overheard, or distractions of any sort. Sit in a comfortable chair in order to help you feel relaxed.

"Use a tape recorder that can be set down rather than hand-held. Have the recorder beside you and make sure it is working and that you know how to record. Then press the record button and forget about the tape recorder. Just let it run of its own accord. This is not dictation. Do not start and stop the recording. If there are long pauses, let them be recorded. If you run out of tape, turn the tape over.

"Begin by breathing deeply and let both your body and your mind relax. Gently close your eyes so that you can go deeply into yourself. If your eyes flutter open, gently close them again. Then when you are ready, in your mind's eye imagine that your father [or mother, spouse, etc.] is sitting in a chair right opposite you face-to-face.

"When you are ready, begin to talk to your father and say everything and anything that comes spontaneously to your mind. But be sure to include your thoughts about your relationship with him, both how it has developed over the years and how, as you see it, it stands between the two of you today.

"Continue until you are finished. There is no right amount of time for this. Take the time that you need. When you are completely finished, turn the tape off. Then bring the tape to the group so that we can listen to it with you."

An audiotaped letter that has been addressed to one or both parents (or, occasionally, to other family members) can be used to express the client's most intense feelings of loss and grief associated with a particular incident or sequence of events. Alternatively, it may express the client's formidable resentment, even murderous rage, in response to his or her perceptions of elusive events. An audiotape may describe all the feelings associated with the ebb and flow of a relationship. Or it may be a listing of all the outrages, injuries, and injustices that a client believes have been perpetrated on him or her in the course of a lifetime by one or the other parent or by the family as a whole.

On the other hand, a tape may be mostly focused on the issues in the current relationship with a parent as it exists in the client's head at this moment. This will acknowledge both the pleasure and chagrin in the current state of affairs, and will also indicate what the client most intends to change or wants to create differently. An audiotape can also in due course be used to begin the cataloging of all the questions regarding self and the family of origin that are currently filling a client's mind and heart. These audiotaped letters are never actually sent to or heard by the parent. They are played selectively in the small group for this "family's" acknowledgment and response. The primary purpose of the exercise is to achieve what has been traditionally called catharsis. This helps the client clear his or her head and focus the vision. In more senses of the word than one, the road ahead comes into sharper relief.

Despite the fact that such clear and mildly hypnotic instructions have been given, the act of audiotaping of even a fantasy letter routinely stirs up great anxiety. Clients have inadvertently turned the sound off, failed to start the tape, not pressed the record button, and simply lost the tape after recording. Some have sat so far from the microphone that nothing was recorded. Some have taken weeks to come upon a tape recorder or have had remarkable difficulty in acquiring a blank tape. Some have written out and dictated copious notes about a parent but not spoken directly to the parent. A few have dictated on airplanes and a few even on busy freeways, cutting the sound on and off as they changed lanes. This exercise has a way of cutting deeply into raw emotionality. The consultant's response to all of these and similar happenings invariably is that the client has done exactly the right thing. Clients should always follow their instincts. They alone know about the inner personal timetable. Admittedly, the consultant and the group will want to explore the matter further with them after the fact.

If the client has been especially anxious about making an assigned tape, this suggests that a related follow-up activity would be beneficial. For example, the client can be asked to listen to the tape alone after it has been completed. Then he or she can add on to the tape all thoughts and feelings that have come up while listening to the original tape. This exercise can be repeated three or four times, as necessary, until the client has adequately distanced and desensitized himself or herself from these particular words and the troubling thoughts and primitive fears that they stir up. Another possibility is to instruct a client to use a yellow marker in imagination when listening to the tape and highlight in the mind and in the memory, whatever seems most crucial.

Observation

As the small group work proceeds, the client is increasingly able to take an observer's stance toward the family of origin and to engage in a more general stock taking. This is facilitated by phone calls or brief visits to the parental home simply to observe what it is like to be there—and to begin to notice who, in truth, actually lives there these days. A range of observations about the family, and the self in relation to it, are noted and reflected upon and subsequently presented to the small group for exploration, clarification and feedback. (This latter part of the exercise is akin to traditional reality testing.) Throughout these experiences of insight and catharsis and reality testing, each group member will be experiencing a relatively consistent response of acknowledgment, empathy, and nurturance from other group members. This can be seen as a corrective emotional experience provided within the new family. Although the client is encouraged to maintain and practice the skill of perceiving from an observer position, the client is not also encouraged to respond emotionally as an observer. He or she is, by contrast, encouraged to practice spontaneous emotional responses within the safety of the small group.

Initiating Negotiations

About this time, the client will be initiating some very preliminary "negotiations about negotiations" with the parents. This may, for example, take the form of addressing parents by their first or given names. This seems like a small thing to do, and certainly it is purely symbolic. Yet it is not unusual for both generations to find this gesture disturbing and disrespectful. Frequently, a client winces at the very thought. Indeed, there is nothing magical about either the act or its outcome. Moreover, it does not need to become a lifelong habit. It is no more than an effective warning shot across the bow, signaling that some kind of engagement is about to begin. It is a highly symbolic act that unfailingly seems to convey a message in shorthand that is rarely missed or misunderstood. Even when the client does not indulge in this exercise openly with the parent, simply practicing within one's own mind and then publicly within the group has a salutary effect. Naturally, where it creates more of an issue, it becomes more of an issue. In this case, clients are encouraged to rehearse this practice in their heads, toward the goal of familiarity with this different way of relating and "perceiving" the parent.

As role-played in the small group (the consultant plays the part of the client and the client becomes the parent), a preparatory dialogue might go something like this:

DAUGHTER: Well, Bob. Have you had any good fishing recently?

FATHER: What did you say?

DAUGHTER: Have you had any good fishing recently?

FATHER: No, I mean did you say "Bob"?

DAUGHTER: Yes, I said "Bob," Bob.

FATHER: Why are you calling me "Bob"?

DAUGHTER: Because I meant you, Bob.

FATHER: But, why are you calling me "Bob"?

DAUGHTER: Funny you should ask me that because I was just thinking about it yesterday. In fact, I think I mentioned to someone yesterday that Bob is one of my very favorite names, although for some reason I hadn't realized that until now. But I do like the sound of it very much, Bob.

FATHER: I don't know that I like the sound of that.

DAUGHTER: You really should like the sound of your own name, Bob.

FATHER: I meant I'm not sure I like you using my name.

DAUGHTER: But that may just be because you're not used to it. Anyway, Bob, how many names are there that are spelled the same forward and backward? Think about it!

Whether or not the client actually ever goes through this exercise with a parent, going through the exercise in his or her head through role-playing in the small group seems to reduce the intimidation to a surprising degree.

Another way in which to set the scene or engage in preliminary negotiations about negotiations shows itself in the following dialogue, as role-played in the small group:

SON: Say, Mom, I have some news for you.

MOTHER: What's that?

SON: Well, although I have not yet made up my mind or made any commitment to it, I am at least toying with the notion of changing the character of our relationship a bit.

MOTHER: I don't understand. What does that mean?

SON: I'm not really sure yet myself what it means. But from what I've heard myself think, maybe it means that I might one day decide to be less your little boy than I've been enjoying in the past. However, remember I am not making any promises yet. Just a thought at this stage.

MOTHER: I still don't know what you mean, John. You're not my little boy. What does that talk mean?

SON: Yes, I know that you know that I am not your little boy. But I'm not sure that I know that yet myself. And if I don't know that I know, you can't know that I know. That in turn means that I can't yet know that you know that I know. That's the bit I might decide to begin working on . . . to see if I can let you know that I know . . . so that I can know that you know that I know. But remember, no commitment yet.

MOTHER: I hope you'll start to make more sense soon.

SON: You've got the message. Yes, I'm on my way to making more sense.

One further illustration may suffice to represent these exercises as they are role-played in the small group.

DAUGHTER: Hello, is that you, Dad?

DAD: Yes, honey. How are you?

DAUGHTER: I'm just fine and I have a fine message for you.

DAD: Oh, yeah? Who is it from?

DAUGHTER: Well, it's from my better self, and as I heard it from my better self, the message is this: You've done a great job about teaching me how to practice in men–women relationships. The bad news or at least the sad news is that now sometime before too long it looks like I'll have to move on to another relationship and leave you. The rehearsal days are coming to a close. I might have to go on stage soon and do a live performance.

DAD: Are you feeling okay, honey?

DAUGHTER: Well, sort of. You know how my first marriage didn't work out too well. I simply hadn't practiced enough or paid enough attention when I was practicing. But I think I will soon be ready to audition again. So I wanted to give you some advance notice. It may be for real next time, so we will both need to be ready for that.

DAD: Honey, do you want to talk to your mother?

DAUGHTER: No, not especially. Anyway, Dad, I'll be talking more about it to you. This is just to get things started.

DAD: Well, you know. I never thought Jack was such a bad guy anyway. Listen, here's your mother.

DAUGHTER: No, he wasn't a bad guy. He was just too much like the sort of guy your wife wouldn't want to marry.

Preparing the Parents

As is obvious from the foregoing paragraphs, these preliminary negotiations begin the preparation of the parents, as well as the son or daughter, for the upcoming political changes. It is crucial to recruit the parents into the process as early as possible and to help them begin preparing themselves emotionally for the new order of things to come. A mutuality of preparation is a key condition of a good outcome. So the client is encouraged to become actively engaged with parents from the beginning, by both taking messages out from the group to them and bringing messages back. From the moment the client first tells the parents that he or she is attending a family of origin group and why, the mutual preparation has begun. The consultant suggests that the parents be identified from the beginning as "consultants to the consultant." After all they are experts on the client, having known him or her longer than anyone else. This may be said somewhat tongue in cheek, but there is also real truth to it. In this way the consultant acknowledges, and does well to constantly remind himself or herself, that the measure of parental goodwill and cooperation, will determine the degree of complication in the program and influence the degree of success or compromise in the final outcome.

Corollary Conversations

At this point in the proceedings, the client will be seeking out corollary conversations with other extended family members, as well as with personal intimates and friends knowledgeable about the lives of each parent. (These conversations are especially necessary when renegotiating with a deceased parent; see Chapter 11.) This information will confirm and supplement, or on occasion call into question and raise new queries about, stories and events already recounted. These forays can be unstructured fishing expeditions. However, they are usually most profitable when the client is already reasonably well informed and has specific questions to ask or matters to clarify. These conversations consistently yield an interesting and idiosyncratic perspective on a parent from someone dealing from an insider position. It can also be very valuable for a client to hear each sibling's perceptions of the family of origin. This will include perceptions of each parent and of the parental marriage, as well as perceptions of the client's place and role in the family of origin.

Preparation of the Agenda

As time goes by, the intensity of the client's feelings about the family reduces and the feelings mellow. In this case, he or she is now ready to begin to prepare a formal agenda of questions for the parents. This is in anticipation of the three-way conversations to be held with the primary triangle in the consultant's office when the time is ripe. To begin with, the client is asked to write out spontaneously at home every and any question that comes to mind for either parent initially, without self-induced censorship, however possible or impossible the question may seem to be. That is, the original agenda consists of everything that comes spontaneously to the mind of the client. This is later read in the group.

The first task of the group is to help the client supplement the agenda with any important matters inadvertently omitted. The second task of the group is to help the client "re-language" the questions in a nonjudgmental way so that they will present a minimum of threat and be likely to yield the maximum of information. (This "re-languaging" process will be described in more detail later.) The client is now being tutored in the art of reframing, a skill that in families where emotional intensity runs high all the time needs to be mastered to the point where it will be internalized and become second nature. One of the most valuable long-term benefits of this kind of therapy is becoming adept at devising alternative meanings to apply to ongoing experiences. As a result, when one "meaning" does not work well for the client, another possibility will be close at hand. That tutorial has now begun.

The Invitation to Parents

The final task facing the client is to prepare the presentation of the invitation to be issued to parents to attend a 2- or 3-day conversation with son or daughter at the consultant's office. The approach that follows (or something similar) has proved to be effective. Different aspects of the invitation, gathered together here, will probably be presented over time:

> "Mother and father, you are being invited to this consultation by me to assist the consultant, since you know me longer and better than any other human being."

In the situation where the parents are strongly negative about the invitation, the client can say, "I am in trouble and my life is in trouble and I need your help." In these circumstances, this is probably the truth, and there are few parents who will not respond to it, even if it takes a little time.

> "The basic reason for the visit is that I want to get to know you from the inside out. This means seeing you through your eyes, from within your shoes, in your own terms, and in your own words. I want to hear your personal narrative in life, including the key moments and events, from earliest memory to the circumstances of your lives today, as well as your hopes and fears for the future.
>
> "I want permission to ask about the private inner personal meanings to you of the sequences of events in your life histories. I don't just want the facts but also the inner meanings. I don't just want to know *about* you, I want to know you directly, face-to-face.
>
> "I value my rich family heritage. I want to hear it and know it and understand it and embrace it directly from the source, which for me is you. You are the richest and most valuable resource of family information and family heritage that exist for me anywhere. You are the living documents. You embody family history, over the generations. But, obviously, you will not live forever.
>
> "So I feel fortunate that you are still available to me today, and I want, with your permission and cooperation, to take advantage of this unparalleled and priceless opportunity. To the extent that you can share your inner self with me, you will be giving to me the richest parental gift possible. This will be a kind of relational gold dust, with which no material or physical gift can compare.
>
> "Most people never come to know much about the inside story

and detail of family roots and heritage. I not only want to know this, I want to know it directly from you. I am going to prepare a lot of questions to ask you, and a few of my questions may seem like an invasion of your privacy. One or two may even seem none of my business. But let me suggest that everything that is you is also some part of me.

"I am most interested in and proud of my family heritage and want to become more familiar with it. [Individuals still feeling burned by unusually abusive or neglectful family backgrounds may instead simply affirm how important and crucial it is to become familiar with the family's history and heritage.]

"In summary, my goal is not to intrude but to learn, not to embarrass but to make contact. I shall receive and hold your information with understanding, respect, and compassion. So I am preparing an agenda of questions for you, some for each of you individually and some for you as a couple.

"So I want to ask you to consider coming here at some mutually convenient time, so that we can have these conversations."

Aspects of this outline can be used informally and repeatedly in the early stages and then more formally again on the actual occasion of the in-office consultation. It is probably clear by now that many of the behaviors in the small group described earlier, are instrumental toward the goal of resolving intergenerational intimidation. The intent is to extinguish the client's learned responses of fear and guilt. These arise as a result of anticipated parental abandonment, rejection, or disapproval in response to failure by the client to meet the letter and sometimes the spirit of parental expectations. Through repeated role playing, in which the consultant plays the part of the "cool client" and the client takes the part of the "feared parent," absurdly playful and "disrespectful" scenes take place. The unthinkable and the unimaginable are not just thought but are actually spoken. Lo and behold, the sky does not fall! This proves to be a compelling psychodynamic event in the life of the client. Fear is not reinforced and begins to be extinguished. For although the actual parents are not physically present in the room, the parents who live in the client's head are very much present, alive, and undoubtedly kicking.

A story from a recent group meeting will illustrate the point. An unmarried professional man in his late 30s began to feel both alienated from and intimidated by his father, now in his late 60s. The parents had divorced when the son was an early teenager, and the client saw his abusive father only episodically from that point on. He rarely saw him since becoming an adult, although this rageful man lived within a few miles of the son. The most immediate obstacle to the son reconnecting with the father was the son's fear of intimidation by this aging man. There was clear evidence of significant anger in the son, but none of this had been accessible to him. Instead, he smiled constantly, even when the painful relationship between him and his father was under discussion. (It should be mentioned that the father had a significant drinking problem.) The assignment was this: the son was instructed to drive by the father's house late one evening and to throw an empty beer can onto the front yard. The beer can was to have a brief message attached saying, "This Bud's for you." Whether by the carrying out of this action or simply by experiencing the fantasy of doing it, the client is likely to begin to feel some of his anger, or at the very least to take a first step in that direction. After depositing the beer can in his father's yard in the dark of the night, the client in this story experienced a new freedom to reach out toward his father in friendship. The client wanted to connect these events, but the group assured him that one following the other was probably just a coincidence.

These kinds of unexpected conversations and transactions do take place between the generations, and lightening seldom strikes and the sky only rarely falls. This is a matter of some delight and relief to the client and the watching members of the small group "family." Important changes begin to occur spontaneously in the inner life and in the relationships with parental introjects. The client becomes desensitized to previous fears about these relationships. More playful, more relaxed, and more versatile responses are associated with previously frightening stimuli. This resolution of intergenerational intimidation is at the very heart of the work of terminating the intergenerational hierarchical boundary and gives a strong impetus in the direction of equality or "peerhood," which results in greater freedom of action and ease of interaction for both generations.

CHAPTER 8

Scheduling the Performance and Contract Negotiating with the Players

> Every bear who's been good
> Is sure of a treat today.
> Lots of marvelous things to eat
> And wonderful games to play.
> Beneath the trees where nobody sees
> They'll run and play as long as they please
> For that's the way Teddy Bears have their picnic.
> —"The Teddy Bear's Picnic"
> Music by John Bratton
> Words by Jimmy Kennedy

Welcoming, Bonding, and Briefing the Parents

When the parents come in with the client to the consultant's office for their first visit, the conversation begins with some light socializing. The chat covers where they have come from, how they got here, how things were back home when they left and how long they plan to stay. This gives them a chance to get over their initial feelings of strangeness and become generally less anxious before the formal proceedings begin. In this way the consultant works toward creating a comfortable and safe atmosphere and seeks to communicate a warm and reassuring welcome. It is made clear from the beginning that the consultant is on the parents' side—at least for today—and that the consultant is of their generation, regardless of actual ages. The intent is to create a connection and a bonding between consultant and parents.

This bonding is a necessary foundation on which everything that is to follow can be built. Should it prove impossible to get a reasonably good connection with the parents, it is advisable to rethink the program. This can be done either by scaling back the original ambition or by slowing down the movement. Occasionally, it is even advisable to hold back the prepared agenda until another time, using this time as an opportunity to develop rapport and to begin building bridges. If something like this should happen, then probably a winking red light has been missed during the prior preparation procedures.

Assuming a steady green light instead, the consultant continues on by debriefing the parents on their thoughts and feelings about being present on this occasion and their degree of comfort in anticipation of the approaching conversations. They are then asked whether they know clearly what the purpose of this meeting is. Invariably the response is "No," or "Well, I've been told something but really don't understand it," or "I maybe do know but I'm not really sure," or "I think I do but I'd like to hear it again." It is an exceptional parent who can say a clean "Yes." So the dynamic of the response is probably more emotional than it is rational. In any event, this provides an opportunity for the second step in the prologue. The consultant now turns to the client and says, "Well, I guess all three of us are wondering what this occasion is about and why you have gathered us all here. So what can you tell us?" The client will then reiterate his or her statement about the purpose, intention, and hope for this meeting. In this deliberately ostentatious way, the client takes responsibility for structuring and guiding the early interaction. This makes it clear that this is his or her business that is now at hand, and not the consultant's.

The Ground Rules for the In-Office Conversations

After clarification of the purpose, the client goes on to explain the three ground rules for these conversations. The ground rules are intended to contribute to a safe atmosphere by clarifying boundaries. By presenting the ground rules the client again takes ownership and focuses the experience directly between the self and the parents. This indicates that the consultant has a peripheral—although, admittedly, probably a useful—role to play.

Taking the Fifth

The first ground rule specifies that while the client has given himself or herself permission to ask any question of any sort on any topic, the parent has a right to decline to respond to any question. At that point the client is permitted one follow-up question. That follow-up question is "Can you tell me why you do not want to respond to this question?" The parent can then choose to respond or to decline to respond to the follow-up question also. If the parent declines, then the matter is closed and the client will immediately move on to the next question. There is an explicit understanding throughout that a parent may not only decline to respond to any question at any time but may do so without presumption of guilt, indeed, without presumption of anything for that matter.

Two-Way Street

The second ground rule is to the effect that this exploration is a two-way street, even though one side has an edge by virtue of having prepared questions. This implies that the parent has an equal right to pose any question of any sort at any time to son or daughter. The client may then in similar fashion respond to the question or decline. If he or she declines to respond, the parent can also ask the follow-up question, "Can you tell me why you do not want to respond to that question?" If the client further declines to respond, the matter is closed. It is clear throughout that either parent can ask any question extemporaneously at any time, since the parents do not have a prepared agenda. They will be specifically asked at the beginning and end of each session if they have any questions or statement to make. The concern here is to demonstrate good faith on the part of the client. Son or daughter will not ask the parents to do something that he or she is not also willing to do.

Confidentiality

The third ground rule defines the matter of confidentiality, and the understanding proposed is this. Each party to the conversations is free to repeat to any other person at any time any comment that he or she makes about the self or any understanding that he or she comes to about the self. On the other hand, all parties commit themselves not to quote any other person speaking on any subject without specific permission. Whether or not others are to be told anything about this meeting, including the fact of the meeting itself, and, if so, which individuals and in what circumstances are issues to be discussed openly at the beginning and resolved fully before the consultation ends. Different families handle the issue of confidentiality in different ways, influenced by the idiosyncrasies of family style and the sensitivities of current family dynamics.

By personally managing the discussion of the ground rules the client takes ownership of the agenda. The consultant is present as a host, a timekeeper, a minutes taker, maybe a prompter, occasionally a referee, and sometimes even an expert witness. But this drama is about the client's life and family, not the consultant's. It is the family's neck and future that are on the line, not the consultant's. The family is here to deal with itself and its own internal dynamics and to review its several individual as well as corporate constructions of reality. From that perspective, everyone else is an outsider. This understanding is established in the early part of the first interview.

The Consultant Sits Down with the Client and the Parents

The three-day in-office visit with the client and the parents (or some representation thereof) is the goal toward which this model of therapy works. It is the climactic event of the entire venture. It is believed that the lasting effectiveness of the psychotherapy program will be influenced more by this event and its outcome than by any other one thing. This is an exercise that is likely to have considerable impact on each of the persons present and upon the various relationships represented in the room, as well as all relationships immediately connected to them. It is likely to be influential for some time to come. Therefore, it is not to be entered into lightly or unadvisedly, but only after considerable planning and scrutiny of the lay of the land as it stretches out in both visible and less visible directions. The consultant needs to have a keen sense of where the bodies are likely to be buried. Over time, he or she develops the skill of tiptoeing through both the tulips and the mine fields and learns how to tell the one from the other. Eventually, even the seat of the pants becomes highly intuitive.

As highlighted earlier, both generations need to be prepared for this "trauma–drama," not just the client. The parents have been initially identified as "consultants to the consultant." They are not presenting themselves as clients, nor will they be seen or treated as such, even if occasionally one of them threatens to slip inadvertently into that role. Since no formal agreement has been entered into with them, the consultant does not assume any formal clinical responsibility for the parents or for their continuing happiness in life. This event has been created for the client's direct benefit, not for the parents'. At the same time, the consultant is also responsible for structuring the overall context of this inquiry, a transaction that at times can assume the character of a friendly deposition, if indeed there is such a thing.

It is important that both parents experience the process as friendly, meaning fundamentally benevolent in intent even in its most poignant and painful moments. It will be kept in mind that the consultant has, after all, encouraged the client to prepare many penetrating and far-reaching questions about the deepest and most sensitive thoughts and feelings, hopes and fears, and memories and anticipations in the life, mind, and heart of each parent. This is likely to include some candid review of the most difficult experiences and painful memories in each parent's life. This cannot but stir up some deep emotions, not all of them pleasant. It is, therefore, the consultant's responsibility to make an early evaluation of just how much inquiry and what depth and speed of inquiry can be sustained and assimilated well by these aging people without unnecessary or lethal damage.

The results of this evaluation will vary noticeably depending on the physical and emotional health, the character of the life story, and the degree of trauma and consequent vulnerability within the person of each parent. It is the consultant's responsibility to be reading moment by moment the impact of the ongoing conversation upon each of these older persons. In light of these considerations, the consultant will turn the psychological or emotional burners either up or down by speeding the process up or slowing it down, encouraging a more detailed explication of particular points or suggesting that some matter be treated either very lightly, be discussed overnight, or, once in a while, even skipped over altogether. A parent's level of comfort or discomfort can be directly evaluated at any given moment. Time-outs are taken as needed. Thus, above all else, the consultant's responsibility as "coach" is to manage the timing, tempo, and speed of the action. He or she will also offer some direct acknowledgment and support to the parents when the occasion calls for it. With rare exceptions, the parents will come to consider the consultant as neutral or at least fair, if not actually "on their side."

The consultant, in fact, functions as a double agent, with the tricky challenge of supporting both parties but doing so in a way that does not contribute to the lasting detriment of either one. The consultant's commitment is to conduct the proceedings in such a way that upon conclusion all three members of the family, while having very different stories to tell about what has transpired, will nonetheless agree that healing has taken place. Such a result is evidence of multidirectional partiality (Boszormenyi-Nagy & Spark, 1973), mixed with some skillful sleight of hand, on the part of the consultant.

If the consultant is not reasonably confident of such an outcome, the planned event should probably not take place, at least not at this time or in the way initially intended. Because of his or her concern for the well-being of the parents, the consultant has previously made clear to the client that he or she will be present "as if" on the parents' side throughout. If the client is not prepared to stand on his or her own feet, wielding the agenda and able to manage these conversations throughout, then he or she is not yet ready to meet in this way with the parents. As for the overall management of this trip, the consultant and client will now have assumed the roles of captain and copilot. The novelty is that the copilot will be asked to fly the plane, even if it does have two VIP's on board.

The captain will offer guidance as needed and in the unlikely event of a loss of oxygen will be ready to assist or take over the controls until things have leveled off. Such a compelling exception is a family scenario in which the client is being willfully pinned down in a destructive psychological corner by a parental coalition that beyond doubt has the emotional resources, if not yet the motivation, to consider some better arrangement. This is a situation in which the consultant might temporarily abandon the more usual neutral position for a more energetic intervention on behalf of the client. This means remaining alert throughout and judging from moment to moment what good thing, if any, can come from this turn (or twist) of events. It is also important that the consultant at no time lose the sense of connection and bonding with the parents. Should that happen. the overall outcome will be in jeopardy.

A Matter of Timing

By now it is clear that the key variable in making a decision to go ahead with this exploratory family surgery using only the mildest anesthesia is the matter of *timing*. The timing must be right for all four parties involved—the client, the parents, and the consultant. Good timing, meaning personal emotional readiness to look and see and say whatever is there, is critical to a good outcome. It can be evaluated from three different perspectives.

Client's Readiness

In the days before this has the client been easily and confidently saying, "Ready?" The consultant may believe the client to be ready, but only the latter, from a subjective awareness of his or her own state of mind, knows for sure. If the client has any continuing reservations that do not quickly resolve with an empathic response of acknowledgment and support, then it is probably better to wait. This is true, perhaps especially so, when the client's hesitation has been in response to parental anxiety. If a client is ready, it means that during the course of preparation the client's primary (if unconscious) loyalty has moved from the previous generation(s) to the consultant, on to the group and the group process as a whole, and finally to the person of the client himself or herself. This shift of primary loyalty is the enabling psychological dynamic that makes the political renegotiation work. It comes to the client's aid in the most frightening of moments. As a final sign of readiness, the client will assume full emotional ownership of the prepared agenda and will be both committed to it and eager to pursue it. If a client balks at any of this, a red flag is flying!

Parents' Readiness

The client's parents must also declare themselves ready. The evidence for this state is naturally more subtle and inferential. For example, if a client reports that a parent finds work demands suddenly overwhelming, even when the visit has been preplanned for weeks or months, the son or daughter should routinely hypothesize unreadiness. Or if a parent has an unexpected and vague illness, again the message may be, "Give me more time to prepare for this." If a parent, even after repeated clear explanations, continues to declare confusion about the request for participation, although not refusing, one must assume that more preliminary negotiation needs to be completed.

Parents frequently feel one or both of two fears. The first is that what is being proposed here is an act of rejection of him or her, a disavowal of family beliefs and values, and an abandonment of the family. The second fear is that this series of meetings has been set up so that through clever psychological detective work the consultant can figure out the various ways in which they have been failures as parents. They are often already wondering how they could have caused the psychological problems that have compelled their son or daughter to come to this guy in the first place. If a parent begins from the premise that seeking psychological help is inherently a sign of extreme personal problems, and therefore of prior parenting failure, this fear will constantly be playing around the edges. Such a parent may require repeated reassurance.

Consultant's Readiness

Last and also least, the consultant, from his or her own perspective, needs to declare, "Ready." First and foremost, this means that the consultant is comfortable with the client and finds him or her trustworthy. The consultant also needs to be satisfied with his or her grasp of family dynamics and history and with the points of particular vulnerability and sensitivity. He or she is already confident about the current general life stability of both generations as they enter this challenge. The consultant is confident that there are no unknown current life events creating an unusual distraction or siphoning off undue energy. (A client will not be encouraged to engage in this renegotiation with parents when his or her marriage is in a state of acute crisis and instability. The same is true for the parental marriage.)

Obviously, the consultant needs to be on good conversational terms with his or her own personal narrative in life in order to be able to stay relaxed and tolerate such wide-ranging explorations by the members of client families. It is not the case that in being relaxed he or she is insensitive or indifferent to what is happening in the room. It is, rather, that the consultant is at a point in his or her life where the client drama is not likely to reflect and activate memories of trauma in the consultant's own life with which he or she has not yet even begun to become acquainted. By having this personal freedom to cross levels of personal consciousness and cross the boundaries of the generations in his or her own family, the consultant can be a guarantor that people actually can and do accomplish this sort of thing and live to tell the story.

These various warnings about readiness on the part of all parties may seem laborious and unduly detailed. But then again, as is often the case when the potential gains are enormous, the potential pitfalls are quite considerable.

The Use of Time

The in-office sessions with parents each last for a double session, approximately 1 hour 45 minutes. There will be either two or three of these sessions, with at least one night between each. The whole event normally takes place within the course of a week. Whether two or three sessions are held depends on the intensity of the family process, the complexity of the agenda, and how slowly the experience will need to go. As a rule, no breaks are taken during a session. An exception is made when either a parent looks unusually tired or overwhelmed or when any party to the proceedings clearly needs an emotional rest or an opportunity to regroup. This calls for a short recess. When parents come from outside the city, they usually stay with son or daughter during the visit. However, when either party is uncomfortable with this arrangement, an alternative is arranged. Sometimes, for example, a client needs physical distance in order to maintain poise in the conversations, or a client's home may be so small, especially if he or she has several children, that it will not be either physically or emotionally comfortable for parents to stay there.

Frequently, a family will be given assignments to complete between sessions. This may include the transmission of information that although important, is not emotionally loaded. By contrast, the client may be asked to pursue with one parent alone some especially sensitive matters that are better dealt with apart from both the spouse and the consultant. The facts of the matter are not likely to be in any way hidden from the spouse. However, the very private inner meanings of the story to the parent to be debriefed may be more candidly revealed if the spouse is not present. An example of this occurred when a daughter began to talk to her father about the possibility that he had had some kind of sexual contact with all four of his daughters many years before. The father became very ashamed and agitated when the subject was first broached. He ran from the office and hid in another room. After some time he recovered and returned. The issue at hand became an assignment to be dealt with by daughter and father between sessions, and all parties agreed to this arrangement. When the debriefing took place at the beginning of the next day, the client took the opportunity to explore this matter to her satisfaction and her father was now able to participate in a way that was useful to both.

In general, a family will be encouraged to spend time together between sessions, in either serious work or in playful recreation. On occasion they will be asked to keep the contact to a minimum, if things are unstable politically or very raw emotionally right at this time. The recommendation from the consultant grows out of the drama of the moment.

If it is called for, the consultant can intervene to support or protect parents in a variety of different ways. The ideal session is one in which, once everyone is into the swing of things, the consultant can lean back and mostly be an observer until it is time to call "time." Sometimes, however, the consultant will intervene very directly. A client can get caught up in the emotionality of the conversation, thereby forfeiting any sense of perspective or distance. The consultant may engage the client directly for a second simply to help him or her ground the self again and regain composure. (This is also an excellent way to protect the parents.) It is an assumption of the theory that any extremely intense emotional reaction to a parent is likely to result in the client having identified or reidentified the self as a disappointed, demanding, angry, or dependent child in relationship to the parent. This is not the desired outcome. When necessary, the consultant may indicate that a given matter has been explored adequately and that any further perusal can do no more than salt old wounds. At times, the consultant will recommend that a given item simply be ignored altogether and skipped over.

From time to time, the consultant will take the emotional blood pressure of the parents and confirm that all the vital signs are good. Infrequently, a parent seems unduly disoriented, and the consultant may suggest a significant reduction of the agenda. The consultant may introduce some innocuous conversation to provide a brief respite.

Before the consultant actually sees the parents in person, his or her perceptions of and judgment about them come from the client's representation of them. Generally speaking, this is accurate and proves to be a reliable guide. Nonetheless, usually the parents are psychologically more attractive than presented. This may be because clients present the early introjected parents whereas the consultant meets the contemporary parents. However, if a son or daughter seriously misreads the readiness and the resources of the parents or if the consultant misreads the information as presented by the client, the proceedings may turn a little sour, calling for some adaptive or remedial action. This is very much the exception rather than the rule, but it does mean that the consultant should without fail be very attentive to this possibility in the early going.

When the ground rules have been explained and other introductory preparations have been completed, the direct conversation between the generations always begins with an invitation to the parents to ask some questions of the client. It has been made clear that there is no question that they cannot ask, even though son or daughter is not obligated to answer. Additionally, parents will be invited to give the client some feedback on how they see the life of son or daughter progressing in general at this time. In some circumstances the client will actually solicit feedback by perhaps asking a question like "What have you thought about my recent marriage [or divorce or remarriage or change of job, etc.]?" The purpose of this very important procedure is quite simply to show good faith. In other words, the parent will not be asked to do anything that son or daughter is not fully prepared to do also. In this way, a conscious effort is made to establish a strong sense of mutuality and reciprocity from the very beginning. This is not just an inquiry into the lives of individuals; this is the unfolding of the story of this family.

CHAPTER 9

Writing the Script: The In-Office Agenda for the Primary Triangle — Part 1. The Parents Speak

> . . . and which is worst of all, continual fear and danger of violent death, and the life of man solitary, poor, nasty, brutish, and short.
>
> — Thomas Hobbes (1588–1679)
> *Leviathan* (Part 1, Chap. 13)

> The colors of the rainbow, so pretty in the sky
> are also on the faces of people going by.
> I see friends shaking hands, saying how do you do;
> they're really saying I love you.
> . . . And I think to myself, what a wonderful world.
> — "What a Wonderful World"
> Recorded by Louis Armstrong
> Lyrics by G. Weiss and B. Thiele

The in-office agenda can be thought of as a play in three acts, introduced by a prologue, concluding with an epilogue.

Prologue: So What Is This Play About? The Parental Narrative

Act One: The Parents' Memories
Scene I — Earliest Memories through Junior High School
Scene II — Junior High School through the Wedding Day
Scene III — The Story of the Parental Marriage: The Normal Developmental Family Experiences

Prologue: So What Is This Play About?
The Parental Narrative

Each human being not only has but, indeed, almost *is* a personal
narrative in life. That is, each person has and is a detailed and
complex story full of specific anecdotes and connected sequences
stretching out over time. Each person is also, of course, a part of the
narrative of the previous generation. From this panoply of experiences one acquires a heritage, forges an identity, and creates a
destiny. All meanings and values in life are constructed around these
sequences of events, including the continuing thread of meaning and
purpose that, however fragile, gives continuity, character, and coher-
ence to a life and that also imposes an ethical evaluation upon it as
well as an assessment of life success.

Since parents are recruited from the class of human beings, each
parent has hundreds of memories or small stories stored in his or her
memory bank or personal library. This multitude of small stories
creates a plethora of individual scenes or snapshots. These are then
connected into acts within the play that is the life of a parent. Within
this unfolding story, a number of alternative organizing principles are
available. These include the principles of love, hate, power, success,
failure, profit, guilt, celebration, suffering and despair. Any one or
any combination of these principles can weave together and unify
these kaleidoscopic fragments into a colorful and patterned whole life
of whatever particular beauty or shabbiness.

Through exploring the detail and the private inner meanings of these many small stories and sequences of events face-to-face with the parent, a son or daughter comes to have a more complete and compassionate picture of the narrative and the state of consciousness and, therefore, the person of the parent. This encourages identification and then forgiveness by the second generation. Recently, the poet Robert Bly (1991) said, "As we get more initiated, the parents get to look more human. We see their woundedness, rather than the wounds we think they gave us." The possibility for an I-Thou relationship (Buber, 1958), rather than a parent–child relationship, is now at hand.

The purpose of exploring personal and family history is not primarily to gain understanding or insight, although that does happen, and certainly is not to establish causal connections. The focus is on contextual thinking, not causal. The purpose is to make accessible in this moment in time deeply felt emotions and deeply emotionalized attitudes that are currently affecting behavior in destructive ways. When the client recreates various scenes from personal and family history, the emotions associated with these scenes and memories tend to show up also. The new information also creates a context for choice on the part of the next generation and through this the possibility of "differentness" and, therfore, differentiation. The creation of a context that holds out and supports this possibility of distinction is the heart of personal authority work. With this prologue in mind, we proceed on with the play.

Act One: The Parents' Memories

Many questions are presented to mother and father. These questions lead to the kind of dialogue illustrated below. Each section of the dialogue represents a different family.

Scene I—Earliest Memories through Junior High School

Family 1

DAUGHTER: Tell me your earliest memory in life. Do you have any preschool memories? What about kindergarten?

MOTHER: I can remember playing in the backyard still unsteady on my feet and running to meet my father and falling down several times. He always came and picked me up and swung me up high. [The daughter later remarked that she had not known about the power of the continuing emotional connection between her mother and her mother's father.]

FATHER: I remember when I was about four going to a day school at a church and soiling my pants one day and being very embarrassed. I still to this day get a little embarrassed when I remember that. [This story gave the daughter some new information about the continuing power of shame in her father's life.]

DAUGHTER: Was it difficult or easy starting first grade? At grade school were you well connected in the peer group or were you an outsider? More of a leader or a follower? Were there any special successes or traumas during grade school? Any problems with discipline or achievement at school or home?

FATHER: I do remember the terror of starting first grade. My father took me to school, but my mother stood at the door weeping; I remember I didn't want to go. However, it was never again as bad as that first day.

MOTHER: I was a real leader at grade school and I loved it. A group of us girls stopped at my home almost every afternoon, and my mother usually had a snack for us. A couple of those girls are still good friends of mine. I don't remember any particular problems.

DAUGHTER: What kind of man was your father, with regard to maleness and masculinity; how would you describe your mother as a woman?

FATHER: My father was a very hard worker; in fact, we didn't see that much of him. He was gone early and came home late. The weekends were the only times that we really ate together. We always had special food at the weekends, and my father would say a long prayer every time.

MOTHER: My mother was a very vivacious person; I think I'm a bit like her. Although things changed a lot when her sister died. She was always very close to her sister, and I think she really missed her. I think too she was a very feminine person. At least she took a lot of pleasure in dressing up at times and looking really pretty. I think my father was really proud of her, although I think sometimes he got a little shy when she dressed up.

DAUGHTER: Have you any memories of your parents' marriage during those years? How did father relate to women and mother to men? What important messages did you get about male–female relationships? How did your parents handle issues of control and decision making in the home? Who exercised the most control?

FATHER: I'd say my mother was probably the boss in our home, at least she did most of the talking. She was certainly the boss with us kids. But there was a time or two when my father would put his foot down. She didn't like it, but if he truly made up his mind about something, there was no changing it. I think I always felt a bit pleased when he did that, although it wasn't too often. Of course, you know your mother has always been the boss in our house.

DAUGHTER: How were your father and mother as parents in those days? How did they express affection and disapproval toward each other and toward you?

MOTHER: I think my parents were really better than average parents, at least they both seemed to genuinely like children. They loved being grandparents, I think you know that.

FATHER: My mother could show affection very easily. But my father left you guessing a bit. I think he loved us alright, but he never said too much about it. He took on the discipline. It was one of those homes where you heard a lot about "wait until your father gets home." But it was mostly a tongue lashing. I only saw him take off his belt two or three times.

DAUGHTER: What do you think today about your role in the family at that time? Were you a favorite with either parent, or the least favored?

FATHER: I don't think my father had any favorites. My mother might have had, but if she did it was Bob. I know it wasn't me.

DAUGHTER: How comfortable were your parents in their own sexuality? What messages did you receive about sex and sexual behavior? How has this teaching affected you?

MOTHER: Actually we got very different messages about sex from our parents. My mother was cautious, I think, but much more comfortable than my father. Now that I think about it, he was probably quite uncomfortable in that whole area. Of course you know, your father doesn't like to talk about it too much either.

DAUGHTER: Is there anything else of importance about the grade school years?

Scene II—Junior High School through the Wedding Day

JUNIOR HIGH YEARS

Family II

SON: Describe your home during the junior high years.

MOTHER: That was a very bad time for me. That was when my

father's drinking was at its worst, and my mother threatened to leave him several times. He lost two good jobs in less than 2 years. I was embarrassed that I couldn't bring any friends home. Things felt very tense at home all the time. In fact I spent a lot of my time at my friend Sally's home.

SON: Describe your overall experience at school during the junior high years.

FATHER: I had a good time, although I kind of wish now that I'd worked harder at that time. It would have been easier in senior high if I had. But, I was very interested in sports then and played something year round. There were no alcohol problems like in your mother's house, the only thing was that my mother had terrible headaches frequently. I was pretty busy with my sports though, and I didn't know much about what was going on.

SON: How do you remember your personal relationships developing with father and mother and brothers and sisters? Any big problems?

FATHER: Well, my father was on the road at that time, Monday through Friday, so we just saw him at the weekends, and I wasn't home too much at the weekends myself. Everything seemed to be okay between the two of them. But that's when my brother wrecked his car. He was in the hospital about five months and that upset everybody. I think he might have been drag racing, although I couldn't get my parents to talk about it. But other than that, no big problems. Just like any other family.

SON: Were you well motivated at school in these years? Did you perform up to your ability? Did you have a best friend?

MOTHER: Well, to be frank I never was much of a student. I think I just always expected to be married. At least that's what I wanted. My friend Jenny was the same. We talked a lot about that. If I were a young person now, I think I would be different.

SON: Now the boy–girl stuff: Did you do much dating? Did you have a steady? Did you do the usual sexual experimentation? Was your sexual development as a teenager fairly ordinary, or unusual in any ways?

FATHER: That's a strange question to ask! Did you make up these questions yourself? Why do you want to know that anyway? Of course, I did everything just like any other teenager.

SON: What was your biggest pleasure and your biggest worry in junior high school?

MOTHER: My biggest worry was getting into senior high school.

My biggest pleasure was being with my friends at the weekend.

Family III

DAUGHTER: As a senior how were things between you and your parents, especially about discipline and control? Were you free to make your own decisions, choose your friends, plan your activities?

FATHER: Well, remember I was in boarding school, dear. So my parents gave their proxy to the school administration. But they weren't a bad lot really. Of course, we did scamper about a bit at night, especially on the weekends. The trick was not to get caught coming in.

DAUGHTER: Which parent was the enforcer? Did they generally agree on things? Did you have a way of getting your own way?

MOTHER: Well, darling, I wouldn't use the word *enforcer*. Although my father was quite a forceful person—still is for that matter. A remarkable man, actually, for his age. Yes, they usually agreed, since my mother never challenged him on anything in public, certainly not in front of the family. I did have a way with him, at least some of the time. I think my father has always been rather partial to women, even to this day.

DAUGHTER: How about your social life at this time. Were you popular with your peer group? Did you find a good balance between social life and school requirements? Does any one achievement stand out during high school?

MOTHER: Well, of course, all my friends lived in the area, and we all went to the same private school together. So we pretty much stuck together right through school. I was quite a good student but never at the top. Once or twice I had difficulties, but I soon had a private tutor and would catch up quite quickly. I must admit, though, I think my social life was a little more important to me than school life. But all that changed once I went to college.

DAUGHTER: Did you have any significant love relationships during your senior high years? How did those come out? Where are those people today? [It is surprising how often an older parent seems to know the current circumstances of someone who had been a special love during the high school years.]

FATHER: I had lots of girlfriends in high school and did a lot of dating, but no significant love relationship, as you put it. I don't think I would have been on for that at that time. I don't know where those girls are now; all happily married, I expect, and raising wonderful families. Actually, I did run into Jill Robinson about a year ago. I can tell you that took me back a bit and brought back some memories.

DAUGHTER: Did anything dramatic happen in the lives of your siblings or the family as a whole in these years?

MOTHER: No, I don't think so. Your Aunt Sharon did go off the deep end a little bit for a while. She was dragged into a psychiatrist every week for some months, I think. In fact, I think she might have spent a few weeks in the hospital, but it didn't seem to affect the family too much. It had to do with being a jilted lover if I remember right. But Sharon always was very touchy. Mother said she took after her grandmother in that regard.

DAUGHTER: When did you start to think about your future at work or college? What were your parents' ambitions for you? Had you any ideas what you might want to do in life? Was graduation a big day?

FATHER: I always knew I'd go to college in the Boston area. That's the family tradition. And I pretty well knew that I'd join my father's business after that. So there wasn't a lot to think about there. And I was quite happy with all that. In fact, it has turned out quite well for all of us. I know some young chaps do have to worry about that sort of thing. So I was quite lucky. Graduation day was a wonderful day. Everyone was there and we had a fine celebration into the wee hours. Of course, we never needed much of an excuse to celebrate.

DAUGHTER: What do you now think was your biggest psychological or emotional issue during high school?

Mother: I don't know that I would call this a psychological problem, but I did worry about my weight quite a lot. I never was very heavy. But I was always rather afraid that I might gain weight suddenly. So I did my best to prevent that.

AFTER HIGH SCHOOL TO WEDDING DAY

Family IV

SON: Now I want to inquire about your life from leaving high school up to your wedding day. This includes the story of the college years. Was college more fun or more work?

FATHER: Well, son, for myself I would say more work. I felt very lucky to be in college and I knew my parents had made a great sacrifice to help me get there. So I was determined to make good on it. I really never thought very much about fun. I felt so lucky just to be there. I still feel very grateful when I think about it, because I know what it cost my parents. I'll always be grateful for that.

Son: What about your first job experience?

Mother: I was actually a year ahead of your dad in college, so while he was just a senior, I went off working. I majored in journalism, so I got a job as an assistant reporter at the newspaper, and I really loved it. It was hard work and the money wasn't very much, but the work itself was very exciting and I think I would have worked for nothing. Mind you, I was glad enough to leave when I got pregnant with you, two years later.

Son: Did you have any significant love relationship prior to meeting each other?

Father: And you expect me to answer that in front of your mother? It's okay, your mother knows all about it anyway. I dated a suite mate of hers. In fact, we went out for about a year before it broke up, and I think partly it broke up because of your mother. I don't mean your mother caused it; I mean I met your mother. I just felt very attracted to her and lost interest in the other girl. Of course, your mother was dating at the time too, so I had a bit of competition. I enjoyed that!

[At this stage in the proceedings, both parents are likely to be very much into the swing of things. By now they are likely to be free-associating into their own stories, with less anxiety and less need for structuring or prompting from the client.]

Son: Were you active at all, either religiously or politically at this time?

Mother: I grew up in a very devout Catholic home, and I did attend church regularly in college. But after I left college, I fell off a bit for a few years. Of course, your father was never very interested. But when you children were small, we started back again, and I persuaded him to come too. Nowadays I find a real comfort in going to church, I don't know why. But I do think that God has watched over this family, and we should all be very thankful. I hope you will get interested, dear.

Son: Tell me about the first time you laid eyes on each other. When and where did you first see the other? Whom did you see when you first looked at him or her? What did you especially notice and respond to in the other, right from the beginning?

Father: Well, I've always thought your mother was a very pretty woman. Still is. The first time I saw her, her eyes really lit up, just like they still do today. That did it for me. And she loved me. I can love anybody who loves me.

Son: How did you get to a first date, and how did that go? How did things evolve into a dating relationship? Who first started talking about marriage? Were you more surprised or more delighted when it became serious?

Mother: Like your father said, I was dating another boy when I met him. And I wasn't that impressed with your father initially. But he was very persistent and he's never been an easy man to say no to. In many ways he reminded me of my own father, although I don't know if that's a good thing or a bad thing. But he had a great sense of humor. And he was always full of ideas about things to do. Does anybody ever know why they get married? I think your father was the first one to talk about marriage, but maybe he got the idea from me. I know I was both surprised and delighted when we got engaged.

Son: Was the courtship easy and relaxed or conflicted and turbulent?

Father: Smooth as velvet. We had a good plan. In the mornings your mother did what she wanted, and in the afternoons I did what she wanted. Worked like a charm. Seriously, though I, refused to get too serious.

Son: As you think back today, who was that person whom you saw and fell in love with? What attracted you? With whom did you fall in love?

Mother: I don't know if I can really answer that. I know I felt safe with your father. I knew I could trust him. That was important to me. My mother really liked him too and that helped. But I don't know if I really knew him at the time.

Son: Okay, so what were the attitudes of both families to your projected marriage? Were both generally favorable or not? If not, how did you deal with this disappointment?

Father: Well, like I said, your mother is very lovable and my family took to her right away. Her mother liked me too, but I don't think her father was quite as sure. I think he wanted somebody who was more responsible or more interested in money or more committed to making money than I was. I think too he thought I was never quite serious enough. But I grew on him over the years and we were quite close by the time he died. If they hadn't liked me—well, I think we would have gone ahead anyway.

Son: Do you have vivid memories of the preparations for the wedding day? Is there anything that stands out about the wedding day itself? What is your memory of your spouse on the wedding day?

MOTHER: Your dad was studying for his final exams, so I did most of the preparations, with a lot of help from my sisters. Mostly it was good fun, except when we couldn't get your dad's attention to help with some of the important decisions. He would just say, "Do it any way you want it." But I didn't think that was a good way to approach a wedding. So I kept after him. The wedding day itself was beautiful. My only bad moment was starting up the church aisle when my father started to sob. I didn't know whether to punch him or hug him. I know I was choking it back too by the time we got to the altar. Not a great way to begin things. Your father looked very handsome in his fancy outfit. He told one joke after another, but I think that was mostly to cover his nervousness. Of course, he'd never admit that.

SON: Where did you go for the honeymoon and how was your experience?

FATHER: Hey, what kind of question is that? None of your damn business! Didn't you have your own honeymoon? Well, it was much like yours, only better. Actually, we had a very nice time, once we recovered from the wedding. It was the first time we were really alone together in weeks.

[Responses to this question have varied all the way from this benign comment, to the mother who said, "Well I realized on the first night of my honeymoon that I had made a dreadful mistake from which I would never recover."]

Scene III—The Story of the Parental Marriage: The Normal Developmental Family Experiences

Family V

DAUGHTER:

"With your permission, I now want to talk to you about the story of your life together in your marriage, clarifying not simply the facts but discussing some of your private inner thoughts and feelings about the events that constitute the story of your marriage.

"First I want to discuss the pregnancies, in particular, your pregnancy with me, and its aftermath.

"I have some questions about child raising, about your beliefs and practices in that regard, and whether these have now changed any.

"Next, I would like to recall the home in which we lived while I was growing up.

"And I want to talk about your jobs and work lives outside the home while I was growing up.

"Next, I want you to reflect on family finances and how that created a context of opportunity (or hardship) for you and for us as a family.

"I'd like to review the matter of the health of the family and of family members over the years, both physical and psychological health.

"I want to explore your memories of your relationships with the in-laws, the special friends in your lives, and then our neighbors.

"I am curious about your understanding and memory of your use of free time, including hobbies.

"What about family vacations and other events and occasions illustrating family rituals?"

The dialogue continues:

DAUGHTER: I also have some questions about your love life, which I want to present in a very open-ended way so that you can say as much or as little as you are comfortable with. First, how did you solve the universal struggle around control and decision making in the marriage?

MOTHER: Well, we certainly had our battles in the early days. In fact we almost came to blows at times. You know your dad was an army officer like his father before him, and he wanted to run the family like a military post. For a few years that was okay with me. But then I began to assert myself more—then we had problems! We had plenty of fights. Then the time came when it just seemed to be worked out. But I wouldn't wish that on anybody. We hurt each other a lot.

DAUGHTER: Every marriage takes some attitude toward how husband and wife should relate to members of the opposite sex. Did you come to any agreement about that? Was this a source of conflict? Did any "third party" relationship ever take on the character of "an affair"?

FATHER: I must admit I've always been a pretty jealous person. And your mother was a woman who could turn heads. I was maybe too anxious about that and tried to control her too much. As far as I'm concerned, if I'd been as faithful to God as I've been to your mother, I'd be the better man for it.

DAUGHTER: Was there ever any conflict of loyalties between your commitment to each other and your commitment to your parents?

MOTHER: The only time was when my father died, and I thought my mother should move in with us, at least for a while. But your dad wouldn't hear of it. I thought he was selfish, and I told him so.

DAUGHTER: Were there any big loyalty conflicts involving close personal friends?

FATHER: The first years we were married, I used to like to play poker with a bunch of guys on Friday nights. Your mother didn't like those guys and didn't like me spending time with them. We had a running battle on that for a while.

DAUGHTER: Any strong differences of opinion about jobs, moves, homes, money, or political or religious beliefs?

MOTHER: Well, you know yourself that we moved a lot. I hated that. But your father had no choice in that if he wanted to keep his job. And each move was toward a promotion. We didn't talk that much about religion or politics. Your dad didn't want me to go back to work at first, but then I think he got to like the little extra money. Funny enough, we had no problems about money in the early years when we didn't have any. The more money, the more disagreements we had.

DAUGHTER: At some point in life every married person wonders, How did I ever get myself into a mess like this? When did you come closest to divorce, and what kept you together?

FATHER: I don't remember ever any talk about divorce, although maybe we thought about it. But things were pretty bad when your mother first wanted to go back to work. I felt I was working hard enough and making enough to provide for my family. She said it wasn't for the money and I came to see that. But I never liked coming home and finding she wasn't home yet. Despite any problems we had, I never felt your mother deliberately tried to hurt me. That's one thing that sure helped me stay there.

DAUGHTER: What nurtured your marriage over the years? What were some of your most difficult times, and what are your best memories?

MOTHER: Neither one of us ever went silent on the other. We always kept talking about things. I think the little country house helped too. We had some wonderful weekends there, both with and without you children. My best memory is when I was pregnant. Your father was always especially good then.

DAUGHTER: Last question, but a difficult one: Do you think looking back over everything, that you would marry this man (or woman) again?

FATHER: Yes, of course. I don't have to think about that.

MOTHER: I think so but you know, dear, you can't possibly know at the time all that might happen.

Scene IV—The Work Life and the Use of Time by Each

Family VI

SON: Are you pleased with the way you've spent your life? Did you spend too much time at work or not enough? Did you choose your work in the first place or ever come to choose it? Would you prefer to have done something else?

FATHER: I think I might better have worked less. I like my work although I think it chose me more than I chose it. A lot of it is just luck, you know, or chance. If I was starting again, I'd like to try something different. I think your mother wishes that she had had a career.

SON: Were you adequately educated and prepared for work and for life? Did you have an adequate opportunity to perform and achieve at work?

MOTHER: My parents felt strongly that it was as important to educate the girls as the boys. I was lucky that way. My professors encouraged me to go to graduate school. In looking back I think I should have done that. I would like to have gone further in my work, but I think you know there were limits to what a woman could do then. Things are much better now.

[For some clients in this generation, an important additional question is: Are you, Mother, pleased with your decision not to work outside the home, and not to pursue a career or profession for yourself? Have you been fully satisfied as a homemaker?]

SON: Are you pleased with the number of children you have had or would you have preferred more or less?

FATHER: I think three was just about right. Of course, we'd have had four if we hadn't lost that baby. That might have been better.

SON: Are you pleased with the way in which you divided your time and energy between work outside and work at home?

MOTHER: You may not know this, but I left my practice for about 4 years when the twins were born. I think things were quite well balanced overall. There were times when I would have preferred part-time, but if you let the practice go down it's hard to build it up again. Sometimes I was too tired in the evenings to be with the children the way I wanted.

SON: Did the division of labor between you two work out in a satisfactory way?

FATHER: I always felt quite busy when at home, but, to be honest, I think your mother carried more than her fair share. I think now I could have done more to help at times, but I didn't see it then. Maybe you'll do better.

SON: Have you any regrets, especially you mother, that you were born at a time when fewer professional work opportunities were available to women?

MOTHER: I think I was an exception actually; there weren't many women in medical school in my day. And there was a lot of discrimination. But I do feel some pride that I helped make it a little easier for the next generation of women.

SON: Have you any thoughts about the importance of work in your life?

FATHER: Oh yes. I'd go nuts without it. In fact, I'm not looking forward to retirement. Although your mother is already working on a list of chores for me. But that's not quite the same. Everybody needs to feel useful and like they're contributing. And everybody wants to be in charge of somebody.

Scene V — *The Parents behind the Parents*

Family VII

DAUGHTER: How would you characterize your experience with your own parents as they became more aged and less competent, more infirm and less independent?

MOTHER: It was really quite painful to watch my father after his stroke. It bothered me the way my mother treated him like he was a child. It was never quite as much fun visiting them after that, more of a strain.

DAUGHTER: How pleasant or uncomfortable was your contact and conversation with your parents in their last years? What expectations and demands did you feel, and how did you cope with these?

FATHER: I quite enjoyed visiting my parents in their last years, but I think I felt distant from them. My father was never very open with his feelings, and he was one of the few people whom I never learned to be open with. My mother expressed her feelings well, but she wasn't so good at listening. I'm not sure she ever realized how much I had changed over the years.

DAUGHTER: To what degree did they grow old gracefully? How did they approach their own deaths, and how did each of them actually die?

MOTHER: My father did very well until the stroke. After that he was just a tragic figure. I think I felt more relief than anything else when he died. You know I think he died just because he didn't want to go on living. My mother might outlive me, although I'm not sure she's very graceful about it. But I have to admire her survivor spirit.

DAUGHTER: Did you have an opportunity to say all the things you wanted to say to each of your parents? Did you receive any inheritance or favorite possessions?

FATHER: To be candid, I felt tongue-tied with my father. There were things I wanted to say, but they wouldn't come out. I don't think they've come out yet. I talked at length to my mother before she died, and I think she died quite peacefully. As you know, we got a little money in mother's will, not much. But those two seascapes that you admire so much in the family room, they came from your grandparents' home. They'll probably be yours some day.

DAUGHTER: Are there ways in which you see them living on in you? Are there ways in which you see them living on in me?

MOTHER: I've been told that I get to look more like my mother every year. I don't know if that's a compliment. I certainly have my father's interest in gardening. I loved to work in the garden with him when I was younger, and he taught me a lot. You're the gardener among our children, so you're like him in that way too.

DAUGHTER: Do you have any persisting regrets about your life with them? Did you say a direct and explicit good-bye to each before their deaths? Do you have a sense of being emotionally complete with each of them now?

FATHER: My one regret is that my father and I never could talk to each other. I think he was proud of me, but I had to guess at it. I felt closer to my mother toward the end, but for a long time I was very distant. I regret that now. With my father, I think we sort of pretended that he wasn't dying until he was gone. With my mother, we talked about it, and she seemed ready. I feel okay about her, but my father, that was a different story.

Act Two: The Parents' Reflections

Scene I—Family Traumas: The Unusual Events

In an earlier section (Act One, Scene III), the client will have discussed with the parents the various challenges and stresses of the sort that occur in the normal life of any family. In the following paragraphs is an exploration of the traumas and the unusual stressful occurrences that are idiosyncratic to the life and history of a particular family and its various members.

One example is the situation where the parents' marriage did not sustain itself, a not unusual occurrence among people who seek out this kind of family-oriented consultation. In pursuing the story of such a marriage, the client will also inquire how the marriage first began to turn sour and how it deteriorated to the point where, whether by unilateral or bilateral decision, divorce was the chosen outcome. The client will seek to discover each parent's personal perceptions of and judgments about these various events. This will include how each parent believes in retrospect that he or she contributed to the problems of the marriage and the decision to end it. This conversation will also make explicit to what extent that turn of events continues to affect the parent in a negative way or to be a source of continuing anger, regret, or guilt.

Sometimes divorced older parents have reached a good resolution with one another over the years and no longer carry intense negative emotionality about each other. They are likely in this instance to be acceptably comfortable in each other's presence and in discussing the history of their life together. In that case, it would always be my first choice to have them attend together for conversations with the client in the consultant's office. On one occasion a son aged 40 was able to bring in both of his parents who had terminated their marriage by divorce 23 years before. He asked of each parent the following questions:

SON:
"In your view, what caused the divorce?

"As you remember it, what effort was made to avoid it, both by you and by your spouse?

"Do you now think the divorce was inevitable?

"If you could go back in time, would you try to stay married or divorce again? If you divorced again, are there any ways in which you would try to do it differently? Would you do it sooner?

"Is there anything about the aftermath of the divorce that you very much regret and would try to do differently?

"Can you think of particular ways in which you contributed to the problems that led to the divorce? Could you have been different?

"Do you think that your marriage was a mistake in the first place and should not have happened?

"Do you see any positive results from the divorce?

"Did any good thing come from the marriage? Was any good purpose served?"

A conversation like this can be of great value to sons or daughters who are still trying to assimilate and make sense of the termination of the parental marriage by divorce. They can offer their own reflections on the parental marriage and also express their own form of regrets with regard to it. But when such an attractive and rare denouement as described above has not been achieved between the parents, the client is more likely to work with each parent separately. Regrettably, this is more often than not the case. It is probably fruitful to include a stepparent at some point in the proceedings but not in the routine processing of the detailed agenda as described here. It is especially valuable to include a stepparent when that stepparent has been unusually active in the client's life or the parent's life or has had a choice vantage point from which to view the family drama.

Having discussed the marriage that has ended in divorce, the parent will be invited to talk about any subsequent courtship(s) and marriage(s) that have transpired. The detail of relevant issues and colorful stories about stepchildren and stepparenting will be reviewed. The extent and way that a stepparent has been both willing and permitted to perform as parent and with what consequences will be acknowledged. In addition, the conversation will review the health history of family members, allowing clarification around such events as miscarriages and abortions and premature deaths of family members. This provides an opportunity to look at all noteworthy loss experiences in the family history. A woman in her late 30s explored with her parents the very private meanings to them of the death of the firstborn child, almost 30 years before, at age 3 years:

DAUGHTER:
"What was it like for each of you when Cecil died?

"How did you grieve for Cecil's death?

"Did you talk very much about it at the time? Have you talked much about it over the years? How do you think it affected each of you and the family?

"Did you talk much about it when your next child was born prematurely and it looked like she might die also? Was that a very frightening time for you? Did you think you were being punished or were just unlucky or what? Were you able to support each other?

"Mother and Dad, I am now returning to you your sadness and deep sense of loss about Cecil's death, since I do not think it will be any longer useful either for me or for you if I continue to carry it."

After acknowledgment of losses mourned and unmourned, a third area of inquiry brings attention to some of the most sensitive matters in the family's history. This will require a gentle and tactful touch and an ambience of compassion and empathy on the part of both the client and the consultant. This will address skeletons in the closet, such as addictive behaviors, premarital pregnancy, extramarital affairs, homosexuality, and physical, sexual, or spiritual abuse. The client now has an opportunity for complete demystification with regard to any matter, real or imagined, that has lived in a shadow land at the back of his or her mind.

This conversation occurred between a daughter in her early 30s and her parents. It had to do with the impact of addictive behaviors (in this case, the abuse of alcohol) on the family.

DAUGHTER:
"Father, do you ever still feel angry about the alcoholism in this marriage and its affects on you? What made you stick around when Mother's drinking got so bad? How did you feel when Mother fell in a stupor and then was confined to bed for months? How did you cope with your anger and frustration at having to care for her as a nurse?

"How did you decide to take on the role of caretaker when Mother was so unbearable? As you reflect on it today, how do you understand your contribution to it and your role in her alcoholism? When do you think you really grieved the loss of your wife? Did you do it more at the time of her fall, or was it more at the time of her death?"

A son in his mid-30s talked to father and mother about his perception of the impact of father's affair on the marriage and on the family. This traumatic event occurred when the son was 15 years old. The questioning went as follows:

SON:
"Mother and Father, I know that this is one of the most sensitive areas we can possibly talk about, and I want to acknowledge and also respect your discomfort when talking about it. I would not bring it up if I did not believe that it is very important for me to do so.

"As a result of Dad's affair, it seems to me that life as we knew it changed dramatically from that moment on and never really recovered. I may have overexaggerated it in my mind, but I feel it is a significant marker, in fact, a turning point in the history of this family. As you both know, we have never ever once talked about it. I know that you know that as children we heard all the arguments at night.

"I've often wondered, why did you stay together? It seems to me, Mother, that you did not forgive Dad for many years. Is that true and, if so, why?

"Dad, do you think it happened like Mother remembers it? Why do you think it happened at all? Do you agree with me that you seemed to become a different person ever after? Did you ever forgive yourself for it? Why could Mother not forgive you?"

Sometime later the conversation continued:

"Mother, can you describe your experience with breast cancer, including your thoughts and your fears? How supportive was Dad during this period? Did this help you to forgive him?"

It should be obvious by now that in discussing the dark side of family history the members are bringing into consciousness at one time the deepest, most poignant, and most painful emotional experiences the family has known. There will, therefore, be both mourning and memory of mourning. Unmourned losses will be named. The client is ready to identify with and participate in the family's grief over any family trauma. This creates one of the most significant opportunities and some of the most moving moments in the client's therapy. Emotional burdens and guilts, unwittingly absorbed by the second generation, will be symbolized in language and consciously released, sometimes returned directly to the source, if it is a parent. The client will decline to continue to carry unresolvable guilts or feelings of remorse belonging to members of previous generations. It is also probable that previously "invisible" intergenerational loyalties will come into the family's consciousness and will be renegotiated.

The scene is now set for the client to be explicit about a previously implicit shift in primary loyalty away from the previous generation and toward the evolving self. This decision is a key initiative in the client's commitment to defining an emotional self that has clear, if porous, boundaries and is not simply an amorphous expression of transgenerational family emotionality. It creates a new mood of voluntariness and choice in the client's emotional life. It also constitutes a giant step in the direction of psychological "peerhood" in relationship to the former parents. To the extent that a given family has had a psychologically complicated history, replete with traumatic losses, the client will spend more time in careful preparation both of the self and the parents for this exposure, for this is likely to be not only one of the most poignant moments but also one of the most distressing aspects of these conversations.

The consultant is highly attentive to the feelings and the well-being of both generations throughout these sequences and minimizes or reframes negative constructions of meaning within the boundary of plausibility. The consultant is focused on a balance of fairness, is providing support where it is most needed, and is ensuring that all parties come out "on their feet" and with no unnecessary bruises. Creating a language for labeling and relabeling experience becomes as important as a good sense of timing in achieving this goal. The consultant's formal clinical knowledge, therapeutic artistry, and personal presence all come together now to facilitate a good outcome. All of these are needed in a situation where emotions are intense, self-esteem is vulnerable, nerves are raw, the stakes are high, and the ramifications are far-reaching. Everybody deserves a rest at this point, and usually a rest is taken.

Scene II—Looking Back: A Retrospective

Scene II and the one to follow, when taken together, are undoubtedly of the greatest long-term significance in their influence on the future life of the client. The client is about to ask a certain pattern of questions sharing a common theme. The answers will give him or her an assessment of how each parent has been coping with that final psychosocial task in life that Erikson (1978) has called the achievement of "integrity versus despair." How the parent copes in this stage of life becomes a powerful imprinting for the next generation. The dominant feeling tone in the parent's life may be on the negative end of the continuum, ranging from disappointment through despair, from hopelessness all the way to cynicism. In this circumstance, it will be essential to make this explicit in the intergenerational consciousness, without in any way further abusing the parent because of it. By making this mood explicit, the client creates a signal opportunity to make a different choice. The client is now offered the possibility of creating a different tone in his or her life than that which characterizes the parent. A core negative emotionality toward life, in an aging parent is at its most pernicious when it expresses itself in ambiguity or some other subtle disguise. It is empowering for a client to grasp that the possibility for a different choice is immediately at hand.

The questions to parents for the retrospective are typically chosen from the following selection:

"Would you choose to be born again into the same family, having the same parents and the same general circumstances in life? If you were to make changes, what are the most important changes you would make in the family and the circumstances into which you were born?

"Would you choose to be your very same self again, with the same body and mind, the same gifts and liabilities? In what ways might you choose to be different?

"Would you choose to spend your life in the same way again, carrying on the very same work, living in the same places, and pursuing the same goals and values?

"Do you think, in retrospect, that your growing-up years in the home and at school properly prepared you to deal with life? Were you adequately prepared and adequately warned?

"As you recall it, were you in charge of your life most of the time or did you feel mostly helpless and at the mercy of circumstances, circumstances that were often unpredictable?

"In retrospect, what person(s) do you think was the most influential in helping you decide your most important life decisions about education and friends and work and love? In short, other than yourself, whom do you hold the most responsible for the way in which your life has turned out, and do you feel more appreciation or resentment for that influence?

"Do you believe that you have had a fair shake in life? Have you been unusually lucky or just average, or was the deck stacked against you?

"Do you think, looking back, that you struggled more or less than an average amount, with fear or sadness? Have you ever felt hopeless enough or discouraged enough to consider ending your life, even briefly in passing?

"Do you think that you have been mostly a success or mostly a failure in life, both in your personal and in your work life? What are the reasons for your answer, either way? Do you take most of the credit or responsibility for that outcome, or do you see strongly contributing or mitigating circumstances? To repeat, do you believe that you succeeded in getting your life pretty well together?

"What achievements first in your work and second in your personal life have given you the greatest pleasure and satisfaction?

"Do you think that your parents came to see you more as a success or as a failure in life? What were the reasons for that judgment? Did you mostly fulfill or mostly disappoint their expectations? Were they more pleased or more disappointed or more surprised by the way your life turned out?

"Pick out any two or three key decisions in your life that you would like to have back again. What are they, and if you had the chance, how might you decide or behave differently?

"What two or three matters have caused you the most personal embarrassment or shame in life?

"What have been the most significant loss experiences in your personal life? How have they affected you? How have you coped with them? How do you stand emotionally in relationship to these losses today?

"What has been the biggest single personal difficulty or challenge in your life that you believe you have mastered or at least managed well? What major crises have you survived in your life? In retrospect, what enabled you to survive them?

"Name two or three persons who have been heroes (or heroines) in your life or people whom you have greatly admired. Can you say why?

"Who have been the two or three closest and most intimate personal friends in your life? What have these relationships meant to you over the years? Have you been able consistently to share your inner life with these persons? Have these persons remained trustworthy throughout?

"Have people treated you overall as well as you have deserved or at least as well as you have treated them? Do you believe that you have been adequately appreciated and acknowledged for your achievements and contributions both in your work life and in your personal and family life?

"Who was your most important spiritual-ethical teacher? When was the time of your greatest spiritual doubt, the darkest night of your soul?

"What particular beliefs or values have sustained you throughout your lifetime and have helped you live to this day? Have these beliefs and values changed much since you were a young adult? Do you believe in God today?

"Has the best moment in your life happened yet? If yes, when was it? If not, when will it be?

"Has your life been worthwhile? Do the story and the outcome of your life make sense to you? Has the effort you've made been worth it?

"Has there been on the whole more joy than pain in your life? Do you see yourself as mostly a happy or mostly an unhappy person?

"*Last question*: As you look back and as you survey the world and your place in it, do you regard this life as fundamentally benevolent and trustworthy or does the world seem to you to be overall more malevolent and untrustworthy?"

One father responded to this last question as follows:

"Well, quite honestly, there's nothing about it that makes any sense to me. You work your butt off and then you're too old to enjoy it. If you can just feel like getting up in the morning, you've

probably had a great day. Your mother says she's going to
heaven. I just hope she'll take me with her."

A second father, at the other end of the continuum, responded as
follows:

"It's been a great life. I've enjoyed almost all of it. I think I was
maybe very lucky or blessed. We got to do most of what we
wanted and to go to most of the places we wanted. We had good
health. We never had a lot of money, but we always had enough.
And our children have all turned out well. What more could we
ask for?"

Scene III—Death and Dying: A Prospective

To Parent:
"We have just been looking mostly backward in time. Now I
would like to look forward into the future with you.
"You are now at an age at which most key decisions in life have
already been made and, indeed, the majority of life has already
been lived. What is it like for you to have reached this age? How
are you negotiating this stage of life with your spouse and vice
versa?
"How are you presently feeling about your own approaching
death?
"I know no one knows but everyone wonders. So, in that
spirit, when do you think you will die, that is, at about what age?
Again, no one knows but everyone wonders. So how do you
think you might die when that time comes? How would you like
to die? Whom would you like to have with you when you die?
[Every aging parent has fantasies about these matters.]
"As you continue in life, whom do you miss the most of those
friends or relatives you have lost to death?
"Do you think you or your spouse is more likely to die first? Do
you have a preference? If you are the one who is left, how will
you handle that loss and what will you do to fill the void? Would
you expect to live for long after your spouse dies? [Alternatively,
where it is appropriate: How has your spouse's death affected
you? Here there can be further questions about the spouse's
illness and death and the experiences of the surviving parent in
regard to this.]
"How would you want or expect your relationship with me to
change, if in any way, if your spouse dies before you?
"Have you any philosophical basis for hope or any religious
faith of any sort, with regard to a continuing existence for

yourself after your physical death? If the answer is yes, on what do you base that hope? If your answer is no, how are you handling your expectation (and fear) that you will in every sense totally cease to exist upon your physical death?

"What do you see as your most important personal legacy or contribution to the world? How do you see yourself living on in your family, especially in me and in my children [as appropriate].

"What expectations or goals, if any, do you still continue to hold for me and my life?

"*Last question*: If you were to have the choice whether to come back again, would you like to live another life on this earth or will once have been enough for you? Why do you feel about this the way that you do?"

The following are responses to this final question:

A MOTHER: "Oh, I'd love to come back; there's so much more I want to do. I know I'd get myself a lot more education and then a lot more things would open up for me. There's so much to learn and so much more I'd like to know about the world and the different people in it. It would be good if I could bring back with me some of the things I've learned this time."

A FATHER: Well, son, let me say this. I think we've really opened up a new line of communication here this week and I want to keep it going. We haven't been very good at talking to each other over the years, but now I really believe we can do better. I think we'll enjoy visiting a whole lot more and we'd like to see more of your children. Maybe that will come easier now."

A SECOND FATHER: "Just to be honest, life's been very hard. I just wouldn't want to do it again if it was going to be anything like this. But I've got to say that your mother and I are both enjoying ourselves now. We've got some good years ahead of us to look forward to. If it could all be like this, I might face it again."

In facing the reality of death and human finiteness together, the two generations can have a profound meeting at the level of spirit. In this moment both generations are aware that regardless of generational and other differences they share together all the fundamental dilemmas of the human experience, culminating in the inevitability of personal death. This sense of shared humanness encourages a mutuality of forgiveness, which penetrates to the deepest level of the human spirit. Residual traces of hierarchical boundaries will dissolve irretrievably.

Here the session ends. The curtain comes down on Act Two. In all probability, both client and parents are ready for a break, a blue sky, and some fresh air. While there is still more business to be transacted, what is in some ways the most telling and compelling event and the one that is often the most far-reaching in its implications has just concluded. For both generations there may be much to absorb and to assimilate—perhaps also to recover from. Each person may want some time alone.

The goal throughout has been to put the parental narrative, with all of its nuances and with the many moods and movements of its music, into language. This in turn creates a consciousness and a context within which the client can grasp the possibility of choosing "differentness" (see Act Three, Scene II). Son or daughter has probably by now caught a glimpse of the self of each parent with a new compassion and appreciation for the faces, words, images, and attitudes of this older man and woman sitting opposite. These parents, like all parents, are also "children" of somebody, and are forever relating to that experience. In Norman Paul's favorite phrase, "We are all in the same leaky boat together." With a winsome shrug, the client acknowledges to himself or herself that this is the same man and woman, now more vulnerable than formidable, more poignant than powerful, who used to be, not so long ago, Daddy and Mommy. The power differential is dissolving right in front of the client's eyes.

In the intimacy of these moments the client embraces different aspects of the humanness of father and mother, levels that transcend biology, social learning, and culture, even maleness and femaleness. Both generations experience and acknowledge their common humanity together, and their shared vulnerability, in the face of all the universal human dilemmas in life and death. This sense of mutuality and reciprocity as human beings for the moment transcends and obliterates the generational boundary, the gender boundary, and finally the hierarchical power boundary. There is often a striking circularity of compassion and forgiveness between the generations, with the unspoken expectation that generations to come will reciprocate in kind. What goes around comes around. From this perspective, differentiation of self is seen not as an end in itself but as a step on the way toward the ultimate goal of family of origin work. That goal is personal autonomy linked with intergenerational adult intimacy, a linkage that becomes both the model for and the dynamic source of all loving relationships in life.

CHAPTER 10

Writing the Script: The In-Office Agenda for the Primary Triangle— Part 2. The Client Responds and the Consultant Reflects

> We hold these truths to be self-evident . . . that [all men] are endowed by their Creator with certain unalienable rights; that among these are life, liberty, and the pursuit of happiness.
>
> — The Preamble to the Declaration of Independence

Act Three: The Client's Declarations

Scene I — Two Special Announcements

It is the start of the third day. By now both client and parents are getting their second, maybe even their third, wind. They are now fairly confident that they will surely live through this experience. After brief socializing and easing back into things, including a debriefing of any interesting happenings since the last visit, the client declares that he or she has two special announcements to make.

What follows is a composite summary showing the kinds of conversations that occur in this sequence of the consultation. A given client will elaborate on a given matter as much as the situation calls for. The consultant will be attentive to see that the message has been unambiguously delivered and clearly and responsively received. If there appears to be fudging going on, then in a tactful fashion the consultant will see to it that the client takes a second and, if need be, a third run at the matter. This is another high-voltage moment in the overall transaction. It needs to be sharply etched so that it will stand out starkly in everyone's memory. It is probably the climactic moment in an evolution that has been going on for months, maybe years. Nonetheless, this is a landmark event in the history of the intergenerational relationships. As such, it deserves a careful marking in the mind. The dialogue will go something like this:

"Mother and Father, I have two things to tell you, and each of these is kind of a good news–bad news situation. Let me present them one at a time.

(*The First Special Announcement:*)
"In the first one, the bad news is that I acknowledge with considerable regret and chagrin that it has taken me a long time to get to this point and to be ready to make this statement. So, the good news is that I am finally 'ready.' By this, I mean finally ready to let you off the hook as 'Mummy and Daddy.' I now take full responsibility for myself and my life and my own well-being throughout the rest of this lifetime."

Parents usually respond with some degree of bemusement or slight amusement at this announcement. Frequently they say things such as:

"Well of course, dear, you have been in charge of your life for a long time. We don't tell you what to do. You've been on your own since you were 12 years old. Your mother and I have always been amazed at how independent you have been. You've never been one who could be told what to do. We brought all of you up to be able to take care of yourselves. Why, this is what we've always wanted, because we won't always be here, you know. . . ."

The conversation continues:

"This means that I am no longer your little boy. You have done a great job of raising me, and now it is over. I do regret taking such a long time and being so slow, but I finally am here and now I am ready. So the good news is that you are off the hook once and for all as 'Mummy and Daddy.' Your parenting work is over, done, complete, finished. The responsibility is fully mine and I now have it completely in my own two hands. I've got it! It's all mine! Yes, I know this feels redundant to you, because you already knew all this. But you see, it has taken me some time to catch up with you and to get to where you are. The good news is that I'm finally here now.

"Yes, I appreciate your statement that you will always go on worrying about me and how I am doing because, as you put it, in some sense I will always be your child. I do appreciate the generosity behind that statement. But I also have to wonder how it is that I manage to keep you thinking and talking like that, even at this late stage. I'm obviously even better at this being-a-child routine than I knew.

"So even though I do not fully understand it, I apologize for it, and I do plan to do better in the future. So even if I do not now understand how it is that I keep you worrying in that fashion, nonetheless I am committed to changing my style and setting you free. There is reason for hope. Of course, if you're not sure of me yet, you can go on pretending to be Mommy and Daddy until you're absolutely convinced that I'm ready for the change.

"Actually, and to be candid about it, when all is said and done, I'm really just looking out for myself. I don't at all mind you worrying about me. It is just that I do not want to go on worrying about you worrying about me. So I have reluctantly decided to give up my little girl status with you. I certainly do not mean to imply that this comes easily to me, for it does not. And you know that you do have and always will have a unique place in my heart. It is just that the 'Mummy-Daddy' thing is about to be over. You've been very patient and I appreciate it. I just cannot bring it off any more. And I wanted you to be among the very first to know."

Occasionally a parent becomes quite upset at this development. The following dialogue illustrates the point.

MOTHER: Well, dear, you just put a knife in my heart . . . and turned it.

FATHER: This is a two-way street you know. What if I was sinking? What would you do then? I hope it never comes to that and we never need it. God forbid that we do, but if we did . . . ?

DAUGHTER: I would reach out with support . . . but it would be because I wanted to and not as a child, not out of obligation.

CONSULTANT: You see this is not at all about you, Mom and Dad. This is all about Jean. It's about a change in her state of mind, her inner consciousness about herself, and the way she sees herself in the world. The only thing that is changing or needs to change for you is your understanding of what is changing for her. Otherwise, you can hold everything the same.

MOTHER: Jean, I thought you always knew that I was there for you, and I'd always be there for you . . . I thought you knew that . . . and I always will.

DAUGHTER: That's fine, Mother, even if I don't need it any more. If you like, I'd be willing to pretend to need it from time to time. Anyway, what's wrong with a little extra insurance? It's just that I probably won't collect on it.

The *second special announcement* is addressed to the opposite sex parent and in the case of a mother and son goes something as follows:

"Mother, I have a second good news–bad news statement for you. The bad news comes first, although frankly it isn't bad news as much as it is sad news, or so it may seem at first. The news is that I have decided, finally decided, that you no longer need to be the first love, the number one woman in my life. I have come to realize that that is no longer fair to you.

"So, I think the time has now come for me to offer that position to someone else. She has been growing on me in recent times, looks a better prospect to succeed you than ever before, and seems increasingly interested in the job. I don't know how much of that is due to her and how much is me, but that really doesn't matter since it is such a pleasing development. You know . . . I think I might have been hoping for something like this all along. Anyway, I wanted you to be at least the second to know."

Alternatively, and as would be consistent with life circumstances, the dialogue might go like this:

Son: Mother, I have decided to give you up as the first love in my life. I do this to clear the decks because I believe that I am now ready to be open to a love relationship, one that might someday develop into a commitment and a marriage. I have learned a great deal in the practice relationship with you. But I don't think I can learn much more from it. I think I am finally ready to move on to the real thing.

Next comes the good news. The good news is that while I am giving you up as number one woman in my life, you do get the number two spot . . . at least until some kid who looks like you comes along.

Mother: That's fine. That's as it should be. I won't resent any woman whom you choose.

When there are children, mother or father may drop yet another place or two in the standings.

Again, the opposite sex parent may protest that son or daughter is misunderstanding the relationship between them, and how it stands now or how it has developed over the years. The client does not need to oppose or contradict this. Instead, he points out that this is his perception of the relationship, and that he is merely signaling an upcoming movement. Anyway, all of this will simply enable him to catch up to where the parent already is. It is not unusual that, even though the language of denial is being spoken, there is both sadness and romance and a strong and poignant sense of loss present in the room. A parent may protest to son or daughter, "I don't know what you are talking about" while simultaneously the tears are glistening in the back of the eyes. The point does not need to be labored. The work is being done. Once in a while, it may be useful to give a parent the title of "Number One Emeritus."

There is usually a sense of loss in both generations and an experience of risk taking in the second generation. Instinctively, son or daughter seems to know that when the parents have been given up directly to their faces as parents in the psychological sense and when the opposite sex parent has been given up explicitly as the first love, neither of these acts can ever be rescinded and neither of the old positions can ever be fully reassumed. These moves are for keeps, and clients move very circumspectly at this point. During the preparation time, the consultant is attentive to see that the client is letting himself or herself in fully on what is happening, as well as the likely consequences.

Following these transactions in the office, one sometimes notices a little courting behavior breaking out between the parents. No doubt this is generated by a mixture of empathy from the watching spouse and a pleasure that the "foreign body" has finally been removed from between them. Obviously, things vary considerably, depending upon the relationships that parents have had with other children, as well as the character of the parental marriage itself. The romance between the client son or daughter and the opposite sex parent can be anywhere on a continuum from very low key all the way up to "hot and heavy." Whatever the degree of voltage being carried, the line itself is invariably "hot."

The consultant can slow the pace down and build in some degree of acknowledgment and support, as is appropriate to the level of trauma being experienced. The client has an ongoing small group to return to; the parent does not. Therefore, the challenge is to create a context in which the client can extricate himself or herself effectively but without unduly wounding the parent. There are occasional and exceptional circumstances, where the process is voluntarily compromised for the sake of the well-being of the parent. That matter is discussed in greater detail later.

Scene II—A Statement of "Personal Differentness"

As part of the prepared agenda, the client will have previously created (that is, worked and reworked) a statement of "personal differentness." He or she now presents this to the parents, indicating differentness from each one in turn. The client begins by explaining that the intention is not to make the parent wrong in any sense or in any regard or for any reason. The parent is A-OK Perfect As-Is. "Differentness" has nothing to do with rightness or wrongness or better or worse. It simply implies being different—and unique. It is the client's intention to declare some of the important aspects of his or her own person that show differentness from either parent, thereby clarifying a number of self-defining distinctions. Taken together, these are differences "that make a difference."

Next, the client proceeds with a litany of all perceivable (or desired) differentnesses from each parent, addressed directly one at a time. This includes some selection from the following topics: self as male or female, self as sexual male or female, self as spouse, self as parent, self as political person, self as religious person, attitudes toward work and money, attitudes toward recreation and hobbies, social and racial attitudes, and just about anything else that comes to mind as relevant.

This is another historic act on the part of the client. He or she has now discovered that being loving does not require being similar and being loyal does not mandate being the same in thought and deed. The discovery, declaration, and celebration of differentness, in detail and in direct eye-to-eye contact with parents, is an important and historic act of differentiation of the self within the family of origin. At the same time, defining a self in terms of differentness, is not an end point but, rather, a step along the way. Nonetheless, it is a crucial step! For the consultant, it is a stirring moment to see a client able to discover and celebrate who the parent is, as the parent defines the self, and simultaneously declare and celebrate a different new self, and do both things within the intimacy of the relationship. *The commitment to wed the drama of differentiation of self with an adult intimacy and sense of belonging within the family of origin constitutes the novelty of the personal authority theory and method.*

The following monologues illustrate the statement of personal differentness as given by a son or daughter to a parent.

DAUGHTER TO FATHER:
"You and I, Dad, are father and daughter, but we are also different. We grew up in different worlds with different physical and social needs and influences. You are a businessman and father. I am a mother, a community and arts organizer. You have had the need and desire to be a successful businessman and provider for your family. I too have identified a strong need, and

that is to express myself creatively, to develop my craft and take pleasure in the work I produce.

"My friends do not come from one socioeconomic group but are Jew and gentile, black and white, rich and poor. I don't feel bound by a specific group's opinion and live a less socially structured life than you. That is not a comparison of which is better, it is the level of living life that works for me. I feel comfortable with many different people and experiences."

SON TO MOTHER:

"How am I different from you? Let me count the ways.

"I am career-focused, and I have not always put family needs above my own personal needs and ambitions.

"I am a risk-taker, and I have been willing to push myself into new and unfamiliar situations, to take a chance to learn something new or to move ahead in my work.

"I am ambitious, and I have felt a strong need to achieve and to be recognized for my accomplishments.

"I am curious and interested in other cultures and peoples who are different from me.

"I need recognition and validation from others to feel successful.

"I am often impatient with other people, especially when I feel they are not meeting my expectations.

"Belief in my own strengths is very important to me, and I do not have strong beliefs in God or in any religion.

"I tend to be demanding and sometimes have unrealistic expectations of the people closest to me.

"I view myself as a liberal with regard to political and social issues."

DAUGHTER TO MOTHER:

"All my life people have told me how much I look like my mother, but we are not so identical in other ways, which is natural and the way it should be.

"First of all, I feel like my life has been much easier, much smoother than yours, Mother, has been. As a child I had more opportunities and a chance for a good education. I know this is what you wanted for me, but sometimes I wonder if I may not be a very strong person because things have been easy for me. I picture you as very strong and tough and me as more easygoing. I know you can handle any problems, but I'm not so sure about my abilities to handle life's hard knocks.

"I also feel that our temperaments are different. I see you as quick to anger or to become frustrated and quick to let the object of your anger or frustration know what's on your mind. I'm not as quick to get angry; I'm more patient and if I'm angry or upset, I'm more apt to hide it. I think your way is more honest, but I will say that sensing your anger or frustration is still something that makes me uncomfortable.

"I know that some of our life's priorities are different. I have really enjoyed my role as homemaker; wife, and mom, staying home with my children, not working after the children were born, and being there for the kids and my husband. I know when I was small you had no choice but to work. But I also know that in recent years when you did not really have to keep on working, you chose to because you are happiest out there in the working world.

"I have really enjoyed my involvement with the children's schools, and I also enjoy the part I play in helping our family become established and secure in our neighborhood, as well as in our family's business."

Son to Father:

"Dad, some of this is superficial. You got your boat, and I want an airplane. You lived part-time in Cancun, and I want the cabin in Colorado. Professionally, I have chosen architecture instead of law. My community service and my profession are fused together, rather than separate commitments. In my spiritual life, I have combined church membership with meditation. I'm not interested in politics, as you were. I admire your life, and I prefer my own."

Scene III—A Statement of Admiration and Appreciation

During the preparation of the agenda, the client will also have composed a statement of admiration to be addressed separately to each parent. In this sequence the client lists everything and anything about the person, behavior, and overall life of the parent that he or she can think of or remember with genuine admiration or appreciation. The only limitation is the degree of imagination and the edge of credibility. The client will have been warmly encouraged to let every good feeling and memory surface, however peripheral or slight. This will include such matters as the way in which the parent worked and provided, the way in which the parent sacrificed money or time or energy or personal ambition on behalf of a child, the nurturance expressed in different ways over the years through the parenting, the ideals or values embodied in the parent's life and person, and acts of parental kindness and courage. This is the time to spend a few moments in unequivocal celebration, acknowledgment, and validation of the person and the life of the parent. The cathartic healing events that have already taken place usually free the client emotionally to commit spontaneously and genuinely to this celebration, with little or nothing blocking the way.

This can be a most memorable moment in the life of a parent. There is no one from whom parents would rather hear acknowledgment and validation than their own former children. No one else can speak favorably with such authority and credibility. No one else is in such a good position to know the full story. Other than the spouse, there is no one else in whom the parent has such an enormous emotional investment. If ever there was a good return hoped for on a long-term investment, this is it! This can be a profoundly life-giving moment in the life of the parent. It makes up for some of the loss experienced earlier. In addition, it has the active ingredients of a healing balm for any wounds that may have been opened, or reopened, in the prior conversations. These words have more power and plausibility since their author is now being perceived more as adult than child. If the client is to err, it should be on the side of generosity! When the context has credibility, both generations like to linger here for a few moments, as if in a flower garden, before moving on. The following are examples of the statement of admiration presented by clients to parents:

DAUGHTER TO MOTHER:

"My respect for you comes from watching you blossom from an unconfident and insecure wife and mother, into a full-fledged woman in her own right. I was there when you studied late into the night after the rest of the family had gone to bed.

"I watched you change from someone very dependent on how others felt about her into a woman who is mature, self-confident, and able to decide for herself what she wants out of life. I'll never forget that."

SON TO FATHER:

"I want you to understand that I am very proud of where I have come from. I have always been very proud and pleased to say that I am your son. I am especially proud of your personal and professional accomplishments. I am very pleased at the efforts you made to insure that I had the opportunities that I needed in order to succeed.

"You have lived a life that not only I but your grandchildren respect. You have set a great example of family commitment and love, and of being ethical in and respected in your business life. When I was young, I found in you both wisdom and a sense of stability."

SON TO MOTHER:

"Mary, growing up I always felt I had freedom to be what I wanted to be and that I had your support for anything that I tried to do. I was always confident that you would be there. You worked hard and gave yourself fully to your family, and I could see that often you did this at the sacrifice of your own needs.

"I admire the way you could give yourself to other people. I especially admire the way you were willing to come here today and deal so openly and honestly with a lot of difficult and sensitive questions."

DAUGHTER TO FATHER:

"Frank, I appreciate your support, both emotional and financial, of my education from high school through college and graduate school. I appreciate your openness to let me choose my majors throughout and move into my own career.

"I very much admire your skill and interest in gardening and in nature, and I learned this from you. I admire your knowledge of antiques and the appreciation for family heritage that you have passed on to me. I admire your knowledge of our European ancestry and very much appreciate the trips we took to Europe and all that you taught me on those trips."

The statement of admiration and appreciation from son or daughter to parent is the conscious act of "re-mythologizing" the person and the life of the parent. By re-mythologizing the parents, the client is now prepared to re-mythologize the self.

Scene IV—The Remaining Years: The Continuing Coevolution of the Intergenerational Relationship

The formal prepared agenda ends with a brief conversation about the character of the relationship as it might be constructed between the two generations during the years that remain to enjoy it. Certain questions now present themselves. How will it be to relate as psychological equals? What are the implications of that? What do the "former parents" themselves expect and want now? How does it look to son or daughter? No effort is made to spell out future behaviors in any detail. There is, rather, a mutual acknowledgment that important changes have occurred. The future will be different, and it will take shape spontaneously over time. The good news is that the changing relationship is trustworthy and will evolve in goodwill. The client puts away the newly completed agenda with a mixture of pleasure and relief. In these closing moments he or she turns formal direction back to the consultant. The consultant, who has been something of a double agent throughout, no longer needs to remain undercover in any sense. There are probably no more secrets or surprises to be managed. If the process has gone well, everyone now has a clear sense of being on the same side and on the inside. At the same time, the consultant can always return to or continue in a stance of strategic reticence when this seems called for.

Scene V—Awarding a Gold Star and Preparing for Reentry

With varying degrees of emphasis, as is appropriate based on the completed experience, the consultant now acknowledges the parents for their courage, their open-mindedness, their responsiveness, their commitment to the task, and their goodwill. They are applauded not only for coming but for being so forthcoming. It is acknowledged that this has not been an easy experience, that it perhaps presented challenges beyond what they had anticipated or in their own minds been prepared for. With but a few exceptions, the parents are awarded a Gold Star, the highest honor available. The consultant assures them that they can offer no richer parental gift than to share the gold dust of their inner life experience with their own flesh and blood.

Now, in conclusion, the consultant asks if the parents have any questions of any sort to ask before leaving. Are they uncertain or confused about any matter? Is there anything at all that they wish to add, take away, query, or clarify? How do they themselves now feel about the experience they have been through? What is their mood, and what is their dominant feeling as they prepare to leave and return home? Have they any as yet unspoken or half-formed question about anything that has been transacted here? Have they a concern about any implication or message of any sort about either one of them or their personal lives or their family's history or their relationship to or their influence upon their son or daughter? Is there any implication or nuance that remains unclear or troublesome? Have they been treated fairly? Is there any other business?

The closing comments focus upon the parents' enjoyment of their time in the city, the trip home, and what they are looking forward to about being home again. The consultant affirms the parents both individually and in their relationship. They are acknowledged for the years they have already lived and all that they have survived in life, and are encouraged to continue to do well in body, mind, and spirit. They are informed that the consultant will be available to them by telephone if they have any troubling or persisting question or concern. Alternatively, this can be routed through son or daughter, if that is preferable. The consultant wishes them well, good health, and peace of mind. If the whole event has gone reasonably well, everyone goes out on a bit of a natural high. The client, of course, will have an opportunity to talk about it all in the next group sessions. The consultant can go jogging or walking, or visit with the spouse.

Crafting the Language for the Questions

Now that the conversations have ended, one can reflect once again on how crucial it is for the client to select and craft a careful language to use to ask the questions, a language that is conducive to a good experience and a peaceful outcome.

In the small group preparations, the client learns to "re-language" his or her questions into a more benign and less threatening form. This is most necessary when the client continues to carry a punitive rage or resentment. The group work first provides an opportunity to defuse the emotion. The next challenge is to find a new way to ask the old question. Some examples follow.

"Dad, why were you such a wimp in your relationship to Mother, letting her push you around all the time? I was so ashamed of you for that."
New language: "Dad, my perception was that you were quite restrained in the use of your power as you negotiated with Mother. Does that fit with your perceptions and did that represent a conscious decision?"

"Mother, I really resented the way you would buttonhole me and force me to listen to all your complaints about Father. You really caught me in the middle. That was a terrible thing to do to a child."
New language: "Mother, my memory may not be fully trustworthy, but it seems to me that as a young teenager you took me into your confidence to an unusual degree, considering my age. You shared some of your more intimate feelings about your marriage, in a way that was quite surprising to me at the time. Do you remember it that way?"

"Dad, you were a real bastard the way you took your belt off and whipped us in your drunken rages and without any good reason. I could have killed you."

New language: "Dad, we have already talked about your problems with alcohol in past years. I seem to recall that sometimes under the influence of alcohol your belt came off rather readily and you punished your children impulsively and sometimes quite enthusiastically. Does that sound familiar as you look back?"

"Mother, nothing about me was ever good enough for you. You criticized me constantly and often brought me to tears. The way I looked and dressed and talked—everything was wrong. All my friends were no good too. I hated you for that."

New language: "Mother, would it be fair for me to say that when I was younger it was difficult for you to take pleasure in your daughter? Was it not a little easier to comment on what was disappointing rather than what might have brought you pleasure? As you might expect, I have had some difficult feelings to resolve within myself as I have remembered some of those scenes. What do you make of that from the vantage point of today?

"Father and Mother, it seemed like you shouted and screamed and fought with each other almost every night of the week. All of us were terrified by the sounds and huddled in one room together. I can't believe that you would treat young children like that or not be more sensitive about it. I don't think you deserved to be parents for behaving that way."

New language: "Mother and Father, it will be no surprise to you that all of us were aware that you went through many difficult moments together as husband and wife in the early years. We heard many of your spirited discussions. Like the others, I observed these scenes with some degree of alarm and apprehension. I'm sure you wondered at times about your readiness to be parents. What do you remember about that?"

Parents have no difficulty in decoding the more refined message, but there is no accusing tone to provoke a shame or a defensiveness that will block any honest acknowledgment and statement of regret. When it goes well, both parties feel cleaner and there is less standing in the way of an intimate relationship.

Epilogue: So What Was That All About?
The Dynamics of the In-Office Consultation

The tragedy–comedy that is the drama of the in-office consultation with the primary triangle can be summarized in six stages:

Establishing the Contract

The first of these six stages is the establishment of a contract between the three parties, and after some initial testing out, an agreement to let the event take place. The main dynamic in this stage is the bonding between the consultant and the parents. The second is the communication of a strong message that the client is taking charge; this is established by the way in which the client presents the ground rules and produces an impressive agenda.

Debriefing Parents

Stage two is the debriefing of parents through extensive questioning, with the prepared agenda as the vehicle. The client tactfully but tenaciously seeks the relevant information and is willing to receive the story patiently and empathically. During this time the stance of son or daughter is one of compassionate listening, including explicit feedback that the information has been received.

Follow-Up Questions

In the third stage, the client responds to what has gone before with a series of questions as needed by way of follow-up to previous answers. First, the client creates some additional questions on the spot in order to get further information that is necessary to fill a vacuum of ignorance or to resolve confusion about any previously unknown fact or event that the parent now chooses to reveal. Second, the client asks a combination of the already prepared and a few newly minted questions, the joint purpose of which is to get clarification when the original information is inconsistent or the meaning is unnecessarily ambiguous. This serves to demystify any uncertain story or vague event.

The third focus of inquiry is of high voltage and so is handled with a matching high level of sensitivity and gentleness. This pertains to parental behaviors over the years that have greatly distressed the client, whether at the time or in recall. (These matters will, of course, have been addressed at great length in the small group preparation in which the client has participated.) The client wants to ventilate these concerns in order to understand better the parental thinking and intention at the time, including the possible pressures under which the parent was then living. So the client may ask a number of questions that begin with an expression such as "What was in your mind when . . ." or "What was your thinking when . . ."

or "What were you hoping to achieve by . . ." or "In retrospect, why do you think you did . . ." or "What was the most difficult thing going on in your life when . . . ?" The client will score a bull's-eye as far as the historical target is concerned, but there should be nothing punitive, judgmental, or blaming about either the way the question is phrased or the tone in which it is asked. Ideally, it will be a neutral and open-ended question the purpose of which is to get a maximum amount of clarification with the minimum of threat.

The fourth aspect of this stage is specific client feedback, volunteered in order to let the parent know just what the client has thought and felt (perhaps still perceives) about a particular behavior by the parent or a historic event in the client's personal history. (The parent may not particularly want to hear this, but the client needs the experience of telling it.) Again, this is presented without willful attempt to judge or blame, although the parent often feels uncomfortable with the feedback. The client may begin this sequence with something like "It is important to me to let you know how I experienced that event, and then I would like to be done with it, once and for all." The primary dynamic or theme in this third stage is the completion of the cathartic release that the client has been experiencing throughout the therapy to date. If the client can handle this part of the conversation in the way that has just been described (success in this is determined by the quality of the prior preparation along with the serendipity of the timing), then this can be a moment of compelling self-actualization. Personal authority is weaving on the client's loom.

Declaration of Independence

The fourth stage is the declaration of independence by the client, reaching its zenith in the statement of personal differentness. Son or daughter has now assumed a new level of personal authority even as, in reciprocal and circular fashion, the parents have been giving up the burdens of parenting. This is now a formal hoisting of the flag of personal identity and authority at this watershed moment in personal history. When the experience goes well, it is a statement of newfound freedom for both generations.

State of the Union

The fifth and final stage (that is, in the ideal scenario) is one of acceptance and mutuality in which no one is trying to change or control anyone else. It is centered in a mutual validation of each generation by the other. A priority of focus is placed on the validation of the lives of the older generation along with an acknowledgment of the mutuality of humanness and, therefore, forgiveness between the two generations, with perhaps a third mentioned in anticipation. Everything that is conceivably admirable or near admirable about the parent is gathered in one place and proclaimed and celebrated. The prevailing mood is one of "differentness with intimacy." This is the new stage in the individual and family life-cycle in action.

Today Parents, Tomorrow the World

A stance of "peerhood" with parents can generalize out toward all parental figures. A client may find it refreshing to seek a social visit with important figures like doctors, lawyers, clergy, teachers, supervisors, bosses, and former therapists. The purpose is to present and hold the self as a peer. Old business can be reviewed, and feedback offered where necessary. Therapeutic style can be discussed with former therapists, acknowledging both the more helpful and the less helpful. Some therapists may want to handle this initiative as residual "unresolved transference," but most will be pleased that they had a hand in such a successful outcome.

Nowhere is this generalization from parents more valuable than in the relationships with spouses, since spouses are inevitably parental figures. This then is one way to resolve the intimacy paradox.

Postscript

A Client Retrospective I

A 43-year-old woman writes and reads this statement to her family of origin group as she prepares to terminate therapy.

Lenses
At thirty-three my lenses were from Nikon and Leica
And like a good girl, aiming to please,
I took pictures of others through wide angles
the bigger picture

A few years later I attached the Nikon to a microscope
where the working of lenses became more complicated
although still pointed away, this time focused on
the smaller picture

Black and white was my only medium
and like a photo left too long in its fix
in a darkroom with the safe light always on,
I showed signs of disappearing

For several years thereafter,
I looked through a lens of tears
alone at night in my dressing room,
absorbed in my mirrored image
and my own sadness

I see now the lie was fighting to break through
the glossy finish of coquilles St. Jacques and trips to France
the house, the pool, the cattle ranch, the swans
When viewed with special light from a new angle
positives were negatives

Honesty and pain, the chemicals in which
new images of self develop,
were new to me.
There soon emerged more shades of grey
And hints of color trying to break through.

At forty-three, I now collect kaleidoscopes
Colliding colors, against mirrors,
One piece moves, the picture shifts,
No returning to what was before;
from broken pieces of glass and found objects
seen in just the right amount of light,
come unlimited possibilities
for exquisite images.

A Client Retrospective II

A 45-year-old male client looks back on his family of origin work, 10 years afterward.

One Client's Experience

"I am a 45-year-old male therapist, writing some 10 years after completing personal authority family of origin work. This experience was and continues to be life-changing for me. From the very first session in which the therapist delivered the lightning bolt about my 'loyalty to my father,' I was nudged, cajoled, and 'paradoxed' into facing my participation in the family of origin drama and into moving toward the healthier position of peerhood with my parents. Because one of my agenda items for therapy was changing my wife, who participated conjointly, the therapist became adept at rebalancing the system. Otherwise she could have experienced it as loaded against her, as a nontherapist woman on her husband's turf with a male therapist.

"The focus was directed and redirected toward family of origin issues for each of us. This took enormous pressure off the marriage and enabled both of us to evolve as individuals as well as spouses. The emphasis on changing behavior through home-work assignments and in-session role plays was especially help-ful, though frustrating to me, a therapist accustomed to ana-lyzing problems *ad nauseum*. The therapist's continual pushing, usually in the form of a paradoxical kind of ploy geared toward our reaching adulthood, was probably the most consistent and growth-producing part of the process. From the early reading of my autobiography, through the tapes made to parents, and finally to the family of origin sessions with parents and siblings, I was never allowed a position of victimhood. Although child-hood grief and anger were acknowledged and affirmed, the overriding message was that I was now a full-fledged participant in the ongoing family process and, as a participant, I was capable of changing my position.

"The in-office sessions with my parents were both enlight-ening and frustrating. The fact that they participated is, to this day, a great comfort and source of self-affirmation for me. However, I had held so strongly to the position of the 'family's therapist' that when my father and mother did not magically change after participating in those sessions, I felt keenly disap-pointed. The continuation of therapy, with much coaching about alternative responses within the family of origin, was essential to keep me working in those relationships, as I do to this day. Repeatedly, I was challenged to return 'home' and practice a different position or response in the family.

"Particularly important was the suggestion that I dialogue separately with my mother and my father, a couple who, after 34 years of marriage, had perfected an amazing ability to fuse completely into one entity. These dialogues allowed me, for the first time in my life, to see each of them as an individual and not just as my parent. Separate interaction was not easy, and the conversations were strained and demanding. The role plays with the therapist enabled me to avoid our persistent attempts at triangulation. I learned, paradoxically, both to be more childlike and playful and to achieve a measure of adult–adult interaction with each of them. I rediscovered, in the process, a great fondness for each of them, which I had not experienced since prior to my adolescence.

"In particular, I was greatly helped by feedback that allowed me to refocus my energy from the position of battler with my mother to one of acceptance and appreciation of her 'craziness' and from the denial of feeling with my father to one of more emotional involvement. When my mother died several years later, I was grateful that I had experienced a different relationship with her and that I had reached more understanding of her as a person and as a woman.

"The general tone of the therapeutic work was playfulness combined with a serious, subtle message to change. I usually had a sense that the therapist's responses and interventions were 'right on.' The playfulness conveyed a sense of optimism, which was vital to me. But there was always an edge to the humor, and for days and weeks (and years) after a session I was 'mystified' or irritated or challenged by a comment or intervention.

"At times, I was infuriated by the therapist's pervasive insistence that I could change and by his refusal to accept excuses, whining, or self-pity. Nonetheless, there also was a feeling, after a time, that he genuinely cared for me and for what happened with my family. One thing that made it possible for me to relinquish so much anger and blame was the therapist's consistent refusal to take sides. In any problematic relationship, there was usually an alternative response modeled to help me out of the position of 'victim.'

"My positive feeling about the therapy does not, however, mean that all the problems in my marriage or family of origin were resolved. I continually go back to the work, in my mind, in my relationships with my wife and with members of my family, especially with my father. In fact, the relationship with my father became quite heated up. The observations of our interaction during the in-office sessions still prove to be useful reference points when he and I become overly entangled. One of the most therapeutic aspects of the entire process was this reinvolvement with my father, with whom I had been so close as a child and whose relationship I had lost later in my life. This reinvolvement contributed greatly to my maturation, finally, into manhood.

"My wife and I still discuss and joke about 'what the therapist said,' and when we get stuck with each other or with our families of origin, the therapy work continues to guide us."

CHAPTER 11

Performing Outdoors: New Life at the Graveyard—Renegotiation with a Deceased Former Parent

(*Enter Ghost.*)

If thou hast any sound or use of voice,
Speak to me.
If there be any good thing to be done
That may to thee do ease and grace to me,
Speak to me.

> —Horatio in *Hamlet*
> (Act 1, Scene 1)

Making the Trip

It is not uncommon that a parent has died before son or daughter is of an age at which political renegotiation is both desirable and possible; not infrequently, client was quite young when the parent died. Sometimes a client has been a little tardy in meeting the challenge, and the parent could not wait any longer. Occasionally, a parent is still alive, but only just, by the time a client first presents himself or herself for therapeutic consultation. Yet in all of these instances, it is remarkable how much renegotiation can take place in response to the client's initiative (Williamson, 1978). Even when the parent is extremely crippled in body or in mind or both, a client can immediately begin to adopt a more attentive observer stance and begin to perceive with a little more emotional distance. In the case of a deceased parent, significant political renegotiation can still occur.

When the parent is already deceased, the client will be reminded that important human relationships do not terminate with a participant's physical death. Relationships continue to live where they have always lived, that is, in the survivor's mind and imagination. Family emotionality is, in fact, often intensified by the grief and other reactions in the period following the death. So it will be clarified to the client, sometimes to his or her surprise, that a parent's death does not mean that the work does not need to be done. Certainly, it does not mean that the work cannot be done. It may be that the relationship has been frozen in time in the client's mind, right where it was at the time of the parent's death. Since no new and unscripted scenes can be played live, a moving picture has become a still portrait. It may well be a portrait in which the eyes seem to turn and follow the client relentlessly around the room. The client often feels immobilized by this. If son or daughter was quite young when father or mother died, the deceased parent may remain a vague or shadowy figure in the adult's mind and, consequently, an enigma. Nonetheless, evidence over the years from observations of clients renegotiating with deceased parents consistently confirms that some extraordinary renegotiation can take place in these relationships.

Some family situations are very accessible to this work, others quite resistant. In the second case, the client needs to show unusual tact and perseverance. The only really essential precondition seems to be adequate motivation and courage on the part of son or daughter. Michael White (1988) has suggested that in dealing with a deceased person, parent or otherwise, certain questions posed to the self can enable one to recover and reexperience lost aspects of the self. As White presents them, these questions go somewhat as follows: What do you know about yourself that comes alive when you think about the deceased person's experience of you? How can you let others know that you have recovered these pleasing and lost aspects of yourself? A subsequent question is, how has knowledge of what you had lost about yourself changed or enriched your life? White has observed that through a ritual like this the client comes to experience "the self as author of the self."

There is, however, one obvious drawback to the work of changing the character of a relationship with a parent who is deceased. The client has no option but to play the parts of both participants, that is, to speak the lines of both. There can be no face-to-face feedback from the voice, eyes, and body language of the parent or from the choreography of the parental dance. The implication is that the client cannot have the satisfaction generated by directly experiencing a parental acknowledgment, empathic or otherwise, of the things that the client needs both to say and to have heard. There is no opportunity for direct reality testing in the usual way. The client cannot poignantly ask, "Why, oh why . . . ?" or "Is it true that . . . ?" and hear the parent respond, "Well, it was like this . . . and I wish it had been otherwise." These questions can still be asked and a new construction of "reality" can result, but the parent cannot be present physically to provide any bricks, for better or worse. This is a big loss, one not to be minimized. Any adult of appropriate age whose mind and heart are open to conversation with parents and whose parents are still alive and accessible should not pass up the chance. *This is undoubtedly one of those few opportunities in life that are not to be missed.*

On the brighter side, the work of a number of clients has shown that quite remarkable renegotiations and resolutions have, in fact, taken place with deceased parents. It can, therefore, be considered to be a possibility that is always at hand for any motivated person. Apart from the challenge of having to speak both lines, the procedures of preparation and implementation are not essentially different for the client working with a deceased parent. The one exception is that this process usually ends up with a more complete good-bye. The experience can be summarized in six steps; which are examined in the following paragraphs.

Screening and Assignment

The client is screened and then assigned to a small group, just as is done with other clients. The screening process will assess the character of the relationship with the deceased parent. This allows for an evaluation of the client's readiness to commit to a transformation of the relationship and the readiness of the surrounding social context to let this happen. Assuming a green light, the client is assigned to a group where the chemistry promises to be good, and the rehearsals begin.

Present Feelings about the Deceased Parent

First the client will identify and acknowledge all the facts about the parent's life that he or she already knows. This includes the client's perception of his or her relationship to the parent and how it ended up and now exists, even if frozen in time. This exploration will identify the various feelings that the client presently carries about the relationship and the parent. This in turn leads to a further discovery and expression of feelings. Conversations with other family members and the friends of the deceased, especially detailed conversation with the surviving parent, can yield rich new information. Therapeutic consultation helps the client prepare these questions for others, including, when necessary, a detailed agenda for debriefing the surviving parent. This leads to further awareness and catharsis.

In dealing with a surviving parent, it is rarely, if ever, ultimately fruitful to express rage directly to the person of the parent. This intensity needs to be resolved in the small group first. From a political and hierarchical perspective, to become enraged means to lose power, presence, and position—that is, authority. Most of the time, expressing rage is a child-to-parent transaction, so that the client has for now forfeited the standing of peer in the relationship.

The course of the drama, however, is different in the case of work with a deceased parent. The obvious advantage of not having the parent physically present to respond with reciprocal anger, hurt, or distress is that the relationship cannot be noticeably injured further by the client's own outrage or outbursts. So some of this can be saved and relived and directly expressed at the gravesite. Even at the graveside, a successful catharsis results in a richer understanding of the person of the parent, and facilitates acceptance and forgiveness.

Preparation of a Graveside Agenda

The third step is the preparation of a detailed agenda that will be taken to the graveside and used there. Sometimes a client will make a dry run to a graveside just to get comfortable with the context and locate the site. (Even a dry run can result in moist eyes. The tape recording made by one client as she wandered around the cemetery begins, "Daddy, I just can't find you," an exquisite comment on the character of their relationship.) The client may visit and spend time at the parent's grave but without engaging in any focused task and without beginning on the agenda under preparation. This is akin to a football team walking around the playing field on the morning of a game with a view to feeling more at home in the setting, or an actor pacing off the stage and projecting the voice into an empty theater.

When the client does later begin to present the prepared agenda, he or she will tape-record the entire proceedings at the graveside. This audiotaping serves two good purposes. First, it means that the group and the consultant are psychologically present to the client at the physical site. This offers emotional support and encouragement from the client's new "family." It also ensures a heightened accountability, encouraging the client to pursue even the more difficult aspects of the prepared agenda. The group is also present both as a guarantor of the experience and as witness to it. The second reason for audio taping is so that a complete and accurate record of what occurs can be brought back to the group for debriefing, review, and feedback. The client may present the entire agenda at one graveside visit or divide it into two or more trips, especially if the location is convenient. Multiple trips allow for a more leisurely and less driven on-site experience. They also encourage the client to relax and ease into the process without feeling the pressure of outside consider-ations of schedule and time. This facilitates a more complete exorcism of any indwelling parental spirit that is ego-alien and incongruent with the authentic self of son or daughter. This is indeed one situation in life where truth encourages freedom.

Initially, many clients feel a little self-conscious at being observed by other visitors while sitting on the ground by a graveside (or other symbolic site) and talking into a tape recorder. This behavior is not perceived as an everyday occurrence, and the reason for it is not immediately obvious to the casual observer. Despite this, the emo-tional power of the occasion usually takes over fairly quickly and preoccupies the client. The surrounding context recedes and is forgotten. (The details of the agenda to be presented at the graveside are described later in this chapter.)

Debriefing and Feedback on the Graveside Visit

In due course, the client returns to the small group from this field trip, complete with audiotapes. To begin with, he or she will describe the experience and its aftermath, including what it was like to do it, what thoughts and feelings came up, what new awarenesses and questions arose, and what sense of contact and response was experienced, if any, from the deceased parent. Any later dreams, daydreams, or other free associations are to be noted and reported. All of this leads to a conclusion about where the client now stands in relation to this parent.

It should be remembered that the members of the small group have been present with the client for some prior period of weeks or months. They have developed intimate relationships reminiscent of family with him or her. So the group now receives and understands this story in the context of previous history, prior experience, and some degree of intimate knowledge of the person of the client. Group members now share their thoughts and feelings and suggestions and questions in response to the experience of the client's visit to the graveside and the recorded "conversations." This feedback usually applauds and validates work well done. It also offers alternate hypotheses and indicates issues that remain unclear or unresolved. In subsequent weeks the client will have the time needed to face and embrace whatever remains as yet unaddressed.

Meeting with the Surviving Parent

In the next step the client invites the surviving parent for an in-office consultation. This follows the guidelines described earlier for in-office consultation. The main difference is that the deceased parent is present in the room only through memory and imagination. For a variety of reasons, including the fact that this is an ongoing relationship with an unwritten future, it has proven more conducive to renegotiate with the deceased parent first. Having already achieved some measure of closure with the deceased parent, the client is strategically placed for the purpose of renegotiation with the survivor. The relationship between the client and the surviving parent has obviously been affected by the fact that the parent's spouse is no longer alive. If the survivor has remarried, a postscript will be added to the prepared agenda. This allows for the story of the second marriage and the client's role within this new triangle.

Assimilation and Termination

All that has transpired so far leads to the concluding phase of this work: assimilation of all that has happened and the termination experience with this new group family. If the client has done well at leaving the family of origin emotionally, he or she will handle leaving the "group family" gracefully also. There is little point in leaving the natural family and parents and then getting stuck with and on the therapy "family" and the consultant. The therapeutic process throughout discourages and minimizes any but transient dependency on the process itself. Everyone stays mindful of the fact that the purpose of the first visit is to get to the last.

A client will sometimes make a second graveside visit some weeks or months after the work has been done. For some this is a validation of their previous work. Where there cannot be a gravesite visit, either because there has been a cremation or for some other less usual reason, this work can be located at some alternative memorial spot recognized as significant by the family or at some symbolic place chosen unilaterally by the client because of a strong identification and association with the life of the deceased parent. This may be a mountainside, a lake, a meadow, an orchard, a beach, or a garden. Clients frequently report having had some kind of mystical experience of the "real presence" of the deceased parent during these pilgrimages to the graveside or some symbolic place. Questions posed to a deceased parent are experienced as having been answered, and new information is frequently received. Obviously, the client takes both the personal and the collective family unconscious mind along on the trip, but just how these phenomena are to be interpreted is left to the personal belief system of the reader.

Detailed Agenda for Graveside Visit with a Deceased Parent

The agenda for a graveside visit regularly has eight parts to it, which are described in the following paragraphs.

"Hello"

The graveside visit begins, not surprisingly, with "Hello." A surprising number of clients begin the renegotiation without any conscious sense of an ongoing relationship with the deceased parent. Consequently, they need to say hello before they feel comfortable going on to say anything else. Following the hello, the client explains the purpose of the visit and briefly identifies the accompanying agenda. Having offered some explanation of purpose, the client solicits the deceased parent's agreement to "participate" in the conversations to follow. In practical terms, this simply means that the client declares the purpose and then sits quietly, listening to the sounds both outside and inside the head. Hearing or feeling no strong objection, the client takes the peacefulness to represent permission. Such a respectful approach can induce a sense of a collaborative relationship and augurs well for what is to follow.

Coming Up to Date

Next the client brings the deceased parent up to date with his or her life. This will highlight specific events since the parent died like graduations, marriages, jobs, births, divorces and any experiences of success or achievement, crisis or trauma, that stand out in the client's mind. The client may then muse about what the parent's likely thoughts and feelings about these different events would be, were he or she present to declare them. The client next talks about the relationship between self and parent as he or she conceives of it today, candidly highlighting both the pluses and the negatives. The parent is now up to date.

Pop Pop, Fizz Fizz

Bringing the parent up to date leads into a soliloquy that lists to the parent all the matters pertaining to the relationship between self and parent that have been a significant source of distress and emotional upset to the client. Whatever sadness, resentment, or rage the client has felt or continues to feel can now be freely (and, if need be, dramatically) expressed. The client has been told that it is okay to "let it all go" at this point. Oh, what a relief it is!

Question Time

Next comes "question time." This is an opportunity to ask everything and anything—however possible or impossible, thinkable or unthinkable, pleasing or frightening—that has ever come to the client's mind about the life of the deceased. These questions are in response to the consultant's advice: "If you have ever thought it, even though you could never previously put it into words, now is the time to mention it." The client asks each question and then remains quiet and thoughtful, listening with a neutral and open mind for a period of time. After noting his or her own free associations and whatever else comes through to consciousness, the client continues with follow-up questions. This is the time to present whatever remains in the client's mind and heart regarding the deceased parent. The client both refers to notes and extemporizes.

Off the Hook as Parent

Son or daughter will now actively and willfully "give up the parent as parent," explaining what this means and the rationale for it. This will be done with sensitivity to the parent's feelings, with an awareness that this would represent an occasion of some considerable emotional loss to him or her if present in person. Nonetheless, there is a sense of finality about the decision and completion about the task.

Personal Differentness

Next the client will present a prepared statement of "personal differentness." This is a simple cataloging of all the ways in which the client experiences the self as different from this parent. It is carefully explained that in declaring differentness there is no evaluation or judgment implied. The parent, even though deceased, is still A-OK Perfect As-Is. Yet in all these ways, both large and small, the client is

different and celebrates that differentness. The statement of differentness is the discovery of the uniqueness of the new and evolving self.

Admiration

Son or daughter will now present a prepared "statement of admiration," just as is done during a live in-office visit. Again, this should be
done slowly, with the client pausing after each statement, waiting
first for an inner acknowledgment of everything that was good about
the parent and then for an inner awareness of the parent's most likely
response.

Good-Bye

There has now been completion of the exorcism of the parent's spirit
from a position of dominance and control within the life of the client.
The client will now say a last good-bye. If not yet quite ready to do so,
as is sometimes the case, the client will leave the site, explaining that
he or she will return in due course to say a final good-bye. In that
circumstance, the client will use the subsequent weeks to assimilate
this experience and prepare the self for the return visit and the
completion. When a demonstrably successful outcome has resulted, it
can be assumed that the client has also said good-bye to the distorted
parental introject, images of which will no longer permeate the
client's mind and relationships by day and by night.

At another level of consciousness and meaning, the client,
having now discovered much more about the real person of the
parent, says good-bye to that "real person" as well. Once in a while
a client will want to hold onto the parent as a continuing guide and
source of nurture in a way that seems malingering, if not malignant.
This will certainly be diminishing of the self and may express a
reluctance to complete the grief process. In this case, the group
members will gently bring this awareness to the client's attention. On
the other hand, occasionally a mature client will report a continuing
sense of the benevolent presence of the spirit of the deceased parent,
which may be experienced as a guide and a support. The character of
this experience is such that it cannot be easily dismissed as pathological. Just how it is to be understood psychologically is again left to the
reader's good judgment.

During the experiences summarized in the preceding paragraphs,
the client may experience intense feelings of loss and grief about the
parent whom he or she once had and has lost. The client accepts the
fact that the parent is dead and simultaneously acknowledges and

celebrates that the client is very much alive. Any part of the client that died with or was buried with the parent will be taken back and restored to the inner self. This willful action makes the boundary and distinction between the two persons crystal clear and irreversibly defined.

Sometimes one or more other family members will accompany the client to the graveside for conversations with the deceased parent. Visits made in the company of the surviving parent can be of particular value. However, the agenda summarized earlier is best completed while in attendance alone at the graveside of the deceased parent. One can speculate about circumstances in which it might be fruitful to have the consultant or even the entire small group accompany the client to the graveside for some part of this process.

In conclusion, work at the graveside has four major dynamics. First is the experience of emotional acknowledgment and catharsis; this frees the client to move to the second part. This is a general validation and celebration of the life and person of both the client and the parent. Third, the client gives up the parent as parent and makes a declaration of the new self. Finally comes the statement of admiration and the good-bye. Obviously, there is a continuum of outcomes, since the extent of the riches and ravages of personal and family history creates a variety of possibilities and limitations. But for most, there is now an inner peace while living with the memory of the deceased parent.

It should be noted that the assignment to complete a relationship with a deceased person through a graveside visit can be used with others besides parents. It has proved effective in completing a relationship with a deceased spouse, a sibling, a prematurely deceased child, or a very close friend. The agenda and the focus vary, but the essential dynamics are the same.

A client's direct and agenda-based conversation with a deceased parent is probably best accomplished while visiting the graveside alone. There is an unrelieved intensity generated by the aloneness that probably facilitates the work. However, there also are occasions when the client does well to seek the company of a surviving parent, a spouse, a close friend, or maybe even the small group and the consultant. The interaction at the graveside can be very informative as well as supportive. Everything depends on the goal of the visit. One thing is certain: if the client actually parks and gets out of the car, the visit is not likely to be uneventful.

What follows is the moving soliloquy of a woman who went to honor and say good-bye to her father, 19 years after his death by his own hand. Instead of going to the graveside she went to sit in a chapel, and she spoke to him there.

Compassion and Honor for the Dead

August 31, 1990

Hello Dad,

We didn't honor you when you died. No one who knew you spoke at your memorial service. It was not a celebration of your life. It was more a brief interval to be endured in a nightmare of horrible shock and pain and bewilderment. We hoped this service marked the end. It was finished—your life, mother's life. There would be no more horrors to endure, no more agonizing decisions, no more visits with you in the hospital.

Now it is 19 years later. This is the anniversary of the day you finally succeeded in killing yourself. And I have come here to honor you and say good-bye.

Last night at an Alanon meeting the subject was forgiveness. I thought of you and about the last year I've spent in therapy, trying to deal with the deaths of you and my mother. What I thought my goal was, was to feel anger and rage at you for this horrendous act you committed, for killing my mother and then yourself. After the anger I could forgive. It hasn't happened, and part of me has felt a failure. But last night I said I don't feel I have to forgive. Forgiveness does not seem to be the issue. Acceptance is the key, acceptance and allowing myself to feel the sadness, the almost unbearable sadness. And then—and then I can let go of it—the event and you, and say good-bye and go on with my life. And so I've accepted what happened, and I've felt the feelings and am feeling them now.

Oh God, I am sad. I miss you. I miss you both. When you died a light went out of my life. There has been a dark place in my heart and soul.

I love you, my father, I love you and want to honor you—and will find a way to do so.

I cannot imagine what your pain must have been like to drive you to such despair and desperation. I am grateful that you finally found your way out of the pain, and I pray that death has brought you peace. I hope you can see me today and know that I am doing well and that your granddaughter is doing very well indeed. You would be so proud of her.

I'm sitting in Rothko Chapel, surrounded by paintings done by a man who must have felt some of what you felt. The paintings are dark and heavy, with no relief or sign of light or hope in them— anger turned inward. Rothko, the artist, killed himself, too.

Here are some scenes or images of you which are still in my mind:

I remember sitting on my bed, packed and ready to return to college after a vacation. I was crying my eyes out because I didn't want to go back. You sat there with me, your arm around me, offering comfort and Kleenex, saying you understood and that it would be okay.

I remember you coming home from work, walking into the kitchen, kissing Mother hello. She was always waiting for you to arrive, and you both seemed glad to see one another.

I remember how every Sunday while Mother, Joan, and I would go to 12 o'clock Mass, you would stay home and fix brunch. You were so proud when you figured out how to bake bacon in the oven.

I remember you ironing your handkerchiefs, taking the dog to Baskin-Robbins and getting her a scoop of vanilla ice cream, you dunking Hydrox cookies or special sugar cookies in your milk.

I admire you for your sharp mind and quick sense of humor;
for your sense of justice;
for your sense of responsibility;
for your sense of family and its importance to you;
for your loyalty to your friends;
for your commitment to pass on your values to your children;
for your love of people;
for your dignity and your privateness.

One of the things which was so sad about your final weeks on earth was that your privateness and dignity were stripped away.

I know that you had a dark side, and I am aware of instances in which it showed. I am aware that some of your admirable characteristics also fell on the dark side, and contributed to your despair.

I accept you as you were—a human being with both good and bad qualities, with both a light and a dark side. I accept that you despaired and in that despair killed my mother and eventually yourself. I accept it and feel my pain surrounding those events.

I honor you as a person who had many wonderful characteristics; who gave much of himself to others; who gave much to me; and who ultimately gave too much away to keep himself alive.

I honor you, Robert Stanley McTavish, as a human being, as a husband and father, as a friend.

I will say good-bye now. Good-bye. May you rest in peace. I love and miss you.

Sharon

CHAPTER 12

Production Problems: Limitations to the Method

The best laid schemes o' mice and men
Gang aft a-gley;
An' lea'e us nought but grief and pain,
For promis'd joy.
— Robert Burns
To a Mouse (Stanza 7)

The Parents as a Source of Limitations

Like any other, the personal authority psychotherapy method works well for those for whom it works well (and is less useful for the rest of the world), which is merely to say that it has its limitations. The source and nature of the limitations are described in the following pages.

Physical and Psychological Problems

When a parent has significant physical and/or psychological problems, these will influence and often compromise the client's program. If a parent is no longer able to speak freely or clearly for physical reasons, obviously this will retard the work. At the extreme, if the parent's mental processes have deteriorated to the point where he or she cannot comprehend language, then the process is most seriously compromised. That is not to say that nothing useful can be done. With enough patience and imagination, it is remarkable how much information can be exchanged, with the relationship changing in response to this.

Nonetheless, in these circumstances the agenda will be modified considerably and the goals will be much more modest. If the parent's physical condition requires that he or she must not experience much stress of any sort, then the dialogue cannot be so freewheeling or persistent. If for physical reasons the parent cannot travel or cannot tolerate sitting for long periods in the consultant's office, then innovations are called for in the choreography of the therapy.

Significant psychological problems on the part of a parent may call for a more far-reaching compromise of therapeutic ambition or assertiveness, at least as far as direct renegotiation is concerned. A parent who is normally anxious and fearful or subject to depression will need to be addressed with considerable sensitivity and tact as the client presents the agenda. A parent who has very limited social support or who is facing or still recovering from a significant emotional loss also represents a situation where the goals of the client may have to be compromised. A parent who is actively schizophrenic is probably unlikely to be able to participate adequately in a bilateral renegotiation. A parent who is given to paranoid perceptions presents a situation where both client and consultant need to select their steps carefully and conduct themselves with both caution and reticence. This may also be true with a parent for whom a conscious identification of self as parent is a key element in self-esteem and a continuing sense of personal worthiness.

The useful guiding principle in all of this is the notion of relational justice and relational ethics (Boszormenyi-Nagy, 1974). This means that the client needs to conduct himself or herself throughout these proceedings in such a way that he or she will achieve a fair balance between personal interest and the interest and well-being of the parent. Through a benevolent triangulation the consultant can contribute to good decision making in this regard by speaking from a more removed position. From there he or she can adjudicate more fairly what a good and necessary compromise would look like. Clients are almost always accurate when they predict during the preparation stages what the parental responses will be should certain initiatives be taken. Guided by this, the consultant can encourage more daring behavior when the client seems to be unduly reluctant to tackle an important issue, or recommend some judicious omissions when the client's residual anger blinds him or her to the possibility of significant injury to a parent.

Alcohol Problems

An alcoholic parent who is still drinking presents another circumstance that is frequently compromising in important ways. Again, the probable lack of integrity, self-esteem, and psychological strength on the part of this parent makes a probing conversation less likely and reduces the bilateral possibilities in the negotiations. The parent may feel very vulnerable and, therefore, limited in the ability to function in this conversation as a peer. This imbalance is itself an ironic turn of events. The parent's responses are likely to be characterized by denial and, therefore, likely to lack credibility and to yield much less useful information. Again, it is not the case that there is absolutely nothing worthwhile to be done. Rather, the idiosyncrasies of the given situation will define the possibilities and will determine the character of the agenda and the dialogue that can be effectively employed. In this circumstance, the client may need more than the normal amount of guidance and support from the consultant.

Psychological Rigidity

A third potentially compromising situation is one in which one or both parents are psychologically rigid and emotionally closed. The behavior of such a parent is likely to be unduly dominating and controlling. This parent is prone to perceive criticism and become defensive when asked even neutral, information-seeking questions if they are asked in sensitive areas of his or her life. If this parent also happens to have strong and conservative religious beliefs, the situation can present an even more formidable challenge. The parent may take exception to the whole enterprise as unethical or as contrary to how it has been "ordained" that things should go between parents and children. Fortunately, most of the time, son or daughter has had ample opportunity during the preparation period to learn playful and paradoxical ways of relating to the more fearful parent, thereby avoiding unfruitful power struggles. This is a plot in which if any party loses its cool, things can get stalemated very quickly, producing an outcome that can freeze over emotionally and not melt for some considerable period of time. This scenario is, therefore, to be avoided if at all possible.

To this end, the client may need to reassure the parent repeatedly that in asking these certain questions he or she is not passing any ethical judgment. He or she can also reassure parents that this conversation is not about determining who is right and who is wrong on any given matter. Since control issues are more likely to be so dominant here, the client is less likely to deal with this issue head-on. The client may prefer to present an act of political change as a fait accompli and let the implications sneak up on the parent over time as the latter becomes ready to acknowledge and absorb them. Certainly, nothing will be forced down the parent's throat, and no immediate verbal agreement will be demanded. It is an expression of the client's higher level of personal authority that he or she no longer needs to insist upon this. The consultant can actively cue and coach the client on all these matters as the agenda moves along.

Parental Divorce

The final situation where a measure of compromise is often required is one in which the client's parents have previously ended their marriage by divorce. As a rule, the client will conduct the in-office conversations with divorced parents one at a time. It is a rare post-divorce relationship in which former spouses can tolerate being present in the same room at the same time and discussing these kinds of sensitive questions with an offspring. The loss of trust and the residual anger and grief generally make this implausible.

Moreover, the agenda includes many additional and specific questions about the character of the failed parental marriage. The answers will indicate how the former marriage and divorce have affected this parent and what for him or her has been the aftermath up to and including this very day. The client will ask the parent if he or she now believes that this outcome could or should have been avoided. It is obvious why very few divorced adults are capable of answering such questions in the presence of the ex-spouse.

Where such a three-way conversation can, in fact, take place, it may be therapeutically valuable not only for the client but also for each of the parents as well. It is, therefore, always to be considered as a possibility even though it may seldom occur. As before, the client will be reminded that he or she is asking questions in a most delicate area of the parents' lives. Son or daughter needs to conduct this aspect of the conversation with a readiness to back off at any moment and a transparent empathy for each parent's feelings. As is true throughout all of these in-office scenes, the goal is to achieve a balance of fairness between what is necessary for the good of the client and what is necessarily not to be pursued for the sake of the good of the parent. The challenge is to manage these matters in such a way that all persons come out feeling equally well treated. There may, appropriately, be a built-in bias in favor of the younger generation. At the same time, there is also a strong awareness that many parents lack the energy and resilience they once had for recovering from such challenges.

The Client as a Source of Limitations

There is one very big difference between the position of the client in these conversations and the position of the parent. The client is engaged in the therapeutic process and is, therefore, both committed and accessible to personal changes in preparation for the in-office consultation. Notwithstanding, the client also may be the source of limitation, even prohibition, in the work. Eleven of these limitations follow:

1. It is obvious that a client with psychotic-level problems cannot participate in the process in the ways described earlier. He or she is invariably in such a one-down position politically and emotionally that this kind of renegotiation is unlikely to take place.

2. A very anxious or dependent client will have a much more difficult time contemplating giving up the parents as parents.

3. A client who is socially isolated will find it difficult to give up the real or imagined source of support represented by parents until someone or something materializes to take their place. Clients who are not and never have been married often find it especially troubling to consider losing the parent as parent.

4. The client who has physical health problems that significantly restrict his or her life and activity, especially if genetically determined, probably cannot establish psychological "peerhood" in the radical sense proposed here.

5. The client who has an acute financial dependency upon parents, probably cannot establish psychological "peerhood."

6. The client with intensely held religious or ethical values may believe that this kind of work is forbidden. For example, such a person may be fervently guided by the admonition "Children, obey your parents. . . . Honour thy father and mother . . . that it may be well with thee, and thou mayest live long on the earth" (Ephesians 6:1-3; Exodus 20:20). Such attitudes of extreme obedience or respect (intimidation) toward parents may have cultural reinforcement, thereby of course underscoring the need for and providing yet more grist for the mill of differentiation.

7. There are some persons who are fervently committed to the posture of being emotionally cut off from the family of origin. Although they may come voluntarily asking for help with their relationships with family, they do not want this kind of help if it means making this kind of overture and change.

8. From time to time there is the client who is so intensely triangulated into the parental relationship that his or her "marriage"

to a parent is currently a more significant source of support than is the spouse. This client is going to think long and hard about the psychological disruption and loss involved in personal authority renegotiations.

9. There is the occasional client who is regularly described as "not being psychologically minded." This may be related to intellect, education, or family culture. But there are also individuals who have created a lifestyle built on a willful commitment "not to know." They will not speculate very much about innermost thoughts, feelings, and personal relationships, especially with regard to early experiences in life. Those who have built a lifestyle based on "not knowing" and who have perhaps in many aspects of life been quite successful with this may not want to know the rich and provocative information likely to emerge from such a wide-ranging agenda. They may not even want to know that they don't know and don't want to know.

10. There are those who have been significantly abused as children, whether it be emotional, physical, or sexual abuse. For these persons, the thought of pursuing intimacy with the offending parent is often distasteful if not repulsive.

11. Last of all, there is a group of psychologically sophisticated people, including some psychotherapists, whose theoretical and professional belief system and identifications do not encourage, and sometimes will not permit, this kind of exploration.

These various client characteristics can constitute formidable limitations. Fortunately, many of these problems will recreate themselves in the small group dynamics. In this case (and if the client stays committed to the process), there is always hope that appropriate modifications can be made in client behavior. Along with this there may be a judicious scaling down of goals or a slowing down of the preparation or the use of a less threatening vocabulary. The client can take more time to get ready or to increase the capacity for forgiveness. In summary, the consultant can encourage whatever nuance or deviation facilitates the maximum good work and the best possible benefit for a given client and family.

Ironically, and as is true of just about every "talking therapy," the more psychologically intact an individual is, the more he or she can gain from this work. Despite this and provided that the idiosyncrasies and limitations of the context are adequately taken into account, a majority of persons who seek out this kind of help make noticeable improvements in their relationships. This is not because of any special genius inherent in the therapeutic method. It is, rather, that families have enormous resources to provide nurturing and healing relationships for one another when they are encouraged to maximize the assets, minimize the liabilities, and mobilize the goodwill.

Reluctance to Making Changes in Family Politics

There are four commonly observable reasons, discussed in the following paragraphs, why people are reluctant to make changes in intergenerational politics.

Intergenerational Intimidation

The first and most compelling reason for a client's reluctance to make changes in intergenerational politics is intergenerational intimidation. In this writer's view, intergenerational intimidation not only influences individual clients but has also influenced the development of theory and method in transgenerational family therapy. By and large, transgenerational family theory has taken the view that the parent remains fully in the role of parent throughout. It is argued that this fundamental hierarchical political structure cannot and should not be challenged. "In this dialogue, however, there is never a reversal of generations; an aging parent, though becoming more dependent or physically incapacitated, still remains a parent. As stated by Spark and Brody [1979], 'in feeling though the adult child may be old himself he remains in the relationship of child to parent'" (Boszormenyi-Nagy & Spark, 1973, p. 224). Framo (1976) supports this position. In my view, taking the position that the parent remains fully in the role of parent is a monumental error! This is a crucial issue and the political perspective taken here is the distinguishing characteristic of this book.

There are two psychological dynamics that make intergenerational intimidation so powerful and pervasive. The first is the fear of suicide, the second the fear of homicide. The fear of suicide is grounded in the fear of rejection by parents if the second generation calls the current political order into question. Even the temporary loss of parental approval and goodwill can be experienced as rejection and, therefore, as life-threatening. Anxiety about rejection conjures up the child's earliest and most primitive fears about abandonment and exposure and, therefore, death if he or she is not accepted and nurtured by parents. Consequently, any questioning of ongoing family politics and dynamics that might incur such a risk is frequently experienced as suicidal behavior.

The second dynamic is the compelling fear that calling the political order into question may result in parental death. This is voiced repeatedly by clients who make remarks such as, "These are old people. They are weak and feeble and close to their own deaths. Why stir things up now? Why upset and distress them in their last days? Why not let them live as long as possible and in peace?" The underlying fear is that any sharp questioning of parents about sensitive matters or any attempt to change the structure of family politics will be so distressing to parents that they may die from shock, hurt, or disappointment. In many instances, the client cannot tolerate the guilt ensuing from such "murderous" thoughts.

Covert Loyalties

A second reason for so much resistance to intergenerational change is the existence of what has been called widespread and covert patterns of "invisible loyalties" between the generations (Boszormenyi-Nagy & Spark, 1973). These, of course, are exercised mostly outside of conscious awareness and are related to fear and guilt at the prospect of not meeting parental expectations, which are transmitted covertly. Invisible loyalties are also related to the powerful dynamics of identification and affection and the ensuing desire to be pleasing to parents. The second generation may also identify consciously with the values and goals of the first so that the motivation born of this identification becomes contemporaneous and functionally autonomous. As Allport (1955) noted a long time ago in describing human motivation, "Whatever drives, drives now."

For all the aforementioned reasons, any criticism of family values and beliefs may be experienced not simply as an attack upon parents but as an attack upon one's inner self. A strong emotional attachment can weld the client to the beliefs, values, and general culture style of previous generations. Any review of these will mobilize deep and intense transgenerational loyalties. This can lead to intense and even violent consequences, all the way from Belfast to Beirut to Baghdad. In fighting either to protect or sustain a particular political order on the local scene, the client may be fighting to carry the flag for the beliefs and values of previous generations. He or she may also be fighting ultimately for the continued existence of the inner self as a construct of these beliefs. The power of this multilevel loyalty motivation can be expressed through organization into small family-like political cells assembled for purposes such as lobbying or terrorist activity.

Unmourned Losses

A third reason for resistance to intergenerational political change is the power of unacknowledged and unmourned losses in previous generations. This emotionality can be transmitted into both the minds and the bodies of the new generation. These subterranean ties of pain and grief weave durable patterns of connectedness with parents. A "sticky emotionality" of this sort does not give up easily.

Fear of Death

The last reason for resistance to change is the universal and understandable human reluctance to face death. The widespread reluctance to face the approaching deaths of aging parents shows itself in the common reluctance to discuss this matter openly with them. Most people prefer to perpetuate the myth that the parents will go on forever. A strong dynamic behind this is the hesitancy to give up the parent as parent. Another reason is that if one openly acknowledges the approaching deaths of aging parents, then one must openly face the inevitability of one's own personal death as simply a matter of a little more time. Most of the time, most people would prefer to think about something else.

The fears of suicide and murder are undoubtedly the most immediate and the most compelling of reasons for reluctance to change family politics. Covert loyalties and unmourned losses are close behind. Fear of death lurks pervasively at both conscious and unconscious levels of the mind. Some aspects of these various fears are quite readily identifiable, other aspects are much more subtle but equally persuasive. Through all of this, the possibility for change is always and immediately at hand. Despite all the reasons for reluctance to change and whether they know it or not, most clients are invariably "trembling on the edge."

PART THREE

Personal Authority Contextual Issues

CHAPTER 13

Personal Authority: The Personal Story

> For you see, in Ireland there is no future, only the past
> happening over and over.
>> —Leon Uris
>> *Trinity* (last line of Epilogue)

It may help explain the theoretical position described in this book if I now describe the personal narrative that is the background to it. A further reason for such a revelation is my belief in the value of congruity and transparency as a healing dynamic for both therapist and client (Framo, 1968, 1990; Jourard, 1971; Rogers, 1961; Skynner, 1981). Finally, I would like to show good faith by documenting that I have not encouraged clients to do things I have not attempted to do for myself.

The Town of Dungannon

I was born in the summer of 1935 in Dungannon, then a town of some 4,000 souls in County Tyrone, Northern Ireland. At that time Dungannon was about equally divided between Protestants and Roman Catholics, the one side known colloquially as the "Prods" and the other as the "Papitches" (from Papist). With few exceptions, the "Papitches" were deliberately confined to clearly demarcated ghettos, which, taken together, constituted scarcely more than one-fifth of the total area of the town. As was generally the case for Protestant children, I had no Roman Catholic friends and few Roman Catholic acquaintances growing up.

Dungannon is about 11 miles from the border with the Republic of Ireland. Ireland was divided some 14 years before my birth into the 6 counties of the predominantly Protestant northeast, which is Ulster, and the 26 counties of the predominantly Roman Catholic south, which is Eire. Northern Ireland (or Ulster) remained an integral part of the United Kingdom, and the other three quarters of the country became an independent republic in 1921 known as the Republic of Ireland. (By and large, it is the accent, the anecdotes, and the ambience of the Republic of Ireland, or Eire, that is known in the United States as "Ireland.") This division of the country, which was implemented as "the solution" to a problem, itself became the greater problem, which has troubled the North of Ireland increasingly ever since with no sign of solution.

When I was growing up, the town of Dungannon was dominated physically, financially, and psychosocially by a linen mill known as "Moygashel," a source of great Irish linen with a proud international reputation. This mill was by far the town's largest employer, bene-factor, and benevolent dictator. Most young men and many young women aspired to a job at "the factory." However, circumstances allowed me to avoid the mill. By aid of a scholarship I was able to attend the local Royal School for Boys, founded in 1614, and, subsequently, college and theological seminary in Belfast, the capital city of Northern Ireland. This, in turn, was the gateway to graduate school in the United States, which I entered in 1961.

I was the last born of six children, three boys and three girls, of whom four survive to this day. The firstborn, a male, died in what were initially somewhat confusing circumstances, ruled at the inquest to be an accidental drowning. At the time of his death in May 1938, Leslie was 17 years old, and I was 2 years 10 months. Before I was born the third born, also a male, died a crib death at the age of 10 months. Three girls and I have survived. My family, although middle-class by the standards of this little town, would in a larger context have been seen as on the boundary between working-class and middle-class, slowly moving into the latter. My parents were pillars of the local Methodist Church, a small but influential and very conservative community in some ways flagrantly fundamentalist in theological, political, and social outlook.

The town boasted two hotels, two cinemas, an occasional mov-able dance hall, a silver band, a volunteer fire department and, by my teenage years, a traveling library. There were two public high schools, one for boys and one for girls, and one of each for Roman

Catholic children, since the church hierarchy required that Roman Catholic children be educated separately. Dungannon is built on a hill, from the top of which can be seen all six counties of Northern Ireland on a rare exceptionally clear day. The ruins of the O'Neill Castle, dating back to Hugh O'Neill, Earl of Tireewn in the 14th century, stand or, rather, continue to fall at the peak of this central hill. In recent years this commanding site was occupied by soldiers of the British Army intentionally to preserve the peace between the partisans and, as it turned out, inadvertently to provide something for the Irish Republican Army to shoot at.

Dungannon is at the heart of County Tyrone, known in the province as "Tyrone among the bushes." It is surrounded by rich farm land and is located 40 miles west of Belfast, which is on the east coast. It is 75 miles from the Giant's Causeway on the Antrim Coast to the north—If not the most beautiful, certainly one of the two most beautiful sights in all of Ireland. (Appropriately enough, the other is in the extreme southwest.) The west coast I would not have known so much about, since that fell within that strange and foreign land known as the Republic of Ireland or, more commonly, the Irish Free State or Eire. The fact that the most northerly tip of the country was in "the South" would not seem odd in Ireland. The terrorists of the Irish Republic Army (sometimes viewed as freedom fighters from another political perspective) were active in the Dungannon area in my early years, as they have continued to be to this day. A depressing cloud of fear and suspicion, defiance and hope, hung heavily in the air. The righteous superiority of the Protestant rulers of the town, ruling with blatant prejudice and by "divine right," was naturally matched by a hostile rebelliousness and a ready willingness to protect terrorists on "the other side."

The political and social focus moved outward a little bit, and there was some mutuality of identification within the divided community during the World War II years in response to the undiscriminating and menacing threat posed by the Third Reich. Catholics and Protestants alike blacked out the light from every window at night lest they provide a marker for enemy aircraft. Both got coupons for food and clothes and sat in closets under stairways with gas masks in hand when the air raid siren sounded. Such was the ambience overall of the town of Dungannon in the late '30s, '40s and early '50s. There were many sorts of intimidation and fear.

The "recent" round of troubles in Northern Ireland began in 1969 with a civil rights march (on behalf of Roman Catholics) from the nearby town of Coalisland into Dungannon. It was led by Bernadette Devlin who lives in Coalisland and who later became Member of

Parliament for the constituency of South Tyrone and Fermanagh, which includes both Coalisland and Dungannon. The march itself was peaceful, although things soon turned very violent. Since that time most of the center of the town has been blown up and then rebuilt several times. Presently, Dungannon looks fresh and refurbished, decorated with large baskets of growing plants and flowers acquired by funds provided from overseas and given to help heal the outer signs and scars of inner and more permanent wounds.

Growing up in Dungannon, with its divided community and located just 10 miles from the border with the Republic of Ireland, and belonging to the smallest Protestant church and born of two parents neither of whom at that time was consistently confident where he or she belonged, I learned to walk the boundary. Out of this grew a preference for a position on the boundary. It became the most comfortable place for me. I do my best work with people on the boundary. To this day I do not respond as well to the highly privileged insider or the undoubting ideologue. It is as difficult for me not to be offended by the narcissism of the former as it is not to be contemptuous of the fearfulness in the latter. But that's my problem.

The Family

Before she became pregnant with me, my mother was warned by the town doctor that she should have no more children, for if she did she would probably lose her own life in the process. With this warning ringing in her ears, as she prepared for my birth, she also prepared herself and her house for her own possible death. For my father's part, the anticipated child was "dedicated to God" before it was born, assuming he or she survived. (As it happens, all three parties survive to this day.)

As mentioned earlier, when I was 2 years and 10 months old, Leslie, the firstborn, died by drowning at the age of 17 years. At first he had simply disappeared, and for some agonizing period of time, no one knew for sure how or to where. Our parents searched the countryside for him day and night. Although a drowning death was known to be a possibility, it was not confirmed until 2 weeks later, when the body was recovered. The coroner later ruled "accidental death by drowning."

In retrospect and after reconstructing as much detail of the story as has been possible, I am convinced there is no evidence or reason to conclude otherwise. There is invariably, however, a complex psychosocial context within which such events occur. For whatever reasons, the family dynamics of that time were such as to generate some persisting doubts about the circumstances contributing to Leslie's death, even if these doubts could hardly be allowed to become as real as words would make them. Indisputably, Leslie's death did result in extraordinary feelings of guilt and inconsolable remorse on the part of my parents. I did not know (that is, remember) anything of Leslie until at age 8 years I was informed about his life and death by some young friends while at play in the neighborhood. When I sought confirmation at home, silence and ambiguity reigned, and remorse abounded. This expressed itself in lowered heads and tears and admonitions not to mention "that name." Many years later I was told the following story, which, if true, would explain a lot. At the site at which Leslie drowned something valuable had been lost from the pharmacy where he worked as a message boy. He was sent to retrieve it but returned empty-handed. He was sent back by someone and told, "Don't come back without it." He did not come back.

Illness

Within just a few months of finding out about Leslie I was put to bed for what turned out to be 18 months with "a heart enlarged like a football" and "four leaking valves." This was surmised to be the result of rheumatic fever, undiagnosed and untreated. The pediatric specialist advised, "Take him home and be good to him. He has about 6 months to live," a comment overhead by the alarmed patient in the next room. As it turned out, the family that had created the context in which this threat to life occurred now went on to create a context in which failure to heal was unthinkable, and a "miraculous" and complete recovery did take place. After 18 months of confinement to bed, I was up and on my way back to complete good health. In retrospect, it is difficult to hold the discovery about Leslie and the subsequent "sickness unto death" as totally unrelated family events. I was now already informally in training to become a family therapist, having experienced the power of secrets and unacknowledged losses in families and the complex way these can be related to health and illness. I had also learned something about the power of the raging sea of family emotionality.

When I was 15 years old (in 1950), my father suffered a massive coronary thrombosis. He could not be moved from the site where it had happened for 48 hours. He was not expected to recover and any attempt to move him was considered dangerous. (At the time of this writing, my father is in his 94th year.) I can still recall the terror of those moments. The fear of losing him and the fear of the consequences in the family of such a loss may well have provided the psychological trigger in the context of genetic predisposition. In any event, within a few months I was confirmed diabetic. A 4-year search for a second "miraculous" cure did not prove as successful as the first, at least not in the way hoped for at that time.

For the last 41 years I have been insulin-dependent. I have learned at an experiential level some things about emotional events in the family as they affect the health of family members and about the powerful connections between emotions and health and between expectations and performance. Learning firsthand about the destructive power of fear and fearfulness in human beings undoubtedly prepared the way for a focus on clear self-definition and personal authority as a route to personal well-being, both physical and psychological. It is hardly a coincidence that in my theoretical view resolving intimidation is presented as the sine qua non of personal authority in life.

Religion

The other factor of some significance in my early years was the fact that a very conservative religious perspective characterized my family's beliefs and values. All of life's experiences were interpreted in light of religious ideas and religious symbols. Discerning and conforming to the "will of God" for one's life, both in general terms and on an everyday basis, was the sustaining reference point for conversation. Competing with love for control at the very heart of this process—as is perhaps true in any closed ideology, whether social, political, or religious—was great fear. Again I became highly sensitized to the negative power of the dynamic of fear in human experience. In time I came to view personal authority (which, of course, includes control of one's thinking process) as an antidote and an alternative to fear.

At age 17 years, I left for college and then seminary. I studied psychology and theology. It is no surprise, given my background, that I was occupied and often preoccupied, with questions of salvation and wholeness, redemption and suffering, disease and personal well-being. I was absorbed by questions pertaining to the relationship between body and mind, between body and mind/spirit, and between beliefs and health. I was curious about the positive and negative dynamics and uses of religious symbols; ideas and values in human health and happiness; the various dynamic patterns of relationship between family process and the health and illness behaviors of individual family members; the promotion of human health and happiness by health professionals, including clergy; and, most important of all, the question of the resolution of fear and fearfulness

Brave New World

In 1961, at age 26, I came to the United States ostensibly to pursue graduate study in the hybrid field of theology and psychology generally known as "pastoral psychology." At that time such a focus for study was not available in any organized way within the United Kingdom. My conscious goal was to complete graduate study and then return to Northern Ireland to be "special" in some as yet unspecified way. From another perspective, it seems clear, in retrospect, that I left Ireland as an alternative to leaving home, maybe also as an alternative to becoming sick again. At the time, I had no idea how to "leave home." So, I moved my body across an ocean, thereby achieving at least physical distance. It is plausible that at some level, not fully in awareness, I was hoping that this would lead to emotional separateness and self-definition as well. Needless to say, I discovered that the parental introjects go along for the ride, in this case, the cruise.

An advantage to being at some physical distance from the parental home is the fact that one does not simultaneously have to deal with the introjects and also deal directly with the "really out there" actual parents. The problem is that these are usually quite different sets of people, which can be confusing if not immobilizing. It can, of course, be argued that, in one sense, the "really out there" parents also exist only as they are experienced in the head. However, it is one thing to relate to parents who have been constructed exclusively out of earlier fixed memories and whose images and behaviors have, therefore, frozen in time. It is quite another thing to perceive and relate to that older man and woman walking around out there constantly active and reactive in the ongoing relationships themselves often wondering who on earth this person is who once was their child. With physical space separating one from the parents, one at least has more energy and courage—whether one conducts this dialogue with or without professional help—to begin to look at the introjects, who will naturally talk back but only with old and familiar lines.

One can then consider a new course of action intended to get these two disparate images of the parents together. The intention is to change inner images in useful ways by renegotiating the current dynamics and, therefore, the contemporary perceptions of the "real" figures of the aging parents. These aging parents are, of course, still that man and woman who used to be "Mommy" and "Daddy."

In my own case, I created a classic cutoff for a few years, perhaps a necessary developmental move, since I was not yet ready for anything more. After a few years, however, I began to visit Ireland once or twice or more each year, and I did this for a number of years. The purpose of these visits (as it turned out) was to see if I could negotiate an emotional leaving so that I could then return emotionally and belong in a different way. Each visit would last 4 or 5 days. The time was spent talking with my parents, both individually and together, and this process was supplemented by conversations with other family members. I discovered that, paradoxically, one can only leave the family of origin emotionally by going back into the very heart of the family and learning to be comfortable there. A potent sign of "having left" is, therefore, the freedom to be present voluntarily and joyfully.

Physical distance and, for some, a period of emotional distance may be necessary developmental steps. Yet an individual will remain uneasy and vulnerable if he or she does not evolve beyond this. As Boszormenyi-Nagy has pointed out, "The resistance to the past is the voice of the past" (Boszormenyi-Nagy & Ulrich, 1981, p. 184). There is considerable plausibility to the idea that one cannot come to feel very much better about one's self than one comes to feel, in the last resort, about one's parents. It is, therefore, of compelling psychological importance to rehabilitate the parents as fully as possible within one's own mind and heart. If nothing else, this is simply enlightened self-interest. In embracing the parents and putting them close to one's heart one is embracing the parent within the self. One is, therefore, integrating within the self system crucial, if previously rejected, aspects of self (Rogers, 1951). This is an important step on the way to wholeness and integrity.

On Returning to the Parental Home

On reflection, four ideas became clear to me about attitudes which I came to adopt that facilitated my work. First of all, by initiating the trips I moved beyond the emotional cutoff with my family of origin. Second, although in the early days I indulged in many fruitless arguments about religious ideas, I finally realized that this was neither useful nor necessary to the goal I had in mind. So, third, instead, playfulness and humor became the order of the day! Perhaps it is only a matter of time before personal identity in life is no longer so closely dependent upon a particular belief system; then, no beliefs will have to be propagated so fiercely or defended so loudly. The differentiation of self takes place at other levels of discourse, relationship, and emotion. Both generations do finally realize that they can believe very differently and still belong together.

Fourth, I became able to acknowledge to my family that I was there talking to them because I needed their help. In the early days I was more inclined to take the stance of a family psychologist: I was someone with special training and special understanding of families and family dynamics, and so I had some questions to ask them and I wanted frank responses. In nice ways they told me to "take a hike," undoubtedly the most appropriate, if at the moment least appreciated, response possible to such an overture. As I became less afraid, I was able to declare the truth: "I'm in trouble and I need your help. I have some questions to ask, because I believe the information will help me."

Family members responded openly and well to this acknowledgment, as family members usually do. I received much useful information as well as emotional encouragement and support not just from my parents but also from my sisters. It became clear at both a relational and an emotional level, that I was now choosing to *belong* to this family. No amount of disagreement about this or that or the other was going to change that fundamental fact. Fear and fearfulness were not going to cast out love. Most persons and most families respond with generosity and delight to such an approach when they experience it as genuine and heartfelt.

Siblings, of course, may be confused or distressed and questioning at several points along the way. As one sister explained to me, she could not understand why I was asking all these upsetting questions and raising all these old painful memories with these aging parents who could do nothing now about the past. They had paid their dues. They should be allowed mercifully to forget the past, and to complete their lives in quietness and peace. Or as a second sister once said:

> "Since you do this sort of thing for a living, I have a question for you. I know it's helpful to you for you to come here for a few days to chat with our parents, and I do believe in what you're doing. But as you may or may not realize, after you fly off they are upset, and we are left here and have to deal with it. Now that

is alright; I am not complaining about that. My question is, do you encourage your patients to do things like this with their parents, and have you found that it usually has worked out well for them? Are their parents upset afterwards, and who helps them to settle down again?"

Another possibility is that a sibling's spouse may become concerned if he or she feels that something noteworthy and intimate is going on within the family and he or she is being excluded. As long as one adopts neither a professional nor a defensive stance, all these events can be grist for the therapeutic mill.

Through these various visits over time, although in rather haphazard fashion, I worked my way through an agenda somewhat like that described in an earlier chapter, used by clients working with their parents. There were lots of hits and misses and plenty of retakes along the way. Some crucial scenes can be recounted briefly; this is intended to show good faith. That is, I do not expect clients to initiate experiences of a sort that I have not gone through myself.

Critical Incidents in Conversations at the Parental Home

On Becoming a Clergyman for Father

A few events stand out in memory as having been markers along the way in the renegotiations with my family of origin. I discovered on one of my trips to my parents' home that long before I was born, my father, as a young man in his 20s, had wanted to become a minister of religion. He had taken some initial steps but, as things turned out, was unable to achieve this goal. For my part, from earliest memory I had always known that I would be a clergyman. It was a given. It now seemed apparent that I had picked up the flag on father's behalf, addressing a disappointment that had begun 15 years before I was born; unwittingly, I had worked toward achieving his unachieved goal. This helped me understand my love–hate relationship with the church at that time. I shared with my father these thoughts as to at least part of what might have been going on with regard to my "call" to religious ministry. I made clear that redressing his disappointment would no longer provide motivation adequate to sustain me. Naturally, he looked at me quizzically, perhaps searching for the hole in my head. Notwithstanding, an intense emotional transaction and renegotiation took place. This resulted in a new clarity of focus and less conflict in my professional life and identity.

In the Matter of Taking Responsibility for Young Children

On another occasion my mother expressed concern because my 7-year-old son, whom she was putting to bed one evening during one of these visits to Ireland, had declined to say any prayers, with the precociously cavalier comment, "I don't go for that Jesus stuff." She explained that were it not for her, he would not be in the world and that she therefore "carried a burden" for him. This was a mandate that had echoed across the generations. I now took the opportunity to explain that this child was totally the responsibility of his own mother and father. Grandma was off the hook. She declined this generous offer and reaffirmed her position of responsibility. I again proposed taking her off the hook. Once again she insisted. I then suggested that she could indeed go on pretending, that is, acting as if she were responsible, if that would bring some pleasure or relief. I promised that only she and I would know the truth; it would be our secret. I offered to brief all other interested parties on their roles and lines in this play. Our eyes met and held for an intense moment. Something critical began to shift in the structure of power between the two generations. The sequelae took some time to heal. Perhaps it could not have been any other way. Anyway, it is long since forgotten.

On Father's Fear of Father

Throughout my growing up years my father had repeatedly shown his extreme fear and intimidation of his father. My grandfather was a retired Belfast Harbour policeman, recipient of the Queen's Police Medal and famous for his physical strength and prowess. One of his tricks, folklore had it, was to twirl 50-pound weights simultaneously on both little fingers. By the time I knew him he was a teddy bear, full of good stories and presents. In college I visited him many Friday afternoons, and as he walked me to the gate he would say, "Fair wind to your wee boat."

Obviously, my father had grown up with a totally different guy and remained very fearful of this old man's disapproval to the day of his death—and beyond. So one day, standing by this old man's graveside in Belfast Cemetery, I was able to ask my father why had he been so intimidated all his life by this old warrior. He had neither a particularly good answer nor much of an understanding of that relationship. The valuable aspect of this conversation was, rather, that making this matter explicit at an important symbolic site made possible a crucial acknowledgment and renegotiation between the two of us. It meant that I would not feel compelled to perpetuate this kind of intimidation into yet another generation. It is scarcely a coincidence that a major explanatory construct in the theory presented in this book is labeled as intergenerational intimidation. (It may also not be entirely a coincidence that my son worked 5 years as a police officer.)

On Mother's Love for Mother

On a similar pilgrimage, my mother and I visited her mother's gravesite at the foot of Mount Slemish in County Antrim, where Saint Patrick is reputed to have tended his sheep and searched in vain for snakes. We freshened the gravesite with some spring flowers. This produced a conducive context for a conversation about this formidable old woman whom my mother still idealized and from whom any outward signs of attention and goodwill had justified considerable effort. This was also a chance to discuss the occasional destructive triangulation involving mother and father and mother's mother that I had observed, though not understood, while growing up and remembered as an adult. Mother was still moved by memory of her mother's goodness and specialness. In yet another guise, intergenerational intimidation was the issue under review once again. It is easy to be intimidated by "goodness," and there is no easy way out. By virtue of what was this old woman so "special"? Why were the memories of her so intense? The act of acknowledging the triangulation that went back a generation in time provided leverage for me to reduce my triangulation in my own parents' marriage. Undoubtedly, all these experiences influenced my thinking about the centrality of intergenerational intimidation and the value of face-to-face conversations in family of origin work.

In the Matter of Not Taking Emotional Responsibility for the Inner Happiness of Aging Parents

Sometime about midway in this work, I received an urgent phone call from one of my sisters. She informed me that Mother would be having an essential surgery within the next week. The physicians had advised the family that she would have no more than a 50–50 chance of survival. My sister simply wanted me "to have this information." Upon reflection, I decided to make an immediate trip to visit my mother before the surgery, rather than wait and perhaps go for a funeral. (No suspense here; my mother, whose mind is still as clear as spring water, has recently celebrated her 91st birthday.) I spent a couple of days chatting in her hospital room. The night before I left, she made a pensive observation. Pointing out the hospital window to the town visible all around, she said:

> "Look at this tired old town of Dungannon. It is full of lorries everywhere, with these young soldiers carrying rifles. This town is old and done—and so am I. All my grandchildren are grown now. None of them need me any more. So now, you just tell me this. Why should I come through this thing [surgery]? Why should I fight this? Why should I go on?"

My response was to say, "You've got me there, Mother. But if you do decide to come through it, I'll be delighted and I'll be back to visit with you some more."

In the context of a family in which great burdens of emotional responsibility moved readily from generation to generation, and often in massive and debilitating proportion, this was an important transaction. There was no denial of the power of the connection or the importance of the relationship between mother and son. Nor was this a denial of or indifference to the power of social and emotional support in relationships. It was, rather, an acknowledgment that no person can take on the burden of the inner emotional responsibility for the personal survival or the will to live or the happiness of anyone else. Managing one life is a full-time job.

A son or daughter can offer physical, emotional, or financial support to an aging parent, as they may come to be needed and as the former has the resources to provide it, without unfairly jeopardizing the self. This is quite different from acting out of an involuntary or self-wounding sense of obligation; it matters not whether this initiative is motivated by guilt, remorse, fear, psychological fusion, or whatever. "Peerhood" means that the parent, even the needy parent, has no longer any power to compel certain responses. What is given can be given freely, and it does not have to be offered at an undue expense to the well-being of the self.

This balancing of indebtedness between the self and a "former parent" is often a delicate, sometimes a poignant, "moment of truth" in human experience. While it does not call for a "loss of self" inspired by guilt, fear, or dependency, neither is this a time for retribution. The adult who has already given up the parent as parent, is now much less likely to be internally or externally cajoled into "playing parent" to an aging or ailing parent now ready to "play child" in complementary fashion. In this scenario, the underlying power status of the parent is frequently protected by the awareness that "only God can let you play God." The more involuntariness and obligation characterize an intergenerational relationship between adults, the less will the generosity and spontaneity of love and tenderness be present.

Honoring Leslie

In the latter days of this work between myself and the members of my family, I requested that arrangements be made so that my three sisters, both parents, and I could all be present in my parents' home for a long afternoon conversation. On this afternoon, with all members present and looking at and acknowledging one another, this family for the first time explicitly and consciously acknowledged that there had been a son and a brother in the family by the name of Leslie, who had died by an accidental drowning in the town of Dungannon in the year of 1938. I took this opportunity to ask every question that had ever entered my mind about Leslie. This included questions as to why my parents had not been able to manage his death emotionally and why it had been held as such a secret. I also raised such extreme possibilities as death by suicide or death by homicide. I became convinced that the death itself was accidental, although not acontextual. However, I believe the raising of all my worst fears and fantasies, while shocking in the moment, was in the long run healing not only for me but for all members of the family. We acknowledged and mourned for and honored Leslie.

"You're British and I'm Irish"

If one is born a Protestant in Northern Ireland, in all likelihood one is "British and not Irish." A conversation about nationality is very likely to go as follows.

QUESTIONER: What nationality are you?
ULSTER PROTESTANT: I'm British.
QUESTIONER: Okay, you're British, but what country do you belong to?
ULSTER PROTESTANT: I'm British and that's all there's to it.

QUESTIONER: Well, I know everyone in the United Kingdom is British, but some people are English and some people are Welsh and some people are Scottish and so on. So what nationality are you?

ULSTER PROTESTANT: I'm British.

QUESTIONER: I know you are British. Are you also Irish?

ULSTER PROTESTANT (*reluctantly*): I'm British and I'm Northern Irish.

QUESTIONER: Okay, so you are Northern Irish. Does that mean that you are Irish?

ULSTER PROTESTANT: I'm British and I'm Northern Irish.

QUESTIONER: I understand that you are British and you are also Northern Irish. So you are Northern Irish. Does that mean that you are Irish?

ULSTER PROTESTANT: I'm not Irish like they're Irish.

So the poignant dilemma of the Ulster Protestant is that he or she cannot as a rule take pride in being Irish and yet has an uneasy and at best ambivalent relationship with the rest of the United Kingdom. To the ruling class English, the Irish are second class, whether Roman Catholic or Protestant, whether north or south. It makes no difference. Over the centuries, the Irish have come to believe this to be so. The conflict in Northern Ireland is not Roman Catholic versus Protestant. It is rather being British versus being Irish. There are powerful and intense cultural differences in history, in heritage, and in values. These differences happen to coincide with and are reinforced by religious differences, giving the mistaken impression of being primarily a conflict of religions. When the symbols of eternity are used to support political and cultural convictions, the stage has been set for profound trouble.

My father was an Orangeman in his early days, which means he was a member of a "Loyal Orange Lodge," the strong, conservative, and pro-British Protestant element in Ulster politics. He and all the members of my family, having lived in Ulster and having lived through "the trouble," are understandably very strongly British in their sense of national identity. Undoubtedly, I would have been the same had I stayed in Ulster. But after I had been living in the United States for more than 20 years and had gone back and toured throughout all parts of Ireland, I finally became Irish. Being an Ulster Protestant, I am Scottish Irish for sure. But Irish nonetheless, and proud of it. From this distance and perspective, "Irish" is indivisible. This cleared the way for me to become a naturalized citizen, after 30 years of residency in the United States. So now I am an Irish American.

This realization led to conversations with my parents and sisters in which each of them in turn declared the self to be British and I declared myself to be Irish, and that is okay. He is British and she is British and I am Irish and we still belong together, and that is okay. This experience represented yet another level of differentiation of self, at a cultural level, combined with the maintenance of an intimate connection. In other words, it was a further opportunity for the exercise of personal authority within the family. Neither identity nor personal authority can be discovered and developed apart from context and apart from culture (McGoldrick, Pearce, & Giordano, 1982).

In my growing up years, a black St. James version of the Holy Bible sitting on an Orange Sash sitting on a Union Jack atop a large drum, constituted all the necessary symbols of political, religious, and cultural life in Northern Ireland. Today, much grief and bloodshed later, Ulster seems to be struggling to adopt a less rigid interpretation of history; in other words, Ulster is flirting with the possibility of creating a different future.

Falling in Love Again with "Former Parents"

On one of my later visits, I sought out an opportunity to acknowledge in each of my parents the attributes and behaviors for which they are most widely appreciated and loved in the family and the community. This took place in the company of the extended family, including grandchildren and their spouses and children. As a centerpiece for my mother, the conversation focused on her remarkable and unfailing charity and kindness to persons in crisis. Because of this quality she had become known in the community as a resource for individuals or families in stress and needing nurturance. I recalled for the family a cherished childhood memory of seeing a Gypsy girl come to the door to sell baskets. My mother predictably declined the baskets, but she sat the girl down on the front step and fed her with milk and sandwiches and encouraged her to eat until she could eat no more. The story symbolized her great quick and kind responsiveness and is a memory from which I have drawn strength.

At the same family gathering, I acknowledged that my father was known both within and without the family for the dominant and transcending courage of his spirit. Over the years he had either mastered or coped with many challenges to life and limb to which a less resilient spirit would surely have succumbed. I mentioned that I have remembered some of these incidents over the years and drew strength from these memories. I also acknowledged both parents for their extraordinary openness of mind and heart in response to the interrogations that I had put them through in recent years. In subsequent years we have had some outstanding family gatherings and picnics, characterized by laughter and celebration. In other words, there was no covert agenda on anybody's part.

From my father's life I learned about the destructive power and impact of fear and intimidation. Learning from his struggles, I was determined to find another way, and eventually resolution of inter-generational intimidation became an important part of personal authority theory. From early days I absorbed from my mother's example the skill of reframing. She had the unusual ability to construct at any time the reality that was most useful to her out of any human situation or set of facts. In retrospect, one of my favorite memories is of her penchant for saying, "You don't really think that. You just think you think that." (That is an intriguing idea. Think about it!) While this tendency was undoubtedly disquieting and invalidating to a child, it was nonetheless magnificent early training for a career in the practice of family therapy, as well as for the management of the dilemmas and paradoxes that characterize every-day life.

Two Observations on the Work

Obviously, there is a continuing evolution of the intergenerational relationship while both generations survive and continue to move through the remaining stages of life, and yet there is this specific developmental task of personal authority to be addressed and achieved at a particular time in personal history. There is a detailed agenda to be covered between the generations. This work can and does get done, and with some sense of completeness and termina-tion. With this perspective in mind, I look back on my own work within the family of origin and am struck by two observations. The first of these is the realization that as one achieves some greater level of personal authority in life, one feels, not unexpectedly, much less controlled by the family of origin. One of the most far-reaching consequences of this, in turn, is that one has much less need to control the surrounding world and everyone in it, especially those within one's own intimate circle. The second observation suggests that there is an ever-widening ripple effect that frequently results from initiating this kind of political change in one's personal relation-ships within the family. I do believe that in most families this ripple effect is generally beneficial to family members in the long run.

Admittedly, just how much change is outside the head and how much is within one's own construction of reality only one never knows for sure, and perhaps they are not even separable. But I have been amazed in recent years, when in attendance at large family picnics, to experience the degree of intimacy and celebration present in my own extended family. It is great news that one's personal narrative in life, including one's family of origin drama, is ultimately a made-up story. A construction of reality that exists only in the individual's mind can be unwritten and rewritten in ways that are more conducive to personal health, intergenerational intimacy, and family celebration. Intergenerational renegotiation inherently offers the possibility of constructing a better story by giving new and multiple perspectives on the same historic events. A new story is always right at hand, willing and ready to be discovered. *History can be rewritten.* That is the attraction of this new stage in family life.

Because a personal history can be rewritten, I regard every client, from his or her very first appearance, as trembling on the edge and teetering on the brink of personal transformation. This is not to play Pollyanna or don rose-colored glasses. While I feel great affection and admiration for my own family of origin, in the fantasy of a repeat journey to this planet I would be tempted to select a path a smidgin more straightfoward and a trifle better endowed. But not at the expense of the good-heartedness of this family.

CHAPTER 14

Personal and Professional Authority in Professional Life

> HAMLET: . . . there are many confines, wards, and
> dungeons, Denmark being one o' the worst.
> ROSENKRANTZ: We think not so, my lord.
> HAMLET: Why, then 'tis none to you; for there is nothing
> either good or bad but thinking makes it so.
>   —*Hamlet* (Act 2, Scene 2)

Murray Bowen has suggested that family of origin issues will recreate themselves not simply in the nuclear family, and especially in the marriage, but also in the client's work setting (Bowen, 1978). Obviously, this can be seen to include the larger social and organizational context of the individual's professional life. *Personal authority is an essential resource for and background to professional identity and authority.* It provides a framework within which I can understand otherwise puzzling aspects of my own professional life, such as when I served as president of the American Association for Marriage and Family Therapy (AAMFT) in the years 1979 and 1980.

The family movement exploded in size and influence within the psychotherapy world in the 1970s. AAMFT was not the primary intellectual source of this movement; nor did its membership include many of the pioneers in family therapy. But by the late 1970s AAMFT did hold the key ground politically. So it sought to come of age as the primary professional organization representing family therapy in the United States, by attempting to more fully professionalize and politicize the discipline by establishing standards for education, clinical training, and practice. At about the same time, certain influential early leaders and pioneers in family therapy who were not active in AAMFT banded together to form a new national group and named it the American Family Therapy Association (AFTA). Initially, the leadership of the new association was not fully aware of the existence, identity, and scope of AAMFT. In time, these became clear. The subsequent view taken was that, yes, AAMFT did exist but it had a history and mandate which, although honorable, were quite different from those of AFTA. AAMFT represented a different discipline, namely, the field of marriage counseling; it was argued that this is indeed something other than family therapy. In truth, historically it *had* been something different, but that time had clearly passed and by the late 1970s marriage counseling had evolved into a subsystem of family therapy. Whether or not this was desirable or just, it was now a fait accompli.

A third view was then offered. While AAMFT might indeed now be a bona fide family therapy organization for the masses, it was not experienced and competent enough to devise and enforce adequate standards on the burgeoning field. A related issue was whether family therapy should be promulgated as a distinct and separate mental health profession or, rather, as a compelling new orientation within the existing mental health disciplines. AAMFT had evolved rapidly, mostly through the energies of persons, often disillusioned, who either were or believed themselves to be disenfranchised in the existing professional political world. It naturally advocated the former position. By contrast, the early leaders of AFTA mostly had strong preexisting discipline-of-origin loyalties to one or the other of the existing mental health disciplines, and in particular, to psychiatry. Finally, there was some understandable residual feeling, that even if AAMFT could do the job, it should not. That mantle, some felt, more properly belonged with the pioneers and their direct and anointed descendants.

It should be acknowledged that unquestionably there have been some unusual historical anomalies and paradoxes in the development of the family therapy field, thereby making it like most everything else in life. To some degree, the head became separated from the body in the family movement, a distortion and dilemma that echoes to this day. In any event, and consistent with their own construction of reality, in 1978 the leadership of AFTA argued to the Department of Health, Education and Welfare (HEW) that AAMFT should not be recognized as the legitimate family organization to serve as the accrediting body for this new discipline. As it turned out, HEW declined this point of view, and AAMFT was duly recognized. As the story continued to unfold, the AFTA leadership read the writing on the wall with varying degrees of disappointment and acceptance, chagrin and relief. AFTA has since continued on its own, now more differentiated, path, becoming an excellent academy of teachers and researchers in family therapy that provides intellectual stimulation and collegial support for its members. (It has also begun to show signs of being more politically sensitive than AAMFT.)

On the other hand, AAMFT has continued growing by leaps and bounds numerically and, therefore, financially and has gone on about the task of "professionalizing the discipline." Its political success has probably been due in part to the fact that, because it had no outstanding intellectual or charismatic leaders, AAMFT discovered its pathway through mostly collegial, collaborative, and democratic negotiations among its leadership. This circumstance built in enough checks and balances so that the goodwill and good sense of the group process usually carried the day. However, in my view, AAMFT has, like most successful movements, since been seduced by its own political success. As a consequence, it has lost much of the vision and some of the idealism that created it, succumbing to the motives and values that tend to characterize any large and successful corporate or trade organization. C'est la vie.

The relevance of this story to personal authority will become clear in the following paragraphs. I chatted with Carl Whitaker at the annual meeting of AAMFT in Houston in the fall of 1978 and explained my dilemma. I was an outsider, and yet I was about to become president of AAMFT at a time when all kinds of ticklish political issues were facing it. I was an outsider to begin with in the sense that I had come from another country and, therefore, was not even a U.S. citizen. I had come from a theological background and so was not initially from a mental health profession. If all that were not enough, I continued, here I was down in Texas of all places, and not on the East Coast where the family of family therapists lived and moved and had its being. I thought I had made my point quite well.

In response, Whitaker simply announced that there is no "inside." Like everything else in life, being on the inside—or the outside, for that matter—is an experience that we create for ourselves. Everybody is on the outside of something, and everybody yearns to be on the inside. It was a helpful moment. Of course we create boundaries in order to be on the inside and identify those who are not. Moreover, although it can be expressed in arrogant and punitive ways, this posture can also be valuable, since without standards there can be no excellence. The useful point is to remember that these boundaries are made by the human mind. So, then, are the emotionalized attitudes associated with them. All of this is central to personal authority and to the way in which personal authority is recreated and expressed in professional life.

The implication of Whitaker's revelation of alternative and more useful construction was salutary. I became committed to the point of view that AAMFT should perceive, hold, and present itself fully as a peer in its relationship to its colleagues within AFTA, many of whom were indeed from the previous generation, both literally and professionally. Yes, indeed, these pioneer leaders of AFTA had paid their dues and deserved their due. At the same time, AAMFT had come of age (was now, appropriately, in its early 40s) and now needed to conduct itself as an adult and a peer. For me, the fact that my thinking and practice in the field of family therapy had been greatly influenced by Murray Bowen, then the founding president of AFTA, added a delightfully ironic touch (or twist) to the whole drama.

Initially, AFTA wanted to have no dealings with AAMFT, but AAMFT refused to participate in this emotional cutoff. During these years I found it well-nigh impossible to persuade Murray Bowen to meet or talk directly about these organizational matters. On one occasion when we did chat, I took the opportunity to ask him a question that interested me. I pointed out that a number of theorists believed that he was strongly within the psychoanalytic tradition and for that reason his theory was not thoroughly systemic. For example, some argued that his theory about the twin forces of separateness and togetherness being in an unending battle was simply the old Freudian dual-drive theory of motivation in modern form. Did he think that this was a fair criticism? After a pause for reflection he replied, "There's Bowen and there's the world. And I'm Bowen." It was a magnificent and memorable response and embodied the most powerful and lasting contribution to the family therapy field by this seminal thinker.

It served to remind me that if I did not hold myself as a peer in relationship to this "professional parent," then I could not represent AAMFT as a peer in its dealings with AFTA. As a result, AAMFT related to AFTA much as an adult son or daughter would do when carrying out the playful strategies, frequently useful in intergenerational political renegotiation, with a reluctant parent. A turning point in this play came at the meeting of the AFTA Board of Directors at the

Ackerman Institute in New York on December 1, 1981. The story of that incident will illustrate the point.

An AAMFT–AFTA Joint Liaison Committee had just met the month before in San Diego at the annual meeting of AAMFT. The joint committee had issued a becomingly modest report calling for just a little more mutual live-and-let-live attitude on the part of these two organizations toward each other. But some important AFTA leaders of that time continued to feel queasy about the possibility that AFTA might unwittingly validate the still-suspect AAMFT as being something it was not or could not or should not be, the particular reason depending on individual perception. In response to the natural absurdity in all of this, the following motion was offered at this meeting of the AFTA Board of Directors.

DATE: December 1, 1981

TO: Board of Directors, AFTA

FROM: Norman Paul, MD, and Donald S. Williamson, PhD

RE: AAMFT–AFTA Joint Liaison Committee.
          Minority Report from San Diego Meeting (11/81)

Two members of the Joint AAMFT–AFTA Liaison Committee (Norman Paul, former nominee for AAMFT President, representing AFTA; Donald Williamson, member of AFTA Board, representing AAMFT) wish to offer to both Boards the following *Minority Report* issuing from the November 1981 meeting of the Joint Liaison Committee.

Minority Report

We have two concerns: First we want to take very seriously the recommendation to the AFTA Board from the AAMFT Board that no action be taken, no agreement be reached, no statement be released which has even the appearance of having the potentiality for being *unnecessarily restrictive* of some future political or other role which AFTA one day might want to exercise in regard to something.

Secondly, we are concerned that no joint statement be agreed to and released from this Board which goes beyond that with which all members of both Boards can feel totally comfortable. Clearly, no creative movement is possible without the *unanimous* agreement of all of the present AFTA leadership. While this may show "internal" fusion, it is surely internal fusion in the interest of "external" individuation.

While the authors of this Minority Report are personally ready to endorse the more radical and progressive position represented by the Joint Committee proposal (San Diego, 11/81), yet we are fearful that this statement, in light of the more general sensibilities among us, may be going too far too fast too soon.

So we have prepared an alternative policy position which we believe will (a) be universally acceptable, (b) meet both conscious and unconscious intentions, and (c) be a statement which is solid enough ground to be built upon in the future. We offer for your consideration the following alternative statement:

"The AAMFT Board and the AFTA Board have mutually agreed to respectfully recognize and herewith publicly acknowledge the nonexistence of each other."

Initially, there was a stunned and uncomprehending silence. Then there came a chuckle or two. Soon the whole room guffawed. The interorganizational friction continued, of course, for a bit, but almost nobody's heart was in it in quite the same way ever again.

The illusion of and hope for differentness between the organizations in the sense of "a difference that makes a difference" gradually evaporated. The good outcome was that there was no cutoff but, instead, a continuing conversation between and within "the family of family therapists." As is true in individual and family life, so also is it true in the professional sphere that letting go of the old love affair with the past brings the freedom to "fall in love with the future." The next breakthrough in the future of the family movement, as it is still affectionately known, will undoubtedly be expressed through another discontinuous leap. Perhaps it will be in a new understanding of "body–mind experience," and result in the evolution of a more organismic and thoroughgoing systemic understanding of human health. This understanding may be more richly contextual in nature, so that body behaviors and health experiences are routinely placed in the context of individual and family emotionality and emotionality is seen against the larger background of spirit and spiritual values. These values are active and influential not only within the individual self and family but within the larger context of culture.

The context of professional life frequently provides an opportunity for further resolution of the important issue of personal authority as it expresses itself through crises in professional identity. If the situation carries any significant voltage, the core issue of intergenerational intimidation will inevitably be present in some form. The moral to be learned from this is the value of constantly referring back to the original sources in the family of origin when conflict arises in the work setting. In this way one has the opportunity to continue locating and relocating and thereby resolving the conflicts at the source, that is, within intergenerational relationships. This enables one to maintain the maximum flexibility of thought and action. Then one can create and enjoy an ambience of playfulness within the larger arena of professional discourse as readily as in one's personal life. Personal authority and professional authority go hand in hand until eventually work is much less a matter of doing than a way of *being*, as they fuse together. At that point yet another evolution becomes possible as the focus shifts from self-as-different to self as an integral and integrated expression of the whole community.

The Future Lies Ahead

The family therapy movement, which initially was about connection and connectedness, can be seen as having represented a renewal of spirit. In the beginning it was a healing antidote to the alienation, separateness, and "psychopathologizing" often encouraged by individual psychology and psychiatry. The focus on relational patterns and interactional language connected persons one to another in families and connected family to family and family to society. The ecological–systemic view reconnected human beings in recursive relationship to nature and to the soil. It also connected psychotherapists to all sorts and conditions of human beings (clients) as it became clear that there are not two kinds of people in the world—the doctors and the patients—but just one, since no objective position outside the system is accessible to anyone. This also brought about organizational connection as individuals were able in this spirit to transcend discipline-of-origin loyalties and move beyond territorial boundaries, coalescing around a new ideal. The new connectedness was around a higher loyalty to a novel way of thinking, believing, and being. Thus, the family movement expressed a new value in psychotherapy.

This new value had a cluster of ethical presuppositions driving it, of which the following are examples: the life shared is preferable to the life lived alone; egalitarian relationships, especially in marriage, are healthier than dominance behaviors; emotional distress should lead to behavioral change in family relationships; parents should form a strong bond together in order to raise healthy children; the individual should have emotional space and free air to breathe within the family of origin; burdens should be rotated around among family members so that no one is chronically scapegoated; families should know how to play as well as to love and work; family emotionality should be acknowledged openly; families should be characterized by gender empathy; and psychological and relational justice is possible in intergenerational relationships.

This new family ethic was indeed an antidote to the more punitive and divisive language about intrapsychic process, individual psychopathology, pejorative diagnoses, and solitary hospitalization. The antidote was about connection, pattern, relational justice, partnership, normalizing, positive connotation, love, and—thanks to the feminists—gender sensitivity. The family systems theory ethos can therefore be seen as an *ethical stance* toward human life and love, and personal well-being and family experience. There is an idealism, however subdued—perhaps even a little romanticism—and a moral vision at the heart of the family ethic. This is one reason why it electrified the field of psychotherapy and "turned on" many young therapists.

But yesterday's revolution can be today's orthodoxy, and yesterday's paradigmatic shift can be today's cliché. As the family therapy discipline has been successfully professionalized, thereby naturally becoming orthodoxy and establishment, the complexity of the evolving structure that has secured these ends has inevitably threatened the life of the spirit of the movement. As to what will come next, one can speculate that it may be a bridging across the biological and psychological boundaries, leading to a thoroughgoing systemic (body–mind–spirit) understanding of human well-being. However, in the absence of a crystal ball, one can fall back on the immortal words of comedian, Mort Sahl who frequently reminded us that "the future lies ahead."

CHAPTER 15

Personal Authority, Professional Authority, and Physical Health

Illness is a wake-up call.
—Bernard Siegel
(unpublished speech, 1989)

There is a substantial and growing body of research literature demonstrating the influential relationships between psychological variables and physical health (Bahnson, 1980; Glaser, Kiecolt-Glaser, Speicher, & Holiday, 1985; Grossarth-Maticek, Bastiaans, & Kanazir, 1985; Justice, 1988). There is some empirical evidence to support the notion that there is a dependent relationship between personal authority and physical health, as measured by the number of physical symptoms reported (Bray, Harvey, & Williamson, 1987). The implication is that the higher the level of personal authority, the fewer the number of physical symptoms. The inference is that better physical health will result from a higher level of personal authority.

Bowen (1960) suggested that one spouse may be dysfunctional in marriage on behalf of the other spouse, who can then be "overfunctional." Historically, in this culture, the woman has been more commonly "chosen" to be the dysfunctional spouse, often in the service of the male. Bowen further suggested that in many instances the dysfunctional spouse is likely to show physical symptoms if the psychological imbalance remains chronic enough for long enough. This chapter proceeds on the assumption that there are influential psychological and contextual relationships between the level of personal authority and the physical health of the individual, as measured by the frequency and the severity of health problems, as well as by the quality of coping with chronic health problems by the individual.

Family dynamics have an enormous influence on the general health of family members (Bloom, Asher, & White, 1978; Christie-Seely, 1984; Doherty & Campbell, 1988; Edelstein & Linn, 1985; Lask, 1979; Lask & Matthew, 1979). Family emotionality has shown itself capable of penetrating most surfaces. At the same time, physical health is negotiated within the confines of the individual's mind and body. When it comes to physical health, the individual's skin is both an immediate and the ultimate boundary. The skin is an unmistakable line of physical definition for the individual self. But it has become evident that physical health can no longer be adequately understood at a level of conceptualization that stays strictly within the individual skin and considers only biomedical data (Williamson & Noel, 1990). Some of the reasons for this far-reaching conclusion are presented in the following paragraphs.

Mind, Emotion, and Physical Health

The Doctor–Patient Relationship

The new and burgeoning field of psychoneuroimmunology has mounting evidence indicating the importance of mind, meaning, and emotion as powerful influences on physical health (Dorian & Garfinkel, 1987; Solomon, 1987; Srensen, Mors, & Skovlund, 1987). The human mind is constantly generating meanings for ongoing experiences—indeed, it seems scarcely able not to do so. The mind makes up meanings around issues of personal health and illness and generates health expectations for the future. There is then a strong impulse to move in the direction of these expectations (Cousins, 1989). This has enormous and far-reaching implications for the construction of language as used by both physicians and psychotherapists to create meanings and, therefore, positive or negative expectations in the patient's mind. Moreover, there is increasing evidence of the effects of positive and negative emotions on the patient's immune system (Dorian & Garfinkel, 1987; Kiecolt-Glaser et al., 1987, 1988).

This information has important implications for the character of the doctor–patient as well as the therapist–client relationship. It suggests that the ideal doctor–patient relationship is less hierarchical and more of a collaborative peer relationship; the defining characteristic is one of consultation and collaboration. Nevertheless, there is evidence that although patients with an internal locus of control do better when given more responsibility for self-management, patients with an external locus of control do better when there is more active guidance from health professionals (Holloway & Rogers, in press). This suggests that in the practice of medicine, as in the practice of psychotherapy, the most effective use of language and relationship is one in which the therapeutic response is tailored to the idiosyncrasies of the individual patient. However, for obvious reasons, a preventive medicine approach will encourage an increasing assumption of responsibility on the part of all patients. The higher the level of personal authority, the greater will be the degree of responsibility assumed by a patient.

In the clinical context, the health professional is the expert. On the other hand, ownership of the life, belongs to the patient. The short- and long-term consequences of all the decisions made about treatment and lifestyle will be expressed in the body of the patient, not the physician. There is wide agreement that the mind and emotion of the patient are very influential in determining the quality of his or her physical health. It follows, therefore, that the patient needs to be in charge of personal health, which means being willing to take responsibility for it. It is hypothesized here that the measure of acceptance of responsibility for physical health relates directly to the level of personal authority within the individual patient.

The Medical Genogram

A family genogram showing all the relevant medical information about the illness experiences and causes of death in prior generations will generate educated guesses about the points of greatest physical susceptibility and the long-term health problems of the individual patient (Rogers, 1990). This can be useful from the perspective of preventive medicine, since it gives the patient an opportunity to make thoughtful decisions about lifestyle, including decisions about diet, exercise, and the management of psychological stress. Again, a critical factor is just how this information is to be conveyed by the health professional. The question posed is: How can language be used to construct a positive reality and healing expectation on the part of the patient?

Information from a medical genogram can easily and inadvertently be used to create negative suggestion and increase fear. It acknowledges a family's health legacies related to cancers, cardiac problems, hypertension, strokes, diabetes, and so forth. Through a good doctor–patient collaboration the patient is motivated to work to transcend the possible consequences of these transgenerational bio-logical family legacies without being frightened out of his or her skin in the process. This is one place where artistry can enter into the crafting of language in primary care medicine, much as it does in psychotherapy.

Family Mythology about Health

Interacting with these biological legacies is the important influence of family mythology about health and illness. Family mythology in-cludes beliefs and values, at both conscious and covert levels of awareness, about the following questions: In this particular family is physical illness permissible? Inevitable? Which family members should be ill and with what, and who should not? How should other family members respond to illness in one of their number? Should a physician be involved in treatment and, if so, when? What constitutes good medical treatment, and how much money and effort should be expended on it? What level of pain or other symptom is acceptable before seeking medical help? What measure of sympathy is to be expressed toward the patient? What speed of recovery is to be expected, or perhaps demanded? In general, what meanings and expectations should one attach to the phenomenon of physical illness in this family?

In some families physical illness is unthinkable and, therefore, for long periods seems rarely to occur. It is simply not part of this family's identity and tradition. By contrast, in other families physical illness is woven into the very fabric of transgenerational family life. In this instance, it is to be expected, sometimes even welcomed as destiny fulfilled. A family member may be "chosen" for illness, if not by a "higher power," then by the family itself. Such a choice frequently denotes specialness. Some anticipate "redemption through suffering" for both self and others. Alternatively, illness can be seen as a punishment that sometimes crosses generational bound-aries. While some feel honored to bear suffering and some are drawn to martyrdom, other families feel inherently flawed or cursed. An additional factor is the power of social learning in the family as young people grow up. Patterns of healthy and unhealthy behaviors are modeled and copied. While the learning of healthy behaviors during the developmental years is applauded and affirmed in some families, in others illness as a response is both expected and rewarded by special attention and sympathy, even gifts. Clearly, the level of personal authority is an important variable in all these family scripts.

As alluded to earlier, if a dysfunctional spouse loses enough of self in a marriage and cannot renegotiate the political–emotional context, he or she may express this distress through physical symptomatology. Alternatively, a child in the same family may show up at the pediatrician's office again and again within a short time period, generating the hypothesis that the child is a red flag signaling the distress in the family. A child's symptom or illness may serve to sustain an uneasy and tenuous connection between parents (Lask & Matthews, 1979; Minuchin, 1978; White, Kolman, Wexler, Polin, & Winter, 1984). It is scarcely too fanciful to suppose that there are people for whom a life-threatening, even terminal, illness is the ultimate outcome of living within a very painful emotional context within which change seems impossible and continued living becomes intolerable. In all these situations the matter of personal authority, or lack thereof, is immediately at issue and may be a predictive variable of wide-ranging significance. The mechanism of the transmission of family mandates about health and illness behaviors is obviously still a mystery. Yet there is compelling evidence from everyday experience that such phenomena, although poorly understood, do regularly happen.

Stress and Health

Addressing the matter from a less esoteric and more empirical perspective, an ever-increasing body of research data showing the deleterious effects of stress on physical health is now available. This includes marital and family stress, as well as work-related stress (Bahnson, 1980; Bloom et al., 1978; Chase & Jackson, 1981; Dorian & Garfinkel, 1987; Glaser et al., 1985). This evidence stands on its own and calls for acknowledgment, whether or not one chooses to interpret and apply it psychodynamically. The implications for the evolution of primary care in medicine deserve to be explored. This is an area where family psychology can make a useful contribution to family medicine.

The Social Support–Social Stress Equation in Health

Recent research also underlines the importance of social support in a patient's life as a neutralizing buffer in the face of psychological stress. Where there is adequate social support, the damaging aspects of this stress can be diminished (Norbeck & Tilden, 1983; Sarason, Sarason, Potter, & Antoni, 1985; Sosa, Kennell, Klaus, Robertson, & Urrutia, 1980). Obviously, the term *social support*, for most people and for most of the time, refers to support from the members of the patient's extended family, supplemented by friends. How social support can be given, especially in the instance of chronic illness, without infantilizing the family member obviously again raises the issue of personal authority.

Families and Health

Finally, the enormous psychological, social, and financial impact of serious physical illness on the family as a whole has been well documented (Doherty & Campbell, 1988). In circular fashion, the family's subsequent level of functioning will, for better or for worse, have its continuing and recursive impact upon the patient. Once again, one cannot have an adequate understanding of the full range of possible therapeutic interventions available if one stays on a purely physical level and stays exclusively within the biological boundary. In many, if not most, instances the physician cannot make an adequate assessment of the etiology or prognosis of an illness and of the best possible therapy without an imaginative inquiry into the social and psychological context of the patient's life, including life in the family. Whether the patient's emotional life and spirit are characterized more by hopefulness or despair is a variable likely to be very influential on the course and outcome of physical health (Justice, 1988; Sagan, 1987). The matrix of relationships that constitute the social life of the patient, with family relationships at the heart of this, is the primary dynamic reference point for either hope or despair.

The Further Implications of These Ideas

This emphasis on the importance of crossing the biological boundary in understanding health in general and on the relevance of personal authority to individual health in particular has further implications, discussed in the following paragraphs.

Toward a Systemic Understanding of Health and Illness

The most important single implication of accepting the relationship between psychological variables and physical health is a recognition of the need for health professionals to develop a thoroughgoing systemic understanding of the processes of health and illness behaviors. Physicians are taught to think systemically about the body. They learn the discipline of consistently doing a "review of systems"; the clinical differential in medical diagnosis requires this. But in practice the boundary usually closes around the body, and the review of systems does not ordinarily include the emotional system, either of the individual or of the family (Williamson & Noel, 1990).

Family therapy theory has taught psychotherapists to place the individual in the context of the family and has taught that the family, as a system, is essentially an emotional system. Yet, by and large, family therapy theory and practice has drawn a boundary around the emotional life, ignoring the biological grounding of all human experience, certainly including health. Psychiatry is the one health discipline where practitioners have been educated sequentially in information pertaining to the health of both body and mind. Most psychiatrists, however, will refer a patient to a "regular physician" if there appears to be a "body problem." The few who do pay attention to the body are less likely to practice, or even be sympathetic to, psychodynamic or "talking therapy." As a result, body and mind have been divided and separated in theory, practice, and education. This is an unfortunate situation with astonishingly deleterious consequences.

Family therapy as a discipline, although committed to a systemic understanding of the phenomena of human life, also participates in splitting apart the conceptualizations of the processes of mind and body. Ideally, a thoroughgoing and comprehensive systemic approach to human health will see the phenomena of body, mind, and spirit as intricately interrelated and interactive. The differential in the differential diagnosis will then include some additional judgment about the dynamic relationship that exists between these various phenomena, in a given patient's presentation. In the exam room the physician will consider whether the presenting symptom began in the body before affecting the emotions or whether a prior emotional stimulus drove, as well as interacted with, the presenting physical symptom. Or whether the processes are now too fused and patterned to permit any such discrimination. Have the behaviors become so circular over time that it is no longer possible to identify any particular point of initiation? Is it even useful to pursue that question, except to clarify the best point or points of immediate intervention?

Whatever the answers to such questions, the treatment implication is the same. A comprehensive systemic approach to human health may not happen today, just as it may not all be carried out by the same person, but there do need to be multilevel interventions into the patient's life for the purpose of helping him or her create, sustain, or recover good physical and mental health. Frequently, this appreciation of system and context will require going beyond the individual patient as a system, even beyond the patient as a member of the

larger emotional system of a family. There will need to be an acknowledgment of the work system, as well as the powerful influence of the
complex health care system with which the patient is interacting. The
larger community of support beyond the extended family may also be
significant in the patient's life. If the primary care physician can learn
to work from a systemic understanding of the individual self and
simultaneously, as needed, place that self in the context of the family
emotional system, then sensitivity to the influences of these larger
systems will usually follow. But this is a tall order!

Consciousness and the Use of Language

A second implication of crossing the biological boundary in understanding health in general follows naturally from the first. This is a
recognition of the need for and huge dividend from a collaborative
body–mind model of practice in family-centered health care. A rich
expression of this is collaboration between family physicians and
family therapists. The most immediate need is to underscore the
importance of a collaborative style of relationship between the
physician and the patient. Certainly, meanings and emotions are a
very crucial part of the health equation. This includes both short-term
and long-term decisions about personal health, at both conscious and
less than conscious levels of awareness. It follows that having good
health intentions and choosing good health practices is something
that cannot be superimposed coercively from the outside. The
problem of compliance is an infamous and widespread dilemma in
medical practice. It will remain so until a genuinely nonhierarchical
and collaborative style of relationship develops in ambulatory care
between physicians and patients.

The doctor–patient relationship, like the psychotherapy relationship, is constructed in language, underscoring the importance of the
use of language in the medical interview. A considerable, if unseen,
amount of injury is caused through the use of inappropriate and
insensitive language in medical conversation, especially in giving
explanation, feedback, and guidance to the patient. It would represent rather an extreme position, but perhaps the only physicians who
should have regular access to direct face-to-face contact with patients
about their health problems are those who have shown acceptable
minimum competence in this most demanding and sophisticated
practice. Other, less significant, medical "procedures" are not attempted without special training. Just as common sense is not nearly
as common as it is presumed to be, neither are these language skills.
Obviously, the majority of physicians can talk in some fashion to

patients, but only a few have developed artistry in the use of language. Yet this is of the essence to good primary care medicine.

The implication is that the conversation of the medical interview can and should be regarded as inherently "therapeutic conversation." Most patients are in an altered state of consciousness. The conversation itself is, therefore, among the most complex, demanding, and far-reaching of interventions; it is not just a pleasant addition. It is still difficult for many physicians to understand that language itself can be a powerful healing intervention, without anything else surgical, chemical, or procedural taking place. Language is as critical an instrument of intervention in primary care medicine as it is in psychotherapy, in some ways even more so in terms of its potential long-term effects on the patient's well-being.

Because it is through the use of language that we label and assimilate, I have described the everyday practice of family medicine as "a call to consciousness" (Williamson & Noel, 1990). In following this encouragement toward consciousness or mindfulness, the family physician who practices continuity of care will over time ask the patient the following sorts of questions: What do you think is wrong with you? What do you think your body is telling you at this time? Why do you think this is happening just now? What does it mean to you to have this sickness? What kind of a recovery do you expect? Do you have the energy and resources to get well or to get well quickly? How do you think your health is going to be in the future? Can you stay well just now? Can we talk together about how your life is going *overall* at this time? (This last question refers to the context of work, the primary love relationship, and other key relationships in the patient's life.) The "call to consciousness" is an invitation to reflect for a moment and ask how life generally is going. What is going on that might be the psychosocial background or context for physical illness or physical symptoms at this time?

The physician need not assert any direct one-to-one causal relationship between a particular emotional circumstance and an illness or symptom. Things are rarely this simple or straightforward in human experience. Systemic thinking acknowledges complexity, synergistic interaction, and pattern. Health is a kaleidoscope of moving variables. Elements can be captured, but the pattern of experience cannot be reproduced under a microscope. The family physician will at times gently draw the patient's attention to the larger life context, which is the backdrop to the concerns bringing him or her to the office today. The patient is encouraged to place health experiences squarely within the emotional life and to be attentive to the unceasing dynamic dialogue between mind and body. In this

way, the "call to consciousness" or awareness is a call to accountability. It is an invitation to the patient to take full responsibility for the
management of all issues related to personal health and well-being. In
that sense it is an expression and an affirmation of personal authority
in the life of the patient. It all begins with an exercise of personal
authority in the context of the relationship to the physician in
attendance, as with other key health professionals in the patient's life.

A story will illustrate the concept of health behavior as multivariate, that is, as pattern. A 37-year-old man enters an exam room
accompanied by a woman. One side of his face looks a little strange,
and he has not recovered full use of one arm. The woman thinks he
had a stroke 48 hours before, although he had also been drinking
heavily that evening and had fallen down. Inquiry reveals that his
father had died after a stroke, and the patient does have high blood
pressure. Now it looks like a small stroke. Is it too late for a CAT scan?
What preventive measures are called for? Blood pressure medication?
Alcohol problem? It all seems straightforward enough. Is this his
wife? Yes, he says, but maybe not for long if she keeps treating him
this way. Then he points his finger angrily and cries out: "I told her
something like this would happen. I warned her. And it will happen
again if she does not change; only it will be worse next time." The
physician knows what she wants to do medically. But in light of these
comments, what else should she do?

Toward a Systemic Orientation to Health Care

Another implication of the systemic perspective on health and illness
is the need to educate health professionals in a thoroughgoing
systemic orientation to health care. It follows that neither primary
care physicians nor psychotherapists should be trained exclusively
within the narrow confines of either the body or the mind. Primary
care medical education at both predoctoral and residency levels
should cross the biological boundary and integrate findings about
human emotionality, motivation, and the individual and family
developmental stages in life. Family doctors should also learn the use
of language to create and sustain a therapeutic relationship and
positive suggestion. Psychotherapists should learn some basic selected knowledge of physiology, anatomy, pharmacology, and the
most common medical complaints, as well as the effects of chronic
illnesses.

A story might help illustrate this point, at least from one side of
it. A few years ago I met in a class with the first-year residents in a
program in family medicine. During the initial orientation month the

new residents were in class each morning, and each afternoon they went out to work in neighborhood health clinics. One morning the class was given the following instructions: "Pick one patient during this afternoon at your clinic, and as he or she leaves the office, pat that person on the shoulder, look him or her directly in the eye, and say, 'Be well.'" A few moments of silence passed. Then a tentative voice asked, "Did you say, 'Be well'?" "Yes, 'Be well.' " A few more moments of uneasy silence passed, and then another voice asked hesitantly, "Do you mean like B-E W-E-L-L?" and spelled out the letters one at a time. What was striking about this interaction was that to the majority of the class this was a novel and unexpected idea. It was uncomfortable to think that the physician would leave his or her purely "objective" and, therefore, neutral—often thought of as professional—stance and become an enthusiastic advocate on behalf of the patient's good health.

Again, at the heart of this recommendation is a call to consciousness and accountability, only this time the call is to both physician and patient. The call to the physician is to be emotionally present and to be a spontaneous advocate of the patient's good health and ability to achieve it. This means the physician will be capable of a more flexible and wider range of responses than simply reassuring, informing, and warning patients of the possibility of present and future malfunction in their bodies. These are all very important functions, but they are not enough, given the potential good influence of the primary care physician in patients' lives.

For their part, psychotherapists, including family therapists, while having no ambition to practice medicine, should be knowledgeable about the everyday symptoms and course of the most common illnesses. The intention is not to diagnosis or treat but to become comfortable in talking to clients and clients' families about their thoughts and expectations, beliefs and values, and experiences and practices with regard to their bodies and their physical health. The psychotherapist can then reinforce the call to consciousness, which is to say, personal authority on the part of the client. The psychotherapist who is knowledgeable can also collaborate more closely and competently and, therefore, more comfortably with the family doctor or other primary care physician. This kind of collaboration can achieve the goal of seeing the family as "a unit of care" from a medical as well as psychological perspective. It will also encourage attentiveness to both individual and family health behaviors. This attention to attitude and motivation may be the single most important precondition of a successful practice of preventive medicine, which at this point is an attractive but elusive ideal.

It is imperative that family therapists inform themselves about the information coming from the new field of psychoneuroimmunology. This can be augmented by more recent information from studies on family dynamics and health as well as from studies on stress as it is buffered and neutralized by social support (National Institute of Mental Health, 1987). Conceivably, this focus on families and health will become an area of special expertise within the field of family therapy. Certainly, it is an arena of inquiry to which family theorists and therapists should be primary contributors. But this requires an enlargement of the usual concept of "systemic" in the family movement. The development of an area of special expertise on families and health within family therapy would make a genuine collaboration between the fields of family therapy and family medicine a feasible proposition. (Let it be noted that the journal *Family Systems Medicine*, founded in 1982 by Donald A. Bloch, MD, and associates, has made an outstanding contribution in this regard.)

Personal Authority and Responsibility for Personal Health Experiences

As has been suggested throughout, the ideas presented in this chapter have strong implications regarding personal responsibility for general health, including physical well-being. This is seen as one core expression of personal authority. The person with a higher level of personal authority will more likely seek out a collaborative relationship and a physician with whom this is available. He or she is less likely to take a helpless, dependent, or victim stance in the face of health needs or crises. This patient will not adopt a simplistic "You're the Doc, Doc, you tell me" posture. As a matter of broad attitude rather than specific detail, this person will take the position that he or she is "creating" all the experiences of his or her own life, including the circumstances of personal health. This is in no way intended to encourage personal blame or guilt for either occurrences or outcomes. Rather, it acknowledges that to the extent that a person gives up personal responsibility for any experience in life, to that degree the person loses a subjective sense of freedom and of self—in short loses personal authority. The vacuum is likely to be replaced with feelings of vulnerability, helplessness, and fear.

The concept of personal authority, as defined earlier, holds the willingness to take responsibility for all of life's experiences as being at the very heart of the matter. Certainly, it is not that one consciously creates all the facts of the story, but one does create all the surrounding meanings and the associated emotions. The degree of personal freedom experienced in the choosing and creating of these meanings is a measure of the individual's level of personal authority and, consequently, overall mental health. This is a boundary that can be constantly tested and expanded.

Reasons for Hesitancy to Change Health Education Practices

The underlying premise of this chapter is that the biggest single problem in health care today is the common practice, with all the consequences that ensue, of splitting body from mind. The most damaging consequence is the resultant perception of bodily processes as functionally autonomous. Unquestionably, mind and spirit can become so disassociated from the body that bodily processes do come to seem to acquire an autonomous or semiautonomous character. The body is then seen as a machine, and problems occur when parts of the machinery warp, break down, or wear out. Fixing the "body machine" can be seen as a matter of oiling or repairing the parts, putting in an additive, slowing the machinery down so the parts can cool, doing a tune-up, deciding if it is just a noise and there is no real problem, scheduling a major overhaul, or deciding to wait and watch and see what happens.

In this view there is no higher level of mind or consciousness controlling this machine, guiding its performance, or influencing its well-being. If the body is indeed a functionally autonomous machine, it follows that there is no particular need for the patient to be conscious about and attentive to this body. By the same token, there is also no medical need for the physician to be conscious of the patient or, for that matter, conscious of himself or herself in the transaction. Fortunately, this sterile view of things is changing in modern medical practice. Family medicine, with its interest in families and health and in the doctor–patient relationship, is in the vanguard. There are, however, obstacles to be overcome in the dynamics of change, and several of the reasons for hesitancy to change medical education practices are addressed in the following paragraphs.

Fear of Consciousness

First there is the universal reluctance in human beings to be "conscious," meaning to be attentive to what one is thinking and feeling at any given moment. Consciousness in this sense is frequently painful or quickly becomes painful if too much time of awareness transpires. It is hard to be still and conscious. Not only do current worries come to mind, but all the stuff still perking in the unconscious starts knocking at the door. This builds on existential anxiety or the fear of death (Becker, 1973; Tillich, 1952). Consequently, there is a great draw to alcohol and other mood-altering drugs (legal or otherwise); to sex, sports, and work; and to television and related entertainment alternatives—all ways of calming both the fear of being what one is and the fear of one day not being at all. Whatever the distinctions of class, creed, color, nationality, wealth, and education, when it comes to matters of life and death, all human beings are in the same leaky boat together. All are subject to the same fears and final outcome. This includes both the patient who is dying and the physician who avoids the dying patient. Any person who is dying is simply dying a little bit ahead of the observer. This aspect of the human dilemma makes it easier to understand why patients, being recruited from the general population, are so frequently reluctant to be conscious about the dynamics of their health.

Where Is the Data, Doc?

Another reason for reluctance to change health practices is the fact that the data supporting powerful connections between body and mind have just become available in adequate amounts in recent years. Health professionals have had to be, and continue to be, on guard against charlatans, quacks, television healers, and the like. It may seem that the only real defense against this is reference to empirically verifiable and replicable data. The physicians of today have to protect themselves not simply from threats to professional self-esteem but from financial threats from litigious patients. The new information has been compounding, but it does take time to garner interest.

Traditional Injunctions

A third obstacle to changing medical pratice is the difficult challenge of changing the character and ethos of traditional medical education. Changing any academic curriculum has been likened to facing the logistical problems involved in moving a graveyard. In medical education the message (slightly caricatured) is the following: "You are the expert and you have the necessary information and know how to interpret it, so tell them what to do. Second, always try to do something, and something biomedical at that. Third, don't stop moving and don't sit down." The injunction to keep moving at all times teaches students to do multiple tasks and attend to several matters simultaneously. This injunction is enormously influential in the everyday choreography of the physician's professional activity. An unfortunate consequence is that the physician learns to split attention in several directions at once and simultaneously to be constantly anticipating the next task. It follows that he or she cannot easily be emotionally present to a given patient, at least not for very long. This poses a great challenge to the doctor–patient relationship.

Communication Skills and Physician Development

A further problem in traditional medical education is the fact that there is rarely much focus placed on the emotional development and maturation of the young physician during these highly significant early years. The presumption is that if the student acquires the necessary information and develops the related clinical and procedural skills, everything else that is necessary will fall into place. It has not yet been adequately recognized that listening and talking effectively to the patient are critical practice skills that do not develop inevitably but can be taught. The acquisition of these skills is directly related to the developmental process in the young physician. This is perhaps the point at which therapeutic psychology can contribute most to everyday medical practice. The slowly evolving collaboration between family therapy and family medicine is providing an encouraging model. (Since the winter of 1990 a Joint Task Force of the American Association for Marriage and Family Therapy and the Society of Teachers of Family Medicine has been meeting to pursue the possibility of nationwide practice collaboration between clinicians in the fields of family therapy and family medicine. This is a promising adventure.)

Too Much to Learn

There is a complication in the more comprehensive and systemic form of medical education being advocated here. This is the fact that the medical student (and later the primary care physician-in-training) is expected to master a huge and ever-increasing body of clinical knowledge. As one senior family medicine faculty member was heard to wryly observe, "The dominant concern of the first-year resident in family medicine is to manage not to kill anybody." Given the incredible demands of a medical education, learning the importance of psychosocial and family information and all the principles about interviewing skills may seem just out of the question. Integration is possible, but it requires great tact and patience.

Personal versus Professional Development

Perhaps the most difficult problem of all in bringing about change is the fact of life that medical students are usually in their early 20s as students and in their middle or late 20s as residents. This means that they are in an early sequence of adult development in their own lives, facing all the issues of young adulthood. As has been suggested earlier, the key sequences in the development of personal authority do not occur until the 30s and early 40s. It does then seem odd to expect young physicians to establish collaborative and peer relationships with a wide range of patients, some of whom are young enough to be "dates" and many of whom are old enough to be parents, sometimes grandparents. The question posed by this dilemma is: How do young physicians elicit and encourage a stance of personal authority in the patient when they are still struggling to acquire this political and emotional stance in life for themselves? There is no easy answer to this question. However, it can be noted that both physicians and psychotherapists learn to practice more skillfully with experience, even though their formal knowledge base may not only not increase much but in some cases will decrease over time. Knowledge that is not regularly useful is forgotten, perhaps in order that "know how" that is essential and works can be acquired.

Is Change Then Possible at All?

In light of these complex obstacles it may be asked, What kinds of change toward systemic and family-oriented care are feasible in primary care practice, if any? It is at just this point that reference to the history and development of clinical training and supervision in the field of psychotherapy, and in family therapy in particular, proves useful.

A Supportive Context for Learning

If a supportive and affirming context for learning can be constructed, medical students and residents can be taught to be open to their own personal feelings. While this statement refers to feelings in general, it focuses especially on difficult feelings about particular kinds of patients and their families. Students can learn that when going into an exam room, they are accompanied psychologically by their own parents (and spouse and children, if there are any). In other words, not only are the patient and the physician in the room together but the members of the families of origin of both parties are emotionally present also. Understandably, this makes for a very complex interaction, especially when one party feels sick, needy, and frightened and the other feels somewhat professionally insecure. If open to personal feelings, a young physician learns also to be open to the patient's feelings about being in this exam room, presenting this complaint at this time. Physicians can learn artistry in language skills—that is, to establish a relationship of empathy and validation.

Establishing such a relationship allows the physician to elicit the inner thoughts and experience of the patient very quickly and to find words to communicate back a measure of understanding and acknowledgment. As young physicians develop personal authority over time, they also become increasingly accessible to a collaborative peer relationship with their patients. This creates the context within which the physician can tactfully encourage and teach the patient how to relate various aspects of physical health to the emotional life, thus illuminating the dynamic relationships between mind and body, and individual and family. Such an understanding supports both the restoration of personal health and the management of chronic illness. It stimulates the patient's motivation that is essential for the effective practice of preventive medicine. The complexity of systemic understanding serves to underscore the importance of an emotionally supportive learning environment for both medical students and residents.

Personal and Professional Authority and the Life Cycle

The physician-in-training can learn about the developmental stages and tasks in the life cycle of both the individual and the family. This knowledge supports the physician in mastering personally the developmental issues involved in young adulthood, including the development of personal authority in life and the evolution of a secure and mature professional authority based on this. All of this facilitates a growing understanding of how specific presenting problems and patterns of physical problems are related to the various developmental stages in life. It also sheds light on the management (or mismanagement) of a given life-cycle task by a patient or family and how this may create a context for the development of physical symptoms. Along with this, the young physician can be acquiring increasing skill and comfort in the use of the self in the doctor–patient relationship to elicit whatever positive healing energy is in the patient and the patient's family. This energy will elicit or create expectations of recovery and good health. Integrating clinical, medical, and psychosocial skills, the physician learns how to use the self as an instrument or medium of healing. He or she is now moving beyond the role of technician, even technical magician, to become a healer in a more profound sense. Personal authority is foundational to all of these experiences.

The desired outcome for the physician is a level of personal authority that will express itself in a reassuring and trust-inducing professional authority, which is a specific expression of personal authority. At the same time, personal authority in the patient encourages the patient to take responsibility for individual health. Ideally, the development of personal and professional authority in the family physician, will be wedded to a thoroughgoing systemic understanding of health and illness behaviors. The family physician can then function as the central consultant and counselor with regard to the overall well-being of the patient and the family. He or she can integrate and interpret all the complex information and recommendations coming from medical specialists and can advise and collaborate with the patient in determining the best course of action.

In summary, the source of personal and professional authority in the family physician is based first on diagnostic skills and on extensive clinical knowledge of biomedical problems and clinical treatments and procedures. This is essential and bedrock—but not enough! Surrounding this is a knowledge of the human nature of the patient-in-context, beginning with the self system and going on to include the larger emotional systems of family and work.

Finally, the family physician as a generalist gradually develops the personal and professional authority to hold himself or herself fully as peer in relation to the practitioners of all of the medical subspecialties who will tend to be hierarchically oriented. Each of these has a great deal more specialized knowledge and expertise in some given area of the practice of medicine. Consequently, these specialists are frequently inclined to adopt a hierarchical position in relation to the family physician. It is essential, then, that the family physician be able to hold himself of herself fully as a peer in relationship to subspecialists in order to be able to exercise a central role as interpreter and counselor to the patient and the family. The family physician who is intimidated by subspecialists will not be able to exercise this role adequately, and both physician and patient will suffer. Obviously, as the young family physician resolves intergenerational intimidation within the personal family of origin, he or she is increasingly better prepared psychologically to handle all issues of professional intimidation as well.

In the matter of families and health, the perspective of personal authority is a useful way to understand both patient behavior and physician behavior and the enormous resources inherent in both.

CHAPTER 16

Personal Authority and Gender Differences: Typecasting

LINDA M. WALSH

> Today, I believe that we will not learn to live responsibly on
> this planet without basic changes in the ways we organize
> human relationships, particularly inside the family, for
> family life provides the metaphors with which we think
> about broader ethical relations. We need to sustain creativity
> with a new and richer sense of complementarity and
> interdependence, and we need to draw on images of
> collaborative caring by both men and women as a model of
> responsibility. We must free these images from the
> connotations of servitude by making and keeping them truly
> elective.
>
> —Mary Catherine Bateson
> *Composing a Life* (p. 114)

> If love is the answer, could you please rephrase the question?
> —Lily Tomlin
> *The Quotable Woman*

This chapter has evolved from two interconnected contexts: the political and
the personal. From the perspective of the political, it is fair to say that because
of insights provided by feminism, and especially because of the feminist
critique of family therapy, gender has become a central and essential
consideration in examining any theory of clinical practice. The personal

*Linda M. Walsh, PhD, is Clinical Assistant Professor, Department of Family Medicine, Baylor
College of Medicine, Houston, Texas.*

context is for me the more complicated. Although I have been a longtime feminist, fighting feminist battles before I even had the language to describe them as such, I have struggled to find ways in which I can incorporate my gender awareness and my feminist values into my professional life and clinical work. In my clinical work I have found that a family of origin approach, especially the theory and practice of Personal Authority in the Family System (PAFS), can be an effective and gender sensitive approach to individuals. This chapter is a first attempt to formulate how gender awareness and feminist values can find successful expression in PAFS theory.

Introduction

There has been much criticism by feminists of systems theory and family therapy for ignoring gender differences and the sociopolitical nature of gender differences in theory and practice. This chapter addresses these issues in relation to Personal Authority in the Family System (PAFS).

Although there is no one single feminist model of family therapy, here or elsewhere, feminism can and does inform many diverse therapeutic approaches. It can inform our understanding of the ways family therapy either perpetuates gender-role stereotyping, to the detriment of both women and men, or enhances our understanding of gender, thereby fostering growth and equality for women and men (Dienhart & Avis, 1991; Luepnitz, 1988; Walters, Carter, Papp, & Silverstein, 1988). Feminists have long focused on the adverse effects of perpetuating hierarchical imbalances for women within the family system. Recently, this focus has turned to the detrimental effects of the hierarchical system on men (Bograd, 1991; Dienhart & Avis, 1991; Meinecke, 1981; Meth & Pasick, 1990).

PAFS can be a gender-sensitive theory and mode of practice of family therapy that addresses the needs of women and men in a sensitive and equitable fashion. Implicit in the PAFS theory is the belief that gender differences are significant and that they are socially constructed in a historical context. The goal of simultaneously achieving personal authority and intimacy with parents and peers is the same for both women and men, although women and men approach the process of achieving personal authority in the family system in ways that are both gendered and individualized.

This chapter will show how PAFS can be a gender-sensitive therapy first by outlining the contributions of feminism, then by surveying the historical, social, and theoretical contexts for the PAFS theory, and then by explicating the gendered nature of the therapeutic process that simultaneously establishes personal authority and intimacy with one's parents. This explication will involve case histories and a discussion of Bowen's transgenerational model and how PAFS differs from it.

Contributions of Feminism

Thanks to the relatively recent and powerful feminist critique of psychotherapy in general and of family therapy in particular, it is now clear that theories of human behavior and development must consider gender to be a central shaping factor in human development and behavior. Gender, like age, is integral to the identity of the individual and to the organization of the family (Goldner, 1985, 1988, Hare-Mustin, 1987). As Goldner (1988) has pointed out, family therapy in general has been slow to undergo the conceptual transformation of the discipline that will come once we acknowledge gender as an organizing principle in the same way we recognize generation and family development.

This failure to acknowledge gender, and the further failure to recognize the hierarchical and patriarchal nature of the gendered relationship as it has been socially constructed in the family system, has resulted in family therapy's continued support of the social and cultural mores that have kept women in a subordinated and disadvantaged position (Goldner, 1985; Goodrich, Rampage, Ellman, & Halstead, 1988; Hare-Mustin, 1978; Taggart, 1985; Walters et al., 1988). It has also kept men locked into a narrow vision of masculine behaviors and traits. By not providing an earlier challenge to the ways men have used and abused their position and power and by not challenging the often inappropriate and ineffectual ways men have learned to respond emotionally, family therapy has missed an opportunity to help men change in meaningful ways (Dienhart & Avis, 1991).

By speaking of gender and hierarchy, rather than generation and hierarchy, feminism illuminates our understanding and demands our recognition of and attention to power issues. These include, but are not necessarily limited to, money, position, education, ownership, opportunity, personal rights, political sanctions, physical and emotional intimidation and abuse, and individual expectations. As Goldner (1988) states, until very recently we have pretended that, or acted as if, the social injustices of patriarchy stopped just short of the nuclear family's door. She writes, "To presume that social hierarchies topple at the domestic portal violates the principle of ecological embeddedness on which our theory depends" (Goldner, 1988, p. 24). Recognition of this denial should lead us to ask why it has been so difficult to separate ourselves as therapists, as women and men, from the hierarchical and patriarchal mainstream sufficiently to devise a theory that advances equality for all. The task is certainly not easy, and the answers are not always obvious.

The founders of the family of origin model were no more sensitive to gender issues than any other of the early family therapy theorists. Fortunately, every model of family therapy (like most social and political sciences) is being reexamined through the feminist lens. The previously accumulated knowledge and learning in these fields is not being discarded to make way for the new but, rather, expanded and liberated from a narrow, androcentric focus to a more complex, multidimensional view. PAFS can and often does provide such a multidimensional view, although we must admit that the multidimensional nature can, if one is not sensitive to gender issues, be overlooked.

A theory that satisfies the feminist requirement that no one in the equation be disempowered will also embody an ecological perspective. It will acknowledge that all entities are interconnected and that change in one will effect change in all the others, although this change may not be obvious or equally distributed. Additionally, it will include a respect for and an appreciation of biodiversity: the more varied a system is, the healthier it will be. An ecological perspective accepts and fosters equality, diversity, and opportunity for all parts of the system, and this allows for multidimensional perspectives and approaches.

It is with this gendered, ecological perspective that the theory of PAFS must be explicated and evaluated. The assumption PAFS makes is that renegotiation with the first generation is an effective way to establish oneself in an equal position in the world generally and in equal positions with significant others. We now need to highlight what feminism has taught us and emphasize that intergenerational renegotiation is at the same time a gendered renegotiation; the individual examines herself or himself in relation to contextualized and gendered roles with each parent and explores the parents' contextualized and gendered roles with their parents.

Implicit in the theory of PAFS is an understanding of the gendered component of hierarchical boundaries, but it is crucial that we make this gendered aspect emphatic and explicit. When we do this the individual in therapy explores her or his identity in relationship to each gendered parent. The nature of the exploration is different with each parent; when complete, the nature of the continued relationship with each parent will be different even though the *difference that makes a difference will no longer rest solely or even primarily on generation or gender but on the ongoing egalitarian interconnection and interdependence* between individuals who have come to accept each other and to be in relationship with each other. This relationship is based on mutuality, respect, and, therefore, equality.

Historical Perspective on Family and "Homelife"

Family therapy and PAFS have not evolved in a vacuum. They have grown out of a social, political, and historical context that is important to acknowledge if we are to understand the current theory. It is not the purpose of this chapter to present a complete historical account of family therapy or gender research but to present some of the more important historical and theoretical developments as they inform an understanding of gender.

We are still working out of the social changes that began in the 19th century. Whereas the home had previously provided the family with the economic means for survival, industrialization assumed this function and contributed greatly to the separation of (1) work from home, (2) men from women, and, eventually, (3) generation from generation.

Previous to the industrial revolution, work was largely a family affair. Although children attended school, they also worked on the farms and ranches and were a necessary and integral aspect of family survival. With industrialization and urbanization, work was defined as something accomplished by men outside the home while women simply remained inside the home to care for young children and the home. Children also left the home for their education and were no longer essential to the production of goods (Aries, 1962; Hareven, 1982). The "cult of domesticity" resulted from a middle-class economic condition that placed women in the home, where their duty was to create a haven for working men and children (Hareven, 1982).

The separation of work from home, men from women, and generation from generation was reflected, for example, in the early family therapy theory and practice of Bowen (1978), Haley (1976), and Minuchin (1974). The hierarchical nature of generation was universally identified while the equally important hierarchy of gender for a long time went unrecognized. This phenomenon is part of what Rachel Hare-Mustin (1987; Hare-Mustin & Marecek, 1988) has called Beta bias (as opposed to Alpha bias, which will be discussed later). It is possible that this gendered hierarchy went unrecognized because to have distinguished gender would have meant "an end to the idealization of family relationships" and an acknowledgment that families are "entities divided against themselves" (Goldner, 1988, p. 27). A validation of generational hierarchy, on the other hand, did not upset the status quo and appeared to be in the natural flow of family life. For a couple to raise children successfully, it was assumed that hierarchies and boundaries had to be established and maintained. The gendered hierarchy of family life thus either remained invisible or was accepted as part of the natural order (see Minuchin's training film *Anorexia Is a Greek Word*) while the generational hierarchy was not only recognized but proclaimed normal and healthy.

With the reentry of women into the workplace in unprecedented numbers in the last few decades has come recognition of the socially constructed beliefs that rationalized women's lower status in the world; when women started to see the tremendous difference in the social, political, economic, and cultural life of the family wrought by these changes, the gendered hierarchy within the generational hierarchy was revealed.

The socially constructed nature of the masculine role in the world was also revealed. If men were no longer "needed" to be the sole providers for the family and if women could compete in most jobs and perform equally well, what special qualities defined manliness and men's roles? It then became apparent that men too suffered from this gendered stratification. Men die earlier than women (Rix, 1990; Meinecke, 1981), suffer from addictions (alcohol, sex, work) more frequently than women, are more cut off from their emotions, and are more socially isolated (Pasick, Gordon, & Meth, 1990). Because men are frequently detached from the responsibilities of the home, they miss out on the rewards of parenting, the closeness and affiliation with children, and the feelings of attachment that caring for a child or spouse can bring. Even housework, long a task many men have considered off-limits, has been found to contribute to the general health and well-being of men who do it (Gottman, 1991).

A Gendered Perspective

Family therapy and PAFS have also evolved in a context of scientific and theoretical development. Although social scientists have long pondered the question of how the sexes are different, there are to date few definitive answers (Gilmore, 1990; Shapiro, 1990). In terms of ability, most will agree that there is much more variance within each sex than there is between the sexes and that the sexes are in general more alike than they are different (McGoldrick, 1989). The biologist's quest for answers has proven equally elusive. There are significant biological differences, not the least of which is the fact that women bear children. The answer to the question of which differences are inevitable, as opposed to socially constructed, however, is still being sought. There are higher levels of testosterone found in boys and men, which can account for increased aggressiveness (Konner, 1982). Recent studies have also shown that men's physiological response to relational discord is longer-lasting and therefore more detrimental to health than is the physiological response to relational discord of women (Gottman, 1991). This could account for some of the very different ways that men and women engage each other, especially in conflict.

There can be little doubt that something happens to boys and girls on their way to adulthood that provokes difference. A recent survey commissioned by the American Association of University Women (1991) of 3,000 children found that at age 9 most girls were assertive, confident, and felt positive about themselves. By the time they reached high school, fewer than one-third of white and Hispanic girls felt good about themselves. Black girls fared better than white and Hispanic girls, presumably because the family and community "sustain high levels of personal importance for black girls" (p. 8), while white girls absorbed the message from their role models at home and at school that they are not valued. Boys also lost some sense of their self-esteem and self-worth but to a far lesser degree than the girls.

Another obvious evidence of differences is revealed in those statistics that show women are twice as likely to become depressed and seek help for their depression (McGoldrick, 1989; Weissman, 1980). Men, on the other hand, are more likely than women to become violent and rageful (Walker, 1980), to suffer severe health disability in later life, and to become alcoholic (Pasick et al., 1990). There are also important differences in the ways women and men communicate (Tannen, 1990; White, 1989). Most therapists would agree that women are more emotionally available and that men act more rationally (Pasick et al., 1990; Walsh, 1989). This last trait has led to the inability of many men to express their feelings and has resulted in significant problems for men. Feelings are disguised as the rational becomes more highly valued. Pasick and colleges (1990) point out that men show a decreased sensitivity to their feelings and to the feelings of others along with an intolerance of or confusion by others' expressions of feelings. Men avoid intimate, committed relationships, use more addictive substances to avoid feelings than do women, and suffer from stress-related illnesses due to their emotional restrictive-ness.

Because there are these observable differences in women's and men's social behavior, the quest for essential distinguishing charac-teristics has continued, and feminist scholars have been prominent in the search (Belenky, Clinchy, Goldberger, & Tarule, 1986; Chodorow, 1978; Gilligan, 1982; Miller, 1976, 1983, 1986; Stiver, 1984; Surrey, 1983). Realizing that standards for human behavior have been based on the observations and testing of males (McGoldrick, 1989), femi-nists have attempted to identify female characteristics and have further asserted that these female characteristics and behaviors are significant, positive, and worthy of independent study. These at-tempts to identify and then to evaluate as positive female character-istics and behaviors have been highlighted in theories of feminine psychology. Rachel Hare-Mustin (1987; Hare-Mustin & Marecek, 1988) has categorized theories by whether or not they take gender into consideration; the two categories are termed Alpha bias or Beta bias. She applies the statistical notion of Alpha and Beta (but not of error) to gender, using the term *Alpha bias* to describe the work of those who find significant differences between men and women and *Beta bias* to describe the work of those who would minimize the differences between women and men. Taking a constructivist posi-tion and believing that there is no absolute reality in any description of gender, Hare-Mustin and Marecek would prefer to have gender described in terms of relationships between women and men, espe-cially relationships that describe domination. The idea of Alpha and Beta bias is, however, a very useful way to differentiate theoretical approaches to therapy.

According to Hare-Mustin and Marecek (1988), Alpha bias exists most obviously in the early psychodynamic approaches of Freud and Jung, in the social sex-role theories of Parsons and Bales (1955), and also in more recent feminist writings. As feminist writers have sought to depathologize and demystify so-called feminine qualities, they have developed theories that enumerate and extol as special those qualities for which women have come to be known, qualities such as emotional responsiveness, intuition, and a willingness and ability to carry the responsibility for maintaining significant relationships. This concept of Alpha bias can also be used to describe the expansion of feminist ideas about the roles of men in families as they relate to the theory and practice of therapy (Bograd, 1991) and the growing body of literature on masculine qualities and characteristics engendered by the relatively new male movement.

One of the most influential of these feminist critics is Jean Baker

Miller, who has helped us develop a gendered perspective in a way that fits with Hare-Mustin's concept of Alpha bias. Miller's important book *Toward a New Psychology of Women* (1976) illuminates the psychosocial differences between men and women. In it Miller redefines heretofore disparaged qualities in women that were based on their subordination, qualities such as the ability to admit to vulnerabilities, helplessness, and weakness; the ability to express emotions; cooperativeness (versus assertiveness); and the capacity to put the care of others before the care of self. These qualities become not only distinctly feminine but also distinctly positive. The dichotomy Miller describes is expressed in the way men and women interact with each other and the way "we force men to center around themselves and women to center around 'the other'" (p. 70). According to Miller, this dichotomy is not merely socially constructed but is the "fundamental form in which women's ties to others are structured" (p. 74). This form is relational and affiliative for women and autonomous for men.

Miller concludes that because women's focus and being are based in relationships, autonomy creates the fear of separation and aloneness. For men, autonomy is a natural outgrowth of their socialization in the dominant group. The therapeutic process is therefore different for men and women, with women needing to identify and make explicit their feelings, even the ever unpopular angry and ambitious feelings, despite the fact that their new responses may meet with negative responses and displeasure from men and other women. This could carry devastating repercussions for some women, and Miller does not deny the social implications of change for women who have been dependent on men for whatever reason. The crucial point Miller makes is that because women occupy a subordinate position in society, they bring a different history and experience to their social and family relationships.

Another important voice in the development of a feminist perspective is that of Nancy Chodorow. In *The Reproduction of Motherhood*, Chodorow (1978) begins by asking the very basic question, Why do women mother? Her answer implicates not the biological, anthropological, or, strictly speaking, learned and cognitive realms but, rather, the realm of learned socialization and social reproduction of motherhood. Based on an object relations model, Chodorow's book examines the ways women mother girls and boys differently and finds the reproduction of mothering (after the period of infancy, when both boys and girls learn the foundations for parenting) to be in the socially sanctioned, deeply felt identification of the mother with the girl child and of the girl child with her mother. Because mothers experience sons as opposite to themselves, mothers stress the differentiation and "propel sons into a sexualized, genitally toned relationship which in turn draws the son into triangular conflicts" (p. 110) and presumably helps him along the road to individuation and separateness. The result of this differential treatment is that girls stay identified with mothers forever and "feel alike in fundamental ways" (p. 110) while boys feel separate and independent if they have a strong male to initiate them into the male world or possibly lost and inadequate if they do not (Bly, 1991).

Chodorow clearly makes the case for a social–contextual explanation of mothering (embedded in Western capitalism): that is, if women continue to mother, they will produce girls who will become mothers, but there is no expectation that this social arrangement will or should change. Therefore, her analysis finally underlines the socially constructed nature of the characteristics of girls and women and of boys and men. Because they are more identified with their mother and for a longer period of time, girls will become women who are concerned with the mothering relationship and who struggle with differentiation, body–ego boundary issues, and an unrealistic view of primary love. Boys, primarily because they are not identified with their mother for a period much beyond the infant stages, will become adults who are differentiated, who are relatively unconcerned with the issues of mothering and child development, and who have less of a problem separating from parents as adults. Girls grow to be better mothers because they are girls and can experience near-total identification with the mother whereas the boy, precisely because he is a boy, cannot. Furthermore, gender identity for women grows out of their continued relationship with women while gender identity for men grows out of their "denial of relationship to their mothers" (Chodorow, 1978, p. 177).

Chodorow points out that the special qualities of empathy and relational capacity developed over time in the primary relationship with mother, as well as the social (and economic) placement of women in the home, are significant differences that make it more difficult for women to differentiate from the primary relationship. Men, on the other hand, are defined by the nonfamilial and the occupational. With fathers frequently absent or only partially present, boys must find identity in role definitions rather than in experienced relationships. As men, it is more difficult for them to function in the relational realm.

This fixed notion of developmental identity carries its own limitations; mothers are still perceived as responsible for the way boys and girls grow to be men and women. Girls' identity with mothers is perceived as responsible for their being less able to differentiate, and absent fathers are perceived as responsible for boys being less able to connect.

Several writers have built on Miller's (1976, 1986) analysis of feminine qualities and characteristics and Chodorow's (1978) analysis of differential development. Most notably, Carol Gilligan (1982) has proposed that women's and men's moral development proceeds along quite different lines, with women developing a moral position based on responsibility that involves care and relationships while men develop a moral position based on fairness that involves competing rights and rules.

As the feminist critique has developed, it has opened the way for further studies on the social construction of masculinity. One new such study by the sociologist David Gilmore (1990) notes that in most societies masculinity, unlike femininity, must be established through ritualistic—and, frequently, harsh—testing; it is not a given. Gender identity for men must be proven in dramatic and public ways. Gilmore sees this as a result of the problematic separation of the male child from his mother, of his conflict between wanting to remain close to the mother and wanting to be independent from her. Society, then, establishes the rules of social conduct to complete and ensure the male's separation from mother. Regression, not castration, is seen as the dominant threat to masculinity. Male identity is, therefore, posited in the tasks men are asked to perform by the society to prove their manliness. These tasks, according to Gilmore, are three: to impregnate women, to protect dependents, and to provide for the home and related kin. These tasks are as significant for what they are as for what they leave out.

Additionally, in carrying out these tasks, which highlight the roles of warrior and hunter, there is an implicit understanding that men are expendable. Men must be prepared to lose their lives or their reputations in the struggle for resources, in confrontation with others, on the battlefield, or in the hunt. The acceptance of men as expendable "represents a moral commitment to defend the society and its core values against all odds" (Gilmore, 1990, p. 224). This concept of the expendability of men is apparent at the global level as well as the familial level.

The *nearly* universal male characteristics, according to Gilmore, are therefore ones that support the ideal of men as defenders and providers. There is little room in this scenario for the expression of feelings, for the possibility of choice in determining one's work and relational roles, and for the creation of close bonds with children and spouses.

Gilmore concludes his study of maleness in various societies with

the interpretation that men *are* both nurturing and generous, sometimes to a fault. The generosity, however, goes more directly to the
society than to a specific person.

> Men nurture their society by shedding their blood, their sweat, and
> their semen, by bringing home food for both child and mother, by
> producing children, and by dying if necessary in faraway places to
> provide a safe haven for their people. This, too, is nurturing in the
> sense of endowing or increasing. However, the necessary personal
> qualities for this male contribution are paradoxically the exact
> opposite of what we Westerners normally consider the nurturing
> personality. (Gilmore, 1990, p. 230)

Although intuitively accurate, this early attempt to reevaluate
masculinity must also certainly be considered limited in scope and
usefulness. It does, however, provide us with a contextualized
understanding of male behavior that looks beyond the simple desire
for male domination as the answer to why men are the way they are.

These theories explicating the cultural construction of gender and
reflecting the Alpha bias have done a great service to women and
men. First, they have framed women's and men's abilities and
qualities in a social context that has helped to explain and define
them. For example, they have acknowledged socially defined feminine qualities and sex-role stereotypes as positive qualities. This not
only validates women and their experience but allows men to accept
and embrace within themselves those feminine characteristics they
would otherwise have denied. Second, feminine characteristics and
behavior are not viewed out of context and are therefore not seen as
inferior (to male) human traits. Male qualities are not seen as existing
purely for the self-aggrandizing preservation of male power but for
more altruistic reasons. The danger, however, is in viewing either sex
with a fixed set of immutable characteristics that prohibit individuals
from stepping outside their historical social positions with one
another, including those of subordination and domination. The
works of Miller, Chodorow, Gilligan, Gilmore, and others like them
help to create a context and a perspective for understanding the
meaningfulness of gender within the PAFS theory and practice.

PAFS and Alpha Bias

By virtue of its acknowledgment that there are differences between
women and men and that the task of differentiating and connecting

with parents and significant others is in some ways different for women and men, PAFS falls into the category of Alpha bias. But PAFS avoids the pitfall of limiting the range of opportunities available to women and men by assuming that both women and men will be able to renegotiate the gendered and generational hierarchy with parents because of the similarities, and regardless of the differences, between them.

Neither women nor men are asked to separate from parents but to connect with them in ways that do not draw the client into old behaviors that have not proven useful or healthy. By behaving differently with parents, men and women are able to see their relationship with parents neither as an entrapment for men nor as life and death dependency for women. In general, for women the most difficult task is to become one's own person in relationship to men as well as women, while for men the most difficult task often is to acknowledge one's early dependency and later interdependency with parents and loved ones, especially the deep attachment to mother (Morris Taggart, personal communication, January 1991).

To acknowledge these differences while moving toward personal authority, however, lets neither women nor men off the hook in the essential business of renegotiating the gendered and generational boundaries. It is expected that both are fully capable of transforming their lives by dealing with issues of power, love, dependency, and autonomy at the source, that is, within the family of origin.

This belief that women and men have the same developmental tasks to renegotiate the hierarchical boundaries is an important aspect of PAFS and gender. The female client, perhaps because of her deep identification with mother, will find her work in identifying different-ness as well as similarities with mother as a way to be in relationship with mother that still allows the client to find and hear her own voice. She will also be asked to explore the power issues with both parents, but especially with father, who may have been romanticized, ideal-ized, feared, or rejected.

Because historically men have learned that women will carry emotional responsibility for relationships, they are able to deny their longing and special relationships with mothers and to romanticize and idealize the distant father and their relationships with fathers (Chodorow, 1978). It is important, then, that in renegotiating with parents the male client acknowledge his special relationship with mother and humanize his father, making the father and his actions and non-actions real and contextualizing each parent's experience. This humanizing of father also demystifies the ideas of maleness established in the father's emotional or physical distance. The following is a summary of one client's therapeutic process as he created an understanding of himself and his relationships in adult life.

Christopher's Story

Christopher grew up in a somewhat traditional American family. His father was a self-made man, making his career first in the financially lucrative investment business and later as a real estate broker when the investment industry began failing. His mother, for most of his childhood and young adulthood, was a homemaker–volunteer who had grown up in a very wealthy family. Christopher had an older and a younger sister. He entered therapy because he was "ambivalent about intimacy," experienced distance in his relationship with his older sister, and was anxious about opening and sustaining a marketing and consultation practice. He had previously been in therapy for brief periods of time. After two individual sessions Christopher joined a small family-of-origin group with two cotherapists.

Christopher's parents divorced after the youngest child had gone to college. Their marriage, although it had begun with hope and high energy, had eventually succumbed to father's work-related absences and mother's alcoholism. By the time Christopher entered therapy, his father had remarried and his mother had committed herself to recovery from her alcohol dependency. His mother had completed her MBA, begun a successful marketing and business consultation practice, and had remarried. Christopher's parents were both highly functioning, successful, and much changed from the earlier personas with whom he had grown up.

Christopher projected self-assurance and confidence in the group; his sense of entitlement and his place in the world rarely seemed in question. On the other hand, although Christopher did moderately well with his practice, he seemed to hold back from pursuing and attaining success. When he was challenged on this matter by the small group, it became apparent that Christopher worried that being more successful than his father might hurt his father in perhaps a life-threatening way. Underlying Christopher's reticence was a fear that he would symbolically overcome his father by becoming more successful than he had become in his later years. Among Christopher's many assignments was one in which he was asked to challenge his father to a game of tennis. This resulted in Christopher's discovery that his father was not as feeble as he had assumed and that his father could handle Christopher's success.

Christopher was also asked to arrange to meet his father in a large and busy shopping mall without designating the exact place. Finding each other without difficulty, father and son appeared to have many similar unspoken ideas. The symbolism of finding his father and the ease with which it was accomplished was not lost on Christopher.

Christopher's mother was the go-getter in the family; if he was in competition with anyone, it was she. Christopher had the unenviable position, therefore, of denying his identity with his father, whom he felt to be somewhat unsuccessful, and denying his identity with his mother, who was alcoholic, female, and clearly successful in everything she undertook, including her own recovery.

Christopher's relationship with his mother was clearly more conflicted than that with his father. He carried the memories of a child with an out-of-control, overpowering, and at times abusive mother. These painful memories interfered with Christopher's ability to see his mother in the context of *her* earlier existence and as the woman she had become and his ability to envision other women noncompetitively and in an intimate relationship.

Christopher's work in therapy involved finding out about both his parents' earlier experiences. He learned to establish boundaries with his mother that allowed him to share his life with her without feeling as though she could or cared to have control over his choices. During the family's in-office visits, Christopher explored his mother's relationship to alcohol, his parents' divorce, and his relationship to each parent, as it had been and as he hoped it would continue to be. Christopher acknowledged his special position of power within the family that reflected the larger social bias and that contributed to his sense of entitlement and distance from his older sister.

Several months after Christopher's therapy ended, he married the woman he had been dating while in the group, and several months after that he admitted his own alcohol and drug dependency and began his recovery in Alcoholics Anonymous. Although during the sessions with his mother he denied that he shared her alcoholism, it is possible that finally being able to identify with her enabled him to identify that part of himself that was also addictive.

The Transgenerational Model and Murray Bowen

Several feminist writers consider intergenerational approaches to be among the more acceptable theoretical positions (Lerner, 1985; Luepnitz, 1988; Walsh & Scheinkman, 1989). Lerner (1985), for instance, recommends that feminists "take Bowen Family Systems Theory and run with it" (p. 36). Though less enthusiastic about Bowen's work, Luepnitz (1988) agrees that, like psychodynamic approaches, the gathering of family data with an eye to changing current relationships with significant family members is important.

Because PAFS has evolved in part from Bowen theory, it is important to discuss that theory and to evaluate the differences in meaning and practice between the two theories. It should be clear, however, from the previous chapters that the goal of PAFS therapy is similar to that of therapy based on Bowen family systems theory. The goal is to create a context where the client can establish a different kind of relationship with parents and peers, one based on equality. The notion of personal authority as "the synthesizing construct between individuation and intimacy" (Williamson, 1982b, p. 310) is the major distinguishing feature of PAFS.

Lerner (1985) points out that the goal of defining oneself apart from others, despite pressure to maintain the status quo, and Bowen's insistence on differentiation in the context of connectedness are at the heart of feminism. Lerner states that Bowen family of origin work and feminism facilitate women's understanding of their roles and struggles through the generations and helps them identify ways in which they are both different from and like those women who preceded them. Lerner also believes that Bowen theory and the use of the genogram are less likely than other family and individual approaches to lead to mother blaming and more likely to "depathologize" women's behavior by viewing it in a social and historical context. "Both feminists and Bowen Theory agree that it is the appreciation of context which allows angry and blaming reactions towards one's mother to be replaced by more empathic and thoughtful ones" (Lerner, 1985, p. 37).

However, since Bowen was not exempt from the prevailing Alpha bias of *his* historical context, there are other problems in his theory. Many of the early writers looked to mothers for the causal link with schizophrenia. Luepnitz (1988) and Walsh and Scheinkman (1989) point out that Bowen saw the mothers' inability to separate from children as based on their own inability to separate from *their* mothers. Thus, "overinvestment" on the part of the mother became, in Bowen's theory, the cause and focus of the child's problems; the transmission of intergenerational pathology was clearly through the maternal line while the fathers' responsibility for the children's development went unexplored. Bowen did not place this struggle with boundary issues within a social and historical context. If he had, he would have seen the problem as one in which women's lives were curtailed by restricted, socially constructed views of gender backed by historical, cultural, constitutional, and legal sanctions (Goodrich et al., 1988; Lerner, 1985; Luepnitz, 1988; McGoldrick, Anderson, & Walsh, 1989; Walters et al., 1988).

In contrast to Bowen theory, the PAFS theory of adult development holds men as well as women accountable for the relationships they maintain with parents and significant others. Each client deals with her or his idiosyncratic position in the family of origin. This means, for instance, that the family dynamics that encouraged a daughter to marry and a son to continue his education are explored as to the meaning and significance for the client's later life and the meaning for each parent. Neither parent is blamed for the client's particular position in life, but each parent is dealt with individually and her or his influence and roles are directly addressed. There is never a focus on causal connections, only an exploration of contexts. And since the questions come out of the client's own emotional life and the answers come out of the parents' emotional life, the questions and answers create a narrative that permits a new construction of reality for the client and possibly for the parents. A father of a client might be asked why he was not available to the family and a mother might be asked why she encouraged a son or daughter to become central in her life. This is done within the social and historical context of each parent's life experience, so there is no doubt about the circumstances surrounding role or occupational choices. The unequal nature of the relationships is made explicit, as are the family's assumptions about female and male roles.

A criticism sometimes made of Bowen theory concerns its tendency to direct the action between clients and parents in a way that keeps the client outside of the emotional field. This can be useful in highly volatile situations but could give the impression that the direct expression of strongly felt emotions is dangerous and reactive (Luepnitz, 1988; Walsh & Scheinkman, 1989). PAFS, on the other hand, highlights the client's emotional life and focuses on the client's experience and meaning.

In the process of achieving PAFS and before the parents are brought into the therapy sessions, the client confronts all the important issues of her or his life. Highly charged and toxic emotional issues—questions of loyalty, unresolved grief and loss, disappointment, and anger—are dealt with in the small group so that clients have an opportunity to detoxify themselves from the harmful effects of those situations, events, and relationships around which they have built meaning. This detoxification process is a necessary preliminary step to opening a new kind of dialogue with parents and can take different forms. On the one hand, the process is a call to clients to become aware of the strong emotions and feelings that they have protected themselves from and to move beyond the fear of destroying themselves, the family, or other important relationships. In the safety of the small group, clients are encouraged to find the voice that expresses their outrage, anger, disappointment, and love and devotion to parents. Having found the voice and the words and having dealt with the emotionality around the meaning of those events, clients can directly address parents (or whoever is significant in their lives if the parents are deceased), with the possibility of a healing outcome for all. The in-office visit also focuses on all the hot issues between the client and parents in a nonjudgmental way. This is the basis on which empathy for parents is fostered and developed.

The small group process and homework assignments in PAFS frequently bypass rational thought and take advantage of the client's willingness to be in a different position vis-à-vis parents. This is a shift from Bowen's highly rational position with clients.

Bowen's approach emphasizes and elevates the rational, (masculine) aspects of personality, leaving the impression that the emotional (feminine) states are less important and less useful for healthy interaction. This is the main (feminist) criticism of Bowen's "Differentiation of Self Scale" (Bowen, 1978; Kerr & Bowen, 1988), which clearly identifies feminine characteristics, such as seeking love and approval, relying on feelings, relatedness, and being for others, at the lower end and masculine characteristics of autonomy, goal-directedness, rational thinking, and being for self at the higher end (Luepnitz, 1988). Because of this polarization, the concept of differentiation does not advance a notion of integration of thought and feeling, of "the ability to tolerate conflict and avoid cutoffs and the capacity both to compete and to collaborate" (Leupnitz, 1988, p. 42). Although differentiation of self is important in PAFS, it is only a step in the important work of establishing empathy and intimacy.

Intimacy, as defined in PAFS, is "voluntary fusion" (Williamson, 1982b, p. 310). Intimacy is different from closeness, which by itself becomes synonymous with fusion. Intimacy must be accompanied by the knowledge and experience of authority, equality, and the ability to choose to be part of an ongoing, interdependent, relationship (Williamson, 1982b).

If equality and peerhood are established with each parent, equality and peerhood cannot help but be established in the marriage. As noted in Chapter 5, shifting hierarchies, both gendered and generational, in the family of origin will create a destabilizing dynamic in the marital relationship. The client will be unable to assume personal authority in one area while maintaining a subordinate position in another.

In PAFS it is not merely assumed that renegotiation with parents will lead to an ability to form healthy, egalitarian relationships with others; within the small group clients are constantly reminded of the similarities between their current circumstances and their relationships within the family of origin. The connection between past and present gives clients an opportunity to try out new behaviors with whoever is creating the greatest upset in their life at the moment or with the person they feel most secure in addressing first. For instance, a client might be able to practice new behaviors with a parent sooner than he or she can with a spouse. The client is encouraged to try these behaviors with both parents and spouse at her or his own pace. For example, a man might be challenged to give up control of a family outing before he is asked to give up control of the family budget, or a woman might be asked to joke with father before she is encouraged to take a stronger position with her husband. The renegotiation in one arena is felt and experienced in the other.

Because men and women *are* different in many ways, their tasks will often be different. Men will learn how to express their emotions directly and deal with parents and others in the feeling arena while women will be asked to participate in the more political realms of everyday life.

The goal of PAFS for the individual is to reconnect with family members in a new way through renegotiation of the hierarchical structure. Renegotiation is the necessary prerequisite for an equitable intimacy. The final in-office visit of parents with client confirms the previous groundwork laid by the client in communications with parents and sets the tone for future interaction with and connection to parents. Through practice, the client learns, with the guidance and support of the therapist and group members, how to carry on a peer conversation with parents. By now the client has established a way of being in the world with peers as well as with parents, which affirms her or his self-worth and equality. This new position becomes the model for the future.

Barbara's Story

Barbara began marital therapy when both she and her husband realized that meaningful, noncombative communication between them had ceased to exist. Barbara worked part-time; Cliff, her second husband, was a successful, highly visible, and influential business executive. Cliff was 10 years older than Barbara and thoroughly invested in his profession. Although he did not object to having three children, he never intended to participate in the day-to-day work of their upbringing, feeling it was his wife's responsibility to raise the children.

Barbara had been in analysis for several years and believed no therapy would be able to cure her of her lifelong depression and inability to effectively express her feelings and desires. As soon as the marriage stabilized and the angry exchanges subsided, Cliff decided to discontinue his involvement in therapy. Barbara, feeling the need for continued support and still experiencing depression, decided to join a small family-of-origin group.

Barbara's family history revealed much to be depressed about. Her father had been physically abusive to each of his three children. She described her mother as critical and ineffective in defending the children against the raging father. Barbara escaped the family home by marrying at an early age, only to find herself in a more dangerously abusive relationship. Barbara was one of the fortunate women to have extricated herself from this type of relationship, she divorced her first husband. Though her relationship to Cliff was not an abusive one, Barbara felt powerless to leave and powerless to assume an equal position.

Therapy for Barbara included many interventions designed to help her interact differently with her parents, her husband, and her children. At first afraid to engage her father on the telephone, Barbara was asked to refer to him in the group not only by his first name but by the name his closest associates might use. She stated that he would refuse to talk to her on the phone and often called her by a name she disliked. Soon after, Barbara began a conversation with her father by telling him a joke, thus assuming a different, more equal stance. Shortly thereafter he began addressing her by her proper name, and a dialogue began between the two.

Barbara's anger at her father was equaled by her anger at her mother for not protecting her as she grew up and for relentlessly criticizing her. Asking Barbara to imagine rolling her invalid mother over the side of a cliff allowed Barbara the opportunity to visualize not only the extent of her anger but also the helplessness and vulnerability that her mother had indeed always felt when around Barbara's father *and* that she now felt with Barbara herself, who was a much brighter, more verbal, and better-educated woman.

On the home front, because Barbara was unable to confront her husband directly, she purchased a life-size punching bag. It was the first time she allowed herself to express any anger, much less a physical display of it. The children also made use of the bag, a practice that visibly lessened the tension in the home. As time went on, Barbara became more comfortable with speaking directly to Cliff and asking for his participation with the children. In the meantime, group members supported, challenged, and acknowledged the many changes Barbara was making in her life and in her relationships.

When Barbara's parents finally came in for the 2-day office visit, Barbara's anger, disappointment, affection, and longing had been exposed and dealt with. She was able to address each parent, exploring with them the circumstances of their upbringing, relationships to their parents, courtship, and marriage. Barbara confronted her father about the early abuse, expressing her feelings about what his anger had meant to her and its effect on her marriage and children. She acknowledged her mother's helplessness in the face of her father's emotional displays, thus connecting and identifying with her mother for the first time in many years.

During the time Barbara was dealing with issues involving her family of origin, her marriage underwent substantial changes. Cliff participated in marital therapy on an "as needed" basis, finding Barbara's changes both exasperating and relieving. He accommodated to her changes, though reluctantly at first. Barbara and Cliff still do not have the "perfect" marriage, but each would agree that the negotiations are more equally balanced and that they have acquired the ability to compromise.

Conclusions

My use of PAFS is based on the belief that gender is important and that women and men come into therapy with very different life experiences and also very similar ones, such as intergenerational intimidation. Women and men are equal in abilities, but they are not similar in the way they interact with others, in the way they present in therapy, in the way they accept or reject therapeutic injunctions, in the way they seek solutions, or in the way they interact with their parents and with their children. PAFS can accommodate these significant differences because it explores the idiosyncratic, contextual, and experiential worlds of the individual.

When a gender-aware therapist addresses these differences while promoting personal authority, both women and men gain a greater appreciation for the characteristics they bring to therapy and to the dialogue with parents. They can choose to identify with either gender to the extent that they are comfortable, and they will be able to choose the kind of gendered individual that they wish to be rather than the kind they formerly assumed that their socialization and cultural background had made them be.

PAFS has grown out of a practice designed to create intimate relationships by humanizing the parents to the client and thus humanizing the individual client. This is different from but not incompatible with the goals of feminism and feminist family therapy which have grown out of the political imperative to establish equality for all individuals within the family system. PAFS theory can and should be compatible and mutually enriching with feminism and with gender awareness. Like other therapies, the personal authority method is as gender-sensitive as is the therapist, male or female, who uses it.

ACKNOWLEDGMENTS

My thanks and appreciation to Terrell Dixon, Cheryl Rampage, Morris Taggart, and Donald Williamson, all of whom provided thoughtful readings, editorial comments and suggestions for this chapter at various stages of its development. All limitations and any mistakes in this initial survey are, of course, my own.

CHAPTER 17

Beyond Personal Authority

For whoever would save his life will lose it . . .
—Matthew (16:25)

Falling in Love with the Future

The goal of personal authority work is to create a congruent consciousness. This means to reconcile and integrate the "strong I" position on the one hand with a commitment to being part of "a pattern that connects" on the other. To achieve this requires a radical psychological–spiritual reconstruction within the family. The therapeutic task is to transform the past in terms of the ways in which it is being constructed and held in the present. *By changing the meanings associated with past events, one can change the intense negative feelings which may be associated with these events.* In this sense, then, personal authority work is about healing the future. Not only is the self a creation in the mind, but we also create and recreate the self moment by moment. Consequently the possibility for transformation is always at hand.

Giving up the need to be parented implies a profound emotional acknowledgment that in the last resort there is no place to go but to the self. The level of meaning, hope, and good purpose required to sustain an integrated human life cannot come from outside the self. Yet, paradoxically, it is by going deeply inside the self that one can learn first to transcend family emotionality and subsequently to make the boundaries of the self more porous. As a result, the client learns to identify more comfortably with all sorts and conditions of human beings, a versatility which is an essential characteristic of the skilled psychotherapist. This transformation begins with a new level of identification with "former parents."

Giving up the need to be parented is a necessary step on the way to acquiring the personal freedom "to choose the future." It is the source of the decision to let go of one's private soap opera and to give up stale and repetitive old stories about a personal history frozen in time. Naturally, by the time they enter their 30s, relatively few people are still actively soliciting parental advice or support. But most people do hold on to the comforting fantasy that when the chips are really and truly down, yes, there is one place to which one can always go. By contrast, the client going through the family of origin experience is preparing the self to give up once and for all this private trysting place where one can always go secretly, in fantasy, to meet with parents. This is the ultimate de-illusionment in life, losing Daddy as King and Mommy as Queen. They are neither all knowing or all good. They can no longer make everything right. It is no longer true that they (and therefore we) will all "live happily ever after."

Nothing will transform a stale old love affair with the past and resolve continuing yearning around what might have been, should have been, or should not have been quite as readily as falling in love with the future. For this means that the client is giving up any lingering residual hope, at whatever level of awareness, that somehow there is a way to turn back the clock, to do life all over again, and to have a different experience and outcome. This is a time to mourn, but after the mourning comes the celebration, and a continuing coevolution between the generations.

When the process goes well, the client has a new freedom and energy not simply in the mind and spirit but even in the flesh and blood as well. (Who knows whether this will affect the genetic coding of the generations to come.) We connect to spirit via our bodies. Before Descartes and Newton nature was alive. But then nature became an orderly machine and the body became a small machine in a dead universe, a machine that can be manipulated and controlled by technology. Frequently, the body is viewed as a biological machine. However, by contrast, the human being sometimes has a subjective awareness of being a field of consciousness almost without boundaries and without limits. So we can fluctuate between seeing the self as a biological machine and experiencing the self as an ever-expanding field of consciousness.

This is analogous to Heisenberg's "uncertainty principle," the dual theory in physics in which it is sometimes more useful to view matter as mass and at other times as energy (Hawking, 1988). As has been true in physics, the more useful way to look at health matters is determined by the character of the immediate context and the purpose to be served. There are acute medical emergencies in which viewing the body as a machine may be the most appropriate response. But most of the time in patient care and in the individual's attitude to personal health, such an approach is woefully inadequate. It falls far short of a systemic understanding of the patterns of health and illness behaviors. In this regard, Chopra (1987) suggests that intelligence and spirit live within and express energy throughout every organ and cell in the body, not simply the cortex. These are stimulating, if still mostly poetic, inferences.

In any event, in personal authority work the client can release out into the blue yonder old pictures of early parental figures previously held rigidly inside the head in punitive, unfavorable and inflexible grimaces and stereotypes. This freeze-frame has become fluid once again; both the individual system and the family system are open. The actors are dancing freely on stage, and there is an ever-present possibility of new lines being spoken, eliciting further new lines in response, so that the final act has not yet been written. This freedom is invaluable since the romance lies in the unpredictable character of the next scene to be played.

This rehabilitation of parents is important since if we do not mythologize and re-mythologize family members, we are likely to "pathologize" them (Campbell, 1988). While child advocacy is an idea that can hardly ever be carried to an extreme, the current cultural focus on the abusing parent, with its mostly unforgiving and harsh stance continuing even in adulthood, is powerful evidence that pathologizing is the likely alternative to re-mythologizing parents. Yet re-mythologizing the self requires a re-mythologizing of the parents. This, in turn, follows the discovery of the story of the family of origin, as it has been understood and constructed within the minds of the parents. Astronauts frequently report that when they get enough physical distance from the earth to see it as a whole, they are deeply moved by both its beauty and its fragility. Something similar happens with the client who gets enough emotional distance to gain perspective on the family as a whole. He or she is usually moved and motivated to sustain the heat of reentry in a very different way.

The client has now created for himself or herself an opportunity to fall in love with his or her own "former parents," but this time in quite another way. This is a relationship of love that is compassionate rather than erotic, one that is voluntary, spontaneous, and psychologically egalitarian. This is agape rather than eros. Its source is a shared sense of mutuality between self and parent, and an awareness by both of being subject to all forms of human vulnerability and frailty and, eventually, physical death itself. By falling in love again, but in a much different way, with one's own flesh and blood, one can also again embrace, but in a very different way, one's own early ideals and youthful dreams.

The client does not have to yet once again recreate the psychological mind-set, the values system, and the emotional coloration of previous generations. This is especially refreshing to know when the previous generation has concluded or is concluding life in a mood of cynicism, moral decay, or psychological and spiritual despair. Paradoxically, falling in love with the future means to feel joy and peace in this present moment. It is an incurable attitude of optimism and celebration toward life itself.

All living beings and, therefore, all problems are interconnected and interdependent and so cannot be solved in isolation. Eastern thinking takes the position that excessive high self-confidence and self-esteem can break the relationship between the self and other people and other living things. This awareness of connection and interdependency is a spiritual awareness. It includes the awareness that certain crucial choices are made at the level of spirit. One example is the willingness to give up one's personal truth, including "truth" about personal history and the seemingly justifiable attendant emotions. By giving up one's personal truth one becomes increasingly agnostic about personal history and, simultaneously, increasingly confident about the personal future. This is not a certitude about the details of future outcomes. It is rather a confidence that one can manage the future well, whatever it brings. These choices create the possibility for both playfulness and joyfulness. Personal truth, which is to say, inner consciousness, is created through the metaphors of language. And so this playfulness is primarily a playfulness with language. Capra (1989) has suggested that "the peak experience is a deepening sense of mystery, which accompanies letting go of certitude." Letting go of certitude about the past is the final step to falling in love with the future.

Personal Authority as Illusion

There is no way to peace. Peace is the way.
    —Thich Nhat Hanh (1990)
    Transformation and Healing

The purpose, then, of this chapter is to present the idea of personal authority as ultimately an illusion, although for a period along the way very well worth believing in and aspiring to. It is human nature to want to be "special" or at least special in some characteristic. Being special means to stand out and apart, which is to say, not just different or differentiated but different in a superior way. This may be why specialness, meaning a differentness defined as superiority over others and groups of others, is the most tenacious illusion and invariably the last to go. This is not to deny that differentiation of self, especially as a step on the way to personal authority, is an important, indeed essential, psychological achievement. But differentiation of self does not guarantee either peace of mind or a sense of fulfillment in life. It simply clears away some of the underbrush obscuring the path by increasing the subjective sense of voluntariness and freedom of choice. Then the question offers itself, How is one to use this personal authority or newfound freedom? To what should one commit this new authoritative self in order to live with a sustained sense of good purpose and personal worth? Each person searches for a place in the sun, seeks a mission, lusts for success, yearns for love, strives for meaning, and does all of this very much like every other person. But now we have entered the domain of spirit. And here the possibility for healing and transformation is always and immediately at hand.

One possible answer is that having achieved a significant measure of personal authority, the next step is to learn to move beyond the strong commitment to protecting the boundaries that define and distinguish the self from the rest of humanity. However, here as with most things in life, timing is of the essence. If a young person tries to lose, deny, or "give up the self" prematurely, psychotic episodes may result. At least as we understand developmental processes in Western culture, it is essential to go through the hard work of creating a self that one is able to experience as existing with some degree of continuity and independence from the rest of the universe. Having achieved this sense of self, the next step may be to consider giving up or "losing" that self in the interest of the greater good. This means giving up the self as the primary and controlling reference point in all choices and for all decisions. It is at this point that a notion like "balance of fairness" in relationships becomes more than simply an impossible dream.

Paradoxically, it is only through giving up some of his or her narcissism that the client can, by empathic imagination cross the generational boundary and get inside the inner world of the parent. Yet it is only by getting inside the world of the parent that the client can discover the person of the parent existing as an independent human being, apart from the role of parent and apart from the person of the client. Finally, it is only through directly experiencing the existence of the parent as separate from the self that the client realizes and deeply feels the existence of the self apart from the parent. These paradoxical and circular sequences can offer some perspective on those otherwise mystifying words "For whoever would save his life will lose it . . ." (Matthew 16:25).

In order to achieve personal authority, one must be focused on the idea for a significant period of time and be occupied, occasionally preoccupied, by the assigned tasks and the flow of the process. But one is only occupied by this goal in order to come to the point where it is no longer very important. Just as one goes to the first interview in psychotherapy in order to get to the last, one does this intergenerational work in order to be done with it. Differentiation of self is neither a useful way of life or a desirable end point. It is, rather, a critical developmental point along the way of life. First, one creates a clear sense of the boundaries to the self and a clear sense of that well-bounded self standing in sharp distinction to all of the rest of the world. This distinguishing of self from all others and all else, begins with the discovery of the self as existing apart from that older man and woman who used to be "Daddy" and "Mummy." One may then move on to be able both to identify with and to find oneself in the face of every other human being (beginning with parents), regardless of all those many things that make us different, sometimes for a brief time even "special." Much of human behavior and certainly most destructive behavior is driven by fear of one sort or another. But the possibility is always at hand to move on through fear, which is grounded in the fear of non-being, to experience love in relationships.

We fear not being wanted and therefore fear abandonment; we fear not belonging and therefore fear being outsiders; we fear ridicule and therefore fear failure; we fear loneliness and therefore fear aloneness; we fear vulnerability and therefore fear ignorance; we fear ordinariness and therefore fear not being special; we fear dependency and therefore fear poverty; we fear helplessness and therefore fear illness; we fear death and therefore fear aging. The development of personal authority within the family of origin seeks to address these many issues and the great seed bed of fearfulness that nourishes them. The purpose behind the mastery of fear is to be free to consider the alternatives. Having celebrated the differentness of the self and reestablished intimacy within the family of origin, one can go beyond this to celebrate the sameness of the self in relationship to every other human being, regardless of circumstances. One can then enjoy the relief and the peacefulness of "ordinariness."

Enjoying the relief of ordinariness does not preclude the possibility of seeking excellence as a goal in whatever happens to be one's sphere of endeavor. It means, rather, that *there are no further controlling or crippling transgenerational mandates that must be honored or fulfilled.* While unconscious drives still have some energy, they are now more familiar, therefore less menacing and less influential. This frees the individual to pursue a reference point for belief, value, and meaning that transcend both the individual self and the individual's extended family.

At this point in the pilgrimage, spirit begins to see all hatred as originating in self-hatred; sees hostility as an attack upon the self; attack as an appeal for help; fear as a yearning for love; blame as generated by guilt; and forgiveness (especially the forgiveness of one's own personal history, with the forgiveness of father and mother as literally at the very heart of it) as finding its source in the forgiveness of the self (Foundation for Inner Peace, 1975, 1985).

In that particular Buddhist meditation tradition known as Vipassana, the sustaining premise says that if the individual human being can give up an attitude of craving in life at one extreme and an attitude of aversion at the other, what is left is the possibility for loving relationships with self and all other human beings (Goenke, 1987, 1991). Then one may be "surprised by joy" (Lewis, 1955). One would not normally speak of Gautama Buddha, the enlightened one from 2,500 years ago, and Murray Bowen, the foundational family systems theorist in the 20th century, within the same breath. (It is worth noting that Kerr & Bowen, 1988, suggest that something akin to systems thinking originated at least 2,500 years ago, although they attribute it to the Greeks living in Ionia in the 6th century B.C.) Yet both the Buddha and Bowen emphasized the importance of taking an objective observer stance in relationships, learning to be "equanimous" or emotionally "nonreactive" to events. Each declared his theory to be a "true science," based on the law of nature. In the Buddha's case, the law of nature is the law of impermanence; for Bowen, the law of nature is the law of evolution. Both developed their theories from naturalistic observation and introspection.

The remarkable difference, however, is that for Bowen the underlying goal is the achievement of a "strong I" position in life, whereas for the Buddha the goal is liberation through resolving all attachments to the "I" or ego. For both, an important goal is awareness, but for the Buddha the ultimate goal is inner peace. He believed that this would, in turn, lead to compassion and outreach toward all living beings. It is only through the resolution of ego attachments, in the Buddha's view, that the "I" finds freedom from suffering. The Buddha emphasized a detached mind but always along with a warm heart. In other words, the enlightened person is simultaneously objective and compassionate. Personal authority theory is an attempt to create a method to pursue this goal.

In the final analysis, personal authority theory is an *ethical stance.* It is about taking personal responsibility for all of life's experiences and outcomes. It says that however recursive and circular human behavior may be, when it comes to ethical evaluation as opposed to psychological understanding, then "the buck stops here" with the individual. This acceptance of responsibility includes acceptance of responsibility for the well-being of the body also. Recognition that our lives are grounded in our physicalness, and embracing responsibility for the well-being of the body, is a spiritual awareness. The recognition that one creates the great majority of one's own pain and suffering in adult life is both astonishing and enlivening. It is energizing to realize how much personal healing is therefore immediately available by one's own hand.

A fascinating distinction was made a few years ago (Weber, 1984) at a meeting between Western psychologists and the Dalai Lama. This distinction suggests that the applied scientist studies nature, as it can be observed outside the self, in order to be able to change it. On the other hand, the mystic seeks to observe and change the self from within. Both of these are aspects of the self, however one's attention may be focused. The one aspect seeks to split the atom while the other seeks to split the inner structure of the ego. If the ego is opened up and dissolved, then in this case, too, great energy is released, but released now for compassion and healing. From this point of view, the evolution of a worldwide consciousness of compassion and partnership is even more important than biological evolution.

A constantly evolving exercise of personal authority within the family system is important—important to the degree that this book has argued that it is the most critical psychosocial task and developmental stage in both individual and family life. But just as is the case with differentiation of self in the family of origin, personal authority work is not the final goal in life nor is it an answer to what is ultimately the more important question.

While it can be stated in many different ways, the more important question in life is, how does one consistently find peace in one's heart and harmony and compassion in one's relationships? This level of experience is psychologically and spiritually *beyond personal authority.* Consciousness is hardly synonymous with meaning, but meaning is certainly at the center of it. How does one create personal meaning in life that transcends the usual human distinctions and divisions of race, creed, nationality, socioeconomic status, education, politics, even distinctions of generation and gender? How does one acquire this quality of good-heartedness, which will surely address the intimacy paradox? Like others, I wish I knew more about how to achieve this. Education and intelligence, power and privilege, health and wealth and beauty; none of these seem to help, often seem to hurt. It may well be that there comes a time in life when the practice of meditation (or certain forms of prayer) will do more than any further historic exploration into the details of the family of origin to resolve continuing anxiety about personal identity and destiny and bring reassurance. When all is said and done, "the buck stops here." Each is on his or her own path and pilgrimage. Bon voyage!

PART FOUR

Personal Authority Research

Personal authority in the family system theory has generated some empirical inquiry and is the source of the Personal Authority in the Family System Questionnaire (PAFS-Q). This work is summarized in the following chapter. So, in the immortal words of Monty Python, "And now for something completely different."

CHAPTER 18

The Personal Authority in the Family System Questionnaire: Assessment of Intergenerational Family Relationships

JAMES H. BRAY

In 1982 Donald Williamson, Paul Malone, and I formed a clinical research team to study the process and outcomes of intergenerational family therapy under development by Williamson. The Intergenerational Family Studies Project began by reviewing Williamson's cases and consultation methods to develop ideas concerning the process of his intervention methods and the outcomes accomplished. We also reviewed the literature on theory, research, and practice methods developed in transgenerational, intergenerational, and multigenerational family therapy approaches. Our review indicated that there was a significant theoretical and clinical literature but virtually no empirical studies in this area and no formal therapy-outcome studies, of any kind, on the methods. In addition, while the concepts were discussed and defined, they were not operationalized so that they could be measured in some quantitative and empirical manner. There were no available instruments or research techniques to measure the outcomes and process of these types of family therapy. Thus, we embarked on a 2-year project to develop a family assessment measure of the concepts and outcomes of intergenerational family therapy and theory. This part of the project culminated in the development of the

James H. Bray, PhD, is Associate Professor, Department of Family Medicine, Baylor College of Medicine, Houston, Texas.

Personal Authority in the Family System Questionnaire (PAFS-Q; Bray, Williamson, & Malone, 1984a, 1984b). After we developed the PAFS-Q we continued with our research on the process and outcomes of consultation methods and intergenerational family theory (Bray, Williamson, & Malone, 1986; Bray, Harvey, & Williamson, 1987; Williamson & Bray, 1988).

The PAFS-Q is a self-report measure that assesses three-generational family relationships identified by intergenerational family theory. The PAFS-Q operationalizes key concepts of intergenerational family theory (Bowen, 1978; Boszormenyi-Nagy & Ulrich, 1981; Williamson, 1981, 1982b; Williamson & Bray, 1985, 1988) into self-enumerated scales for use in research and clinical practice. The PAFS-Q assesses each individual in the family's self-reported perceptions of intergenerational family relationships. A person describes *current* relationships with parents in the family of origin, spouse or current significant dyadic relationship, and children. Current perceptions of family relationships are more important than historical viewpoints and memories of relationships in intergenerational family theory (Williamson & Bray, 1988).

There are three versions of the PAFS-Q. Version A is for adults with children, version B for adults without children. Versions A and B were developed in our initial research project (Bray et al., 1984a). Version C is a modification of version B for college students, older adolescents, and young adults without children and was developed by Bray and Harvey (1989). This chapter primarily discusses versions A and B and draws from previous work found in Bray et al. (1984a, 1984b) and Bray and Williamson (1987). The PAFS-Q is the only published instrument that measures intergenerational family relationships for research and clinical purposes (Grotevant & Carlson, 1989).

Key Concepts

The key concepts and behaviors measured by the PAFS-Q include individuation, emotional fusion, triangulation, intimacy, isolation, personal authority, and intergenerational intimidation. These concepts and behaviors apply to the family of origin and the current nuclear family as well. The following paragraph contain descriptions of the concepts used in the development of the PAFS-Q. These concepts have undergone an evolution through our work, and the current descriptions are found elsewhere in this volume. These definitions are provided to help the reader understand the conceptualizations used in the development of the PAFS-Q.

We defined *individuation* similarly to the concept of differentiation of self by Bowen (1978). It lies at one end of a continuum with *emotional fusion* at the opposite end. Individuation is a process by which a person differentiates within his or her relational contexts (Bowen, 1978; Karpel, 1976). The primary contexts are the family of origin and the nuclear family. Individuation is observed by an individual's ability to function in an autonomous and self-directed manner without being controlled, impaired, or feeling unduly responsible for significant others (Bowen, 1978; Kerr, 1981). Emotional fusion refers to diminished autonomous functioning in relationships, more emotional reactivity in interactions, and the tendency to take undue responsibility for others or to avoid taking responsibility for oneself. Emotional fusion reflects unresolved emotional attachments to the family of origin (Bowen, 1978).

Triangulation is a process of dealing with emotional fusion in which two people "engage" a third person to diffuse tension in the dyad through diversion, collusion, or scapegoating of the third person. Triangulation is related to fusion in that both indicate a lack of differentiation of self. However, they are different processes. Emotional fusion occurs between two people, triangulation between three. Fusion is often experienced as positive, although the effects of being in an emotionally fused relationship are not always constructive (e.g., decreased emotional and/or physical functioning). Triangulation is generally experienced as stressful by at least one person in the triad; he or she feels pulled between the two others. Fusion and triangulation were previously viewed as the same process; however, our research indicates that these are distinct but related concepts.

Intimacy is defined as voluntary closeness with distinct boundaries to the self (Lewis, Beavers, Gossett, & Phillips, 1975; Williamson, 1981). Closeness that lacks boundaries and is not perceived as voluntary reflects emotional fusion rather than intimacy. Intimacy includes trust, love–fondness, self-disclosure, and commitment (Larzelere & Huston, 1980; Peplau, 1982). Intimate relationships are characterized by mutual respect and freely initiated self-disclosure, while the individuation of the participants is maintained. *Isolation* is at the opposite end of the continuum from intimacy. Relational intimacy includes both intergenerational intimacy within the family of origin and intimacy with peers, particularly with one's spouse or significant other.

Personal Authority in the Family System (PAFS) is a synthesizing construct that represents the inherent tension between differentiation and intimacy within the family of origin and recreated in other important personal relationships. PAFS is a continuum with personal authority at one end and *intergenerational intimidation* at the other. PAFS includes being a differentiated person (Bowen, 1978; Karpel, 1976; Kerr, 1981), in whom increased control is exercised over individual destiny and choice of personal health and well-being. PAFS includes reconnection and belongingness to the family of origin while simultaneously acting from a differentiated position *within* the family of origin. PAFS further implies relating to all human beings, including one's parents, as peers in the basic human experience (Williamson, 1981, 1982b).

Intergenerational intimidation is the opposite pole of personal authority and reflects a lack of individuation and adult intimacy and the presence of the intergenerational power hierarchy between parents and their offspring. Intergenerational intimidation comes from the dependency of children on their parents and their perception of parents as the fundamental source of their selves. Intergenerational intimidation is reflected by family processes such as triangulation (Bowen, 1978) and covert loyalties (Boszormenyi-Nagy & Ulrich, 1981). Boszormenyi-Nagy argues that children have both conscious and unconscious loyalties to their parents that are expressed through perceived expectations and parental mandates. Children also may protect their parents by finding ways to exonerate them of misdeeds or failures, for example, by not "showing them up" in their life functioning (Harvey & Bray, 1991). Therefore, intergenerational intimidation constitutes an obstacle to offspring's development of autonomous and effective functioning as they progress into adulthood.

Intergenerational family theory predicts that interactional patterns are reproduced from generation to generation (Bowen, 1978) through social learning with parents, grandparents, and other significant family members (Bandura, 1977; Williamson & Bray, 1988). These patterns are often maintained because of loyalty to previous generations (Boszormenyi-Nagy & Ulrich, 1981). Thus, it is hypothesized that levels of personal authority, individuation, and intimacy in relationships with parents are reproduced in relationships with spouses and significant others (Harvey & Bray, 1991; Harvey, Curry, & Bray, 1991). PAFS is not a personality construct but a set of interpersonal skills and interactional behavior patterns that are observed in family interactions and other significant interpersonal relationships (Bray et al., 1984a).

Questionnaire Development

A pool of items that measure the key concepts of intergenerational family theory was developed. The items were based on the relevant literature and our clinical experience. Some items were drawn from previously developed instruments; items from these measures were reworded and rescaled to meet the design of the current instrument.

The initial versions of the PAFS-Q were evaluated empirically to determine the reliability and validity of the scales. This was an interactive process in which the specific items and scales were evaluated in several studies for internal consistency, reliability, and content and construct validity. Bray et al. (1984a, 1984b, 1987) present a detailed description of the procedures and results of these studies.

The final version of the PAFS-Q (version A) contains 132 items grouped into eight nonoverlapping scales. The following paragraph contains descriptions and sample items from each scale.

1. *Spousal Fusion–Individuation*: Items measure the degree to which a person operates in an emotionally fused or individuated manner in relationship with the spouse or significant other. Items are scaled so that larger scores indicate more individuation. (Examples: I often get so emotional with my mate that I cannot think straight; I worry that my mate cannot take care of himself or herself when I am not around.)

2. *Intergenerational Fusion–Individuation*: Items measure the degree to which a person operates in an emotionally fused or individuated manner with parents. Items are scaled so that larger scores indicate more individuation. (Examples: I am usually able to disagree with my parents without losing my temper; My present-day problems would be fewer or less severe if my parents had acted or behaved differently.)

3. *Spousal Intimacy*: Items assess the degree of intimacy and satisfaction with the mate or significant other. Items are scaled so that larger scores indicate more intimacy. (Examples: My mate and I frequently talk together about the significant events in our lives; My mate and I have mutual respect for each other.)

4. *Intergenerational Intimacy*: Items assess the degree of intimacy and satisfaction with parents. Items are answered separately for mother and father. Items are scaled so that larger scores indicate more intimacy. (Examples: I share my true feelings with my parents about the significant events in my life; I can trust my parents with things we share.)

5. *Nuclear Family Triangulation*: Items measure triangulation between spouses and their children (these items are completed only by people who have children). Items are scaled so that larger scores indicate less triangulation. (Examples: Children's problems [behavior, school, physical illness] sometimes coincide with marital conflict

or other stress in families. In your view how often does this happen in your family?; It feels like my children cannot get emotionally close to me without moving away from my mate.)

6. *Intergenerational Triangulation*: Items measure triangulation between a person and his or her parents. Items are scaled so that larger scores indicate less triangulation. (Examples: When your parents are having a significant problem in their marriage, to what extent do you feel **personally** responsible to provide a solution to their problem?; How **comfortable** would you be dining and having intimate conversation with one parent?)

7. *Intergenerational Intimidation*: Items assess the degree of personal intimidation experienced by an individual in relation to his or her parents. Items are scaled so that larger scores indicate less intimidation. (Examples: How often do you think of yourself as your mother and/or father's "little boy/girl"?; How often do you feel you must modify your behavior to meet your parents' expectations concerning your work, marriage, parenting, appearance, lifestyle?)

8. *Personal Authority*: The scale measures the interactional aspects of personal authority as defined by Williamson (1982b). Items reflect topics of conversation that require an intimate interaction with a parent while maintaining an individuated stance. Items are scaled so that larger scores indicate more personal authority. (Examples: How comfortable are you talking to your mother and father about **family secrets**, both real and imagined, and about skeletons in the family closet?; How comfortable are you talking **face to face** with your father and mother to make explicit with them that you are not responsible for their survival or happiness in life and that you are not working to meet goals and achievements in life which have been passed on from them [or prior generations] to you?)

Items on the Intergenerational Intimacy, Intergenerational Triangulation, and Intergenerational Intimidation scales are answered separately for mother and father, although the responses for mother and father are summed for each question to calculate the total score for each scale. The items on the Intergenerational Fusion–Individuation scale are answered for *parents* without separating responses for mother and father. This format was used to pull for fusion in the relationship with the parents.

All items are rated on a 5-point Likert scale. Version A contains all scales and is intended for use by individuals with children. All items except those on the Nuclear Family Triangulation scale are designed for married or unmarried people. Version B is intended for individuals without children; it is identical with version A except it does not contain the Nuclear Family Triangulation scale. Version C also does not include the Nuclear Family Triangulation scale and is modified for a college or adolescent population. A separate paper (Bray & Harvey, 1989) describes the development of Version C.

Norms for the PAFS-Q

The PAFS-Q was standardized on nonclinical (N = 100 to 712) and clinical (N = 62 and 83) samples (Bray & Harvey, 1989; Bray et al., 1984a, 1984b, 1986, 1987). Means and standard deviations for these groups are provided in the manual (Bray et al., 1984b) and in the Bray and Harvey (1989) paper for version C. A clinic group completed the PAFS-Q twice after completing intergenerational family therapy (Bray et al., 1986). The first completion was in reference to their present functioning, and the second completion was in reference to functioning before therapy. Means and standard deviations for the clinic group's PAFS-Q scores are provided for both time periods. Means, standard deviations, and interscale correlations for version C are provided in Bray and Harvey (1989). There are separate statistics for male (N – 345) and female (N = 367) undergraduates for version C.

Reliability

Reliability of the PAFS-Q has been demonstrated in several studies. In the Bray et al. (1984a) study alpha coefficients for a sample of nonclinical adults (N = 90) ranged from .82 to .95 at a first testing and from .80 to .95 at a second testing, with means of .90 and .89, respectively. Internal consistency coefficients for empirically derived factors ranged from .74 to .96 (N = 400; Bray et al., 1984a). In a clinical sample, reliability estimates ranged from .77 to .96 (N = 80; Bray et al., 1987). Version C has comparable alpha coefficients, which ranged from .97 to .85 (N = 321) and from .73 to .92 (N = 712) in two samples of undergraduate college students. In a clinical sample of undergraduates, alpha coefficients ranged from .75 to .92 (N = 62; Bray & Harvey, 1989). Test–retest reliability was acceptable for all scales except Intergenerational Fusion in a sample of 90 nonclinical adults (range .55 to .95, with mean of .75; Bray et al., 1984a). Version C demonstrated 2-month test–retest reliabilities ranging from .56 to .80 (N = 321; Bray & Harvey, 1989). The Intergenerational Intimidation scale had a test–retest reliability of .56, while the remaining scale reliabilities were above .66. Anderson and Fleming (1986a, 1986b) and

Fleming and Anderson (1986) found that the Intergenerational Fusion–Individuation, Intergenerational Triangulation, and Intergenerational Intimacy scales had internal consistencies of .76, .87, and .94, respectively, in a sample of college students.

Validity

The PAFS-Q correlates with other measures of family functioning to a moderate degree but also reflects unique aspects of family functioning. In a nonclinical sample, correlations between PAFS-Q scales and the Adaptability scale of the Family Adaptability and Cohesion Evaluation Scales (FACES; Olson, Bell, & Portner, 1978) were generally low (Bray et al., 1984a). The Spousal Intimacy and Intergenerational Intimacy scales correlated significantly with the FACES Cohesion scale, and several PAFS-Q scales correlated significantly with the Dyadic Adjustment Scale (DAS; Spanier, 1976).

In a clinical sample there were significant correlations between all but the Intergenerational Intimacy scale of the PAFS-Q scales and the Symptom Index, which measures physical and psychosomatic symptoms and stress (Bray et al., 1987). Correlations were also found between scales of the PAFS-Q and the Family Adaptability and Cohesion Evaluation Scales II (FACES II; Olson, Portner, & Bell, 1982) and the DAS. These correlations replicated the findings from the previous study (Bray et al., 1984a, 1984b). In a multiple regression analysis using the family process measures (PAFS-Q, FACES II, DAS) to predict health distress (Symptom Index; Sheely, 1982), PAFS-Q scores accounted for a significant amount of the variance over and above the other two measures. These findings also indicate that the PAFS-Q assesses aspects of family process not assessed by FACES II or the DAS. The results show that individuals who are more individuated from parents and spouse (higher Intergenerational Fusion–Individuation and Spousal Fusion–Individuation) report fewer health problems (Bray et al., 1987). In another study the PAFS-Q scores of college students were correlated with measures of life stress and health distress. In this study better health was predicted by less life stress, less intergenerational intimidation, less personal authority, and more individuation with parents and the significant other (Bray et al., 1987). We hypothesize that the finding that lower scores on the Personal Authority scale predict better health supports Williamson's (1982b) developmental theory that lack of personal authority is age-appropriate prior to the fourth decade of life.

A factor analysis of the PAFS-Q from 400 nonclinical adults supported a seven-factor solution (an eighth factor, representative of Nuclear Family Triangulation, was found for scores of persons with children). The conceptual scales were generally supported by the factor analysis. The major exception was an overlap of items from the Spousal Fusion–Individuation scale with items from the Spousal Intimacy scale. However, this finding supports the conceptualization of intimacy including aspects of individuation.

The PAFS-Q has been used in studies investigating intergenerational family processes, marital relations, career issues, and health issues in both psychological and medical contexts (Anderson & Fleming, 1986a, 1986b; Bayer & Day, 1987; Carpenter, 1990; Cebik, 1988; Curry, 1986; Day, 1988; deGruy et al., 1989; de la Sota, 1985; Ecker, 1989; Fleming & Anderson, 1986; Gilkey, 1988; Harvey & Bray, 1991; Harvey et al., 1991; Kinnier, Brigman, & Noble, 1990; McCollum, Schumm, & Russell, 1988; McCreanor, 1988; Quick, 1987; Reeve, 1988; Rogers, 1985; St. Clair, 1984; Weiner, 1990). More extensive norms for clinical and nonclinical couples and families are currently under development. In addition, further validity studies that compare PAFS-Q scales with behavioral observations of families are in progress.

Interpretation of PAFS-Q Scale Scores

An individual's or group's scale scores can be compared to the mean scale scores from the normative samples to facilitate interpretation. The mean scale scores from the study by Bray et al. (1984a) are normative scores from a nonclinical population. Means from a clinical sample are provided in Bray et al. (1984b, 1986).

Profile Types

A highly differentiated person will report high intimacy, high individuation, and high personal authority but low triangulation and low intimidation (Bray & Williamson, 1987). A report of high intimacy and high intimidation and low individuation reflects the classic pattern of fused or undifferentiated relationships. Often these people are happy or satisfied with the relationship, but there are problems with dependency, lack of autonomy, and physical or psychological symptoms. Conversely, reports of low intimacy and low individuation or of low intimacy and high intimidation indicate an emotional cutoff with the family of origin. These profiles are useful to keep in mind when assessing family functioning. Currently there are no cutoff points or categories for the PAFS-Q. An analysis of the profile using all the scores is employed to assess the family system (Bray & Williamson, 1987).

Bayer and Day (1987) developed a couple typology using the PAFS-Q that generally supports these profile types. They did a cluster analysis on PAFS-Q scores from 103 couples and then examined differences in marital intimacy and adjustment across the clusters. The analysis indicated four distinct clusters: (1) contemporary—male intergenerationally intimate, (2) contemporary—female intergenerationally intimate, (3) male intergenerationally distressed, and (4) female intergenerationally distressed.

Cluster 1 (contemporary—male intergenerationally intimate) reflects subjects who had equal, highly differentiated spouses. Males had high scores on intergenerational intimacy and individuation. Couples in this cluster reported high marital intimacy and adjustment.

Cluster 2 (contemporary—female intergenerationally intimate) reflect subjects who had good levels of individuation similar to those of their spouses. Females had high scores on intergenerational intimacy and personal authority. Couples in this cluster reported good marital adjustment and intimacy.

Cluster 3 (male intergenerationally distressed) reflects couples in which male spouses reported low personal authority, high intimidation, and low intergenerational intimacy. Female spouses had average individuation scores, low personal authority, and high intimidation scores. Couples in this cluster reported low marital intimacy and adjustment.

Cluster 4 (female intergenerationally distressed) reflects couples in which female spouses reported low levels of personal authority and high intergenerational intimidation. Males had average levels of individuation. Couples reported lower levels of marital adjustment.

It is important to use other sources of information for evaluation of intergenerational relationships. Comparison of responses on the PAFS-Q with other measures, such as the Dyadic Adjustment Scale, Marital Satisfaction Inventory, or Family Assessment Device, can provide a more complete picture of marital and family functioning. In addition, it is always essential to use the PAFS-Q with clinical interviewing and evaluation.

Clinical Applications

The PAFS-Q has multiple applications in the consultation and therapeutic process (Bray & Williamson, 1987). The questionnaire is useful as an assessment device to measure current family functioning. The PAFS-Q may be administered at the beginning of therapy or when family of origin issues are a primary focus. Comparison of similarities and differences in scores from various family members provides important perceptions of family functioning. Having couples share their responses on the PAFS-Q helps both partners understand not only current nuclear family perceptions but also the differences between family of origin relationships. In addition, discussion of individual questions and responses can serve as a stimulus for exploration of family of origin issues. The PAFS-Q given at different points in therapy can serve as a measure of change and self-evaluation. The PAFS-Q is also useful as an intervention tool to help clients begin to think about the current status of their intergenerational family relationships. Taking the PAFS-Q is usually not a neutral experience; this process usually stimulates considerable thought about family of origin relationships.

Research and Theory Applications

The PAFS-Q has been used in several studies to empirically evaluate aspects of intergenerational family theory (Bray et al., 1987; Harvey & Bray, 1991; Harvey et al., 1991). In each paper intergenerational family theory was evaluated to determine the ability of the theory to predict health, illness, psychological distress in adult and college-age populations. Intergenerational family theory proposes that the interactional processes of individuation–intimacy and fusion–intimidation are primary influences on the life stress and the psychological and physical health or illness of family members. In addition, the theory hypothesizes that these family patterns are transmitted to subsequent generations and that *current* intergenerational relationships directly and indirectly affect the quality of intimate relationships and psychological health of parents' offspring.

Bray et al. (1987) conducted two studies with the PAFS-Q that investigated the theory and measurement of intergenerational family processes and their relationship to life stress and health distress. In the first study self-reports of relationships in the family of origin and current nuclear family were used to predict health and illness in an adult clinical sample. Family process variables from the PAFS-Q accounted for 53% of the variance in health distress. Measures of family of origin relationships accounted for significant portions of the variance in health distress beyond that accounted for by nuclear family relationships. In the second study life stress and self-reports of family of origin and peer relationships on the PAFS-Q and life stress were used to predict health and illness in a nonclinical college-aged sample. Family process variables accounted for a significant amount of variance in health distress over and above the amount accounted for by life stress. These studies also found the PAFS-Q is reliable and support the validity of the measure.

Harvey and Bray (1991) conducted an explicit test of the multi-causal model of intergenerational relationships and health in interge-nerational family theory using structural equation analysis. On two separate occasions 319 college students were administered a battery of questionnaires. Results for the first administration indicated that the degree of individuation and intimacy in intergenerational and peer relationships directly influenced subjects' health-related behav-iors, accounting for 30% of the variance in this factor. Intergenera-tional intimidation and fusion directly influenced the level of health distress, and the complete causal model accounted for 35% of the variance in this factor. The degree of intimacy and individuation in peer relationships was found to directly influence subjects' level of psychological distress. The intergenerational family factors were found to directly influence life stress, but these factors had separate direct effects on health distress beyond life stress. The complete causal model accounted for 73% of the variance in the psychological distress factor.

Harvey et al. (1991) extended and replicated the findings of the two previous studies by simultaneously evaluating intergenerational family theory using causal modeling and structural equation analysis in a sample of middle-aged adults and their college-aged offspring. Individuation and intimacy were significant predictors of health distress and psychological distress for both mothers and fathers. Parents' relational patterns of individuation and intimacy directly and indirectly influenced their offspring's family relationship patterns, providing partial support for the intergenerational transmission of family patterns. Important differences between relational patterns of mothers and their children and fathers and their children were also found. Mothers' intergenerational and nuclear family relationships had stronger influences on their children's relationships and adjust-ment than did fathers' relationships. These studies provide some empirical support for this theory and its importance in predicting health and psychological functioning.

The research by Anderson and Fleming (1986a, 1986b) and Fleming and Anderson (1986) further supports the validity of the PAFS-Q and the theory underlying its development. Their research indicates that college students who report lower levels of intergen-erational fusion and triangulation have better ego identity, more autonomy, greater self-esteem, mastery, and fewer reported health problems. Similarly, deGruy et al. (1989) found that patients with somatization disorder reported less spousal and intergenerational intimacy, more intergenerational fusion and triangulation, and more nuclear family triangulation.

The PAFS-Q was used in an evaluation of the intergenerational consultation process designed by Williamson (1982b) to help people change significant relationships in the three-generational family system (Bray et al., 1986). Clients who participated in the consultation process were compared to clients who participated in systems-oriented marital therapy. The results indicate that clients who participated in the intergenerational consultation process reported significantly greater increase in personal authority and decrease in intergenerational triangulation than clients who participated in systems-oriented marital therapy. People in the latter group showed significantly more positive change on the Spousal Intimacy scale than did subjects in the intergenerational family therapy group. There were no differences between the groups in reported change in presenting problems, satisfaction with therapy, or helpfulness of therapy. Persons who had their parents in the office for consultation also reported significantly more change in personal authority and less intergenerational intimidation than clients who did not have their parents in the office for consultation.

Summary and Future Work

The PAFS-Q is a reliable and valid measure of intergenerational family relationships and processes. It is the only published instrument that attempts to measure concepts developed from intergenerational family theory (Grotevant & Carlson, 1989). The theory that the PAFS-Q is based on is gaining empirical support and will need some revisions based on the results of these studies. Future work on this theory needs to consider the new developments in epistemology, constructivism, and the feminist critique of family system theory. It is apparent from the research that there are gender differences in the differentiation process.

As with all self-report instruments, there are limitations to the usefulness of the PAFS-Q in both research and clinical settings. It is important to use multiple methods and sources of data to assess these important concepts. We are currently developing a behavioral observation system to further assess these concepts in research projects. In addition, we hope that the development of a behavioral observation system will help students learn about these concepts and will facilitate more accurate assessment of families in clinical practice. In the near future we plan to revise and update the PAFS-Q. In both our studies and others there has been useful feedback that will be used to revise the PAFS-Q and improve its psychometric properties. Of particular importance is the need to modify the instrument for easier application to the multiple family structures (e.g., single-parent, stepfamilies) and variety of family experiences that currently exist in our society.

ACKNOWLEDGMENTS

Work on this chapter was partially supported by NIH grant RO1 HD22642 from the National Institute of Child Health and Human Development.

References

Allport, G. (1940). Motivation in personality. *Psychological Review, 47,* 533–554.

Allport, G. (1955). *Becoming: Basic considerations for a psychology of personality.* New Haven, CT: Yale University Press.

American Association of University Women. (1991). *Shortchanging girls, shortchanging America* (a nationwide poll to assess self-esteem, educational experiences, interest in math and science, and career aspirations of girls and boys ages 9–15). Washington, DC: Greenberg-Lake, The Analysis Group, Inc.

Anderson, S. A., & Fleming, W. M. (1986a). Late adolescents' home-leaving strategies: Predicting ego identity and college adjustment. *Adolescence, 21,* 453–459.

Anderson, S. A., & Fleming, W. M. (1986b). Late adolescents' identity formation: Individuation from the family of origin. *Adolescence, 21,* 785–796.

Anonymous. (1972). Towards the differentiation of a self in one's own family. In J. Framo (Ed.), *Family interaction: A dialogue between family researchers and family therapists* (pp. 111–166). New York: Springer.

Aries, P. (1962). *Centuries of childhood.* New York: Knopf.

Bahnson, C. B. (1980). Stress and cancer: The state of the art. *Psychosomatics, 21*(12), 975–981.

Bandura, A. (1977). *Social-learning theory.* Englewood Cliffs, NJ: Prentice-Hall.

Barker, P. (1981). *Basic family therapy.* Baltimore: University Park Press.

Bayer, J. P., & Day, J. D. (1987). *A couple typology based on differentiation and its predictive ability for marital intimacy and adjustment.* Unpublished manuscript, Department of Psychology, Texas Woman's University, Denton, TX.

Becker, E. (1973). *The denial of death.* New York: The Free Press.

Belenky, M. F., Clinchy, B. M., Goldberger, N. R., & Tarule, J. M. (1986). *Women's ways of knowing: The development of self, voice and mind.* New York: Basic Books.

Bloom, B. L., Asher, S. J., & White, S. W. (1978). Marital disruption as a stressor: A review and analysis. *Psychological Bulletin, 85,* 867–894.

Bly, R. (1991, March). Speaking free form at "A Gathering of Men" workshop sponsored by Men's Council of Houston, TX.

Bograd, M. (Ed.). (1991). Feminist approaches for men in family therapy. *Feminist Family Therapy, 2*(3/4).

Boszormenyi-Nagy, I. (1974). Ethical and practical implications of intergenerational family therapy. *Psychotherapy Psychosomatics, 24,* 261–268.

Boszormenyi-Nagy, I., & Krasner, B. R. (1980). Trust based therapy: A contextual approach. *American Journal of Psychiatry, 137,* 767–775.

Boszormenyi-Nagy, I., & Krasner, B. R. (1986). *Between give and take.* New York: Brunner/Mazel.

Boszormenyi-Nagy, I., & Spark, G. (1973). *Invisible loyalties.* New York: Harper & Row.

Boszormenyi-Nagy, I., & Ulrich, D. (1981). Contextual family therapy. In A. S. Gurman & D. P. Kniskern (Eds.), *Handbook of family therapy* (pp. 159–186). New York: Brunner/Mazel.

Bowen, M. (1960). A family concept of schizophrenia. In D. D. Jackson (Ed.), *The ideology of schizophrenia* (p. 369). New York: Basic Books.

Bowen, M. (1966). The use of family theory in clinical practice. *Comprehensive Psychiatry, 7,* 345–374.

Bowen, M. (1976). Theory in the practice of psychotherapy. In P. J. Guerin (Ed.), *Family therapy: Theory and practice* (pp. 42–90). New York: Gardner Press.

Bowen, M. (1978). *Family therapy in clinical practice.* New York: Jason Aronson.

Bray, J. H. & Harvey, D. M. (1989). *Development of the college student version of the Personal Authority in the Family System Questionnaire.* Manuscript submitted for publication.

Bray, J. H., Harvey, D. M., & Williamson, D. S. (1987). Intergenerational family relationships: An evaluation of theory and measurement. *Psychotherapy, 24,* 516–528.

Bray, J. H., & Williamson, D. S. (1987). Assessment of intergenerational family relationships. In A. J. Hovestadt & M. Fine (Eds.), *Family of origin therapy: Application in clinical practice (Family therapy collections,* pp. 31–44). Rockville, MD: Aspen Press.

Bray, J. H., Williamson, D. S., & Malone, P. E. (1984a). Personal authority in the family system: Development of a questionnaire to measure personal authority in intergenerational family processes. *Journal of Marital and Family Therapy, 10,* 167–178.

Bray, J. H., Williamson, D. S., & Malone, P. E. (1984b). *Manual for the Personal Authority in the Family System Questionnaire.* Houston: Houston Family Institute. (Manual may be obtained from James H. Bray, 5510 Greenbriar, Houston, TX 77005.)

Bray, J. H., Williamson, D. S., & Malone, P. E. (1986). An evaluation of the effects of intergenerational consultation process to increase personal authority in the family system. *Family Process, 25,* 423–436.

Buber, M. (1958). *I and Thou.* New York: Scribner.

Campbell, J., with Bill Moyers (1988). *The power of myth.* New York: Doubleday.

Capra, F. (1989, August). Author's notes from Dr. Capra's part of unpublished speech *Social construction of reality: How we create values and beliefs,* Institute given at "Creativity and Consciousness: Meeting the Challenge of the 90's," 27th annual conference of the Association of Humanistic Psychology, Stanford University, Stanford, CA.

Carpenter, M. C. (1990). *A test of Bowen family systems theory: The relationship of differentiation of self and chronic anxiety.* Unpublished doctoral dissertation, University of Maryland College Park.

Carter, E. A., & McGoldrick, M. (Eds.).(1989). *The changing family life cycle: A framework for family therapy.* Boston: Allyn & Bacon.

Cebik, R. J. (1988). Adult male maturity and the attainment of personal authority in the family system. *Dynamic Psychotherapy, 6,* 29–36.

Chase, H. P., & Jackson, G. G. (1981). Stress and sugar control in children with IDDM. *Journal of Pediatrics, 93,* 1011–1013.

Chodorow, N. (1978). *The reproduction of mothering: Psychoanalysis and the sociology of gender.* Berkeley: University of California Press.

Chopra, D. (1987). *Creating health: Beyond prevention, toward perfection.* Boston: Houghton Mifflin.

Chopra, D. (1989). *Quantum healing: Exploring the frontiers of mind/body medicine.* New York: Bantam Books.

Christie-Seely, J. (Ed.). (1984). *Working with the family in primary care: A systems approach to health and illness.* New York: Praeger.

Cohler, B. J., & Geyer, S. (1982). Psychological autonomy and interdependence within the family. In F. Walsh (Ed.), *Normal family processes* (pp. 196–228). New York: Guilford Press.

Combrinck-Graham, L. (1985). A developmental model for family systems. *Family Process, 24*(2), 139–150.

Cousins, N. (1989), *Head first.* New York: Dutton.

Curry, C. J. (1986). *Intergenerational family processes of college students and their parents: Determinants of physical and psychological well-being.* Unpublished doctoral dissertation, University of Texas, Austin, TX.

Day, L. H. (1988). *Intergenerational distancing and its relationship to individual, family and occupational functioning: A partial test of Bowen theory.* Unpublished doctoral dissertation, College of Human Ecology, Kansas State University, Manhattan, KS.

deGruy, F. V., Dickinson, P., Dickinson, L., Mullins, H. C., Baker, W., & Blackmon, D. (1989). The families of patients with somatization disorder. *Family Medicine, 21,* 438–442.

Deikman, A. (1989, August). *The cult of the spiritual.* Paper presented at the 27th annual conference of the Association for Humanistic Psychology, Stanford University, Stanford, CA.

de la Sota, E. M. (1985). *Perceived family relationships of college males and females and their effect on psychological adjustment and capacity for intimacy and achievement.* Unpublished doctoral dissertation, University of Texas, Austin, TX.

Dell, P. (1989). Violence and the systemic view; The problem of power. *Family Process, 28*(1), 1–14.

Dell, P. F., & Goolishian, H. A. (1981). Order through fluctuation: An evolutionary epistemology for human systems. *Australian Journal of Family Therapy, 2,* 175–184.

Dienhart, A., & Avis, J. M. (1991). Men in therapy: Exploring feminist-informed alternatives. *Journal of Feminist Family Therapy, 2*(3/4), 25–51.

Doherty, W. J., & Campbell, T. L. (1988). *Families and health.* Newbury Park, CA: Sage Publications.

Doherty, W. J., & Colangelo, N. (1984). The family FIRO model: A modest proposal for organizing family treatment. *Journal of Marital and Family Therapy, 10,* 19–29.

Doherty, W. J., Colangelo, N., Green, A. M., & Hoffman, G. S. (1985). Emphases of the major family therapy models: A family FIRO analysis. *Journal of Marital and Family Therapy, 11,* 299–303.

Dorian, B., & Garfinkel, P. E. (1987). Stress, immunity and illness. *Psychological Medicine, 17,* 393–407.

Ecker, S. L. (1989). *Intergenerational family relationships as perceived by adult children of alcoholics.* Unpublished doctoral dissertation, Department of Family and Child Development, Virginia Polytechnic Institute and State University, Blacksburg, VA.

Edelstein, J., & Linn, M. W. (1985). The influence of the family on control of diabetes. *Social Science and Medicine, 21*(5), 541–544.

Eisler, R. (1987). *The chalice and the blade.* New York: Harper & Row.

Erickson, M. H., & Rossi, E. L. (1979). *Hypnotherapy: An exploratory casebook.* New York: Halsted Press.

Erikson, E. H. (1968). *Identity: Youth and crisis.* New York: Norton.

Erikson, E. H. (1978). Reflections on Dr. Borg's life cycle. In E. H. Erikson, *Adulthood* (pp. 1–31). New York: Norton.

Erikson, E. H. (1982). *The life cycle completed: A review.* New York: Norton.

Fisch, R., Weakland, J. H. & Segal, L. (1982). *The tactics of change: Doing therapy briefly.* San Francisco: Jossey-Bass.

Fleming, W. M., & Anderson, S. A. (1986). Individuation from the family of origin and personal adjustment in late adolescence. *Journal of Marital and Family Therapy, 12,* 311–315.

Foundation for Inner Peace. (1975, 1985). *A course in miracles.* Tiburon, CA: Foundation for Inner Peace.

Framo, J. L. (1968). My families, my family. *Voices, 4,* 18–27.

Framo, J. L. (Ed.). (1972). *Family interaction: A dialogue between family researchers and family therapists.* New York: Springer.

Framo, J. L. (1976). Family of origin as a therapeutic resource for adults in marital and family therapy: You can and should go home again. *Family Process, 15,* 193–210.

Framo, J. L. (1981). The integration of marital therapy with sessions with family-of-origin. In A. S. Gurman & D. P. Kniskern (Eds.), *Handbook of family therapy* (pp. 133–158). New York: Brunner/Mazel.

Framo, J. L. (1990). The question never asked: "Dad, who are we to each other?" *Contemporary Family Therapy, 12*(3), 219–221.

Freud, S. (1930). Civilization and Its Discontents. In J. Strachey (Ed. & Trans.), *The standard edition of the complete psychological works of Sigmund Freud* (Vol. 21, pp. 64–145). London: Hogarth Press.

Gilkey, J. K. (1988). *From their daughters' eyes: Parent/daughter relationships and college adjustment in young women.* Unpublished doctoral dissertation, Virginia Polytechnic Institute and State University, Blacksburg, VA.

Gilligan, C. (1982). *In a different voice.* Cambridge, MA: Harvard University Press.

Gillis-Donovan, J. (1991, Summer). Common misunderstandings. *AFTA Newsletter, 44,* 7–14.

Gilmore, D. (1990). *Manhood in the making: Cultural concepts of masculinity.* New Haven, CT: Yale University Press.

Glantz, K., & Pearce, J. (1989). *Exiles From Eden. Psychotherapy from an evolutionary perspective.* New York: Norton.

Glaser, R., Kiecolt-Glaser, J. K., Speicher, C. E., & Holliday, J. E. (1985). Stress, loneliness, and changes in herpesvirus latency. *Journal of Behavioral Medicine, 8*(3), 249–260.

Goenke, N. S. (1987, February). The ten-day course, Vipassana Meditation Center, Santa Rosa, CA.

Goenke, N. S. (1991, April). The ten-day course, Southwest Vipassana Meditation Center, Dallas, TX.

Goldner, V. (1985). Feminism and family therapy. *Family Process, 24,* 31–47.

Goldner, V. (1988). Generation and gender: Normative and covert hierarchies. *Family Process, 27,* 17–31.

Goodrich, T. J., Rampage, C., Ellman, B., & Halstead, K. (1988). *Feminist family therapy: A casebook.* New York: Norton.

Gottman, J. M. (1991). Predicting the longitudinal course of marriages. *Journal of Marital and Family Therapy, 17*(1), 3–7.

Gray, T. (1751). Elegy written on a gravestone in a country churchyard in England.

Grossarth-Maticek, R., Bastiaans, J., & Kanazir, D. T. (1985). Psychosocial factors as strong predictors of mortality from cancer, ischaemic heart disease and stroke: The Yugoslav prospective study. *Journal of Psychosomatic Research, 29*(2), 167–176.

Grotevant, H. D., & Carlson, C. I. (1989). *Family assessment: A guide to methods and measures.* New York: Guilford Press.

Gurman, A. S., & Kniskern, D. P. (Eds.). (1981). *Handbook of family therapy.* New York: Brunner/Mazel.

Haley, J. (1963). *Strategies of psychotherapy.* New York: Grune & Stratton.

Haley, J. (1976). *Problem-solving therapy.* San Francisco: Jossey-Bass.

Haley, J. (1980). *Leaving home: Therapy with disturbed young people.* New York: McGraw-Hill.

Hare-Mustin, R. T. (1978). A feminist approach to family therapy. *Family Process, 17,* 181–194.

Hare-Mustin, R. T. (1987). The problem of gender in family therapy theory. *Family Process, 26*(3), 15–27.

Hare-Mustin, R. T., & Marecek, J. (1988). The meaning of difference: Gender theory, postmodernism, and psychology. *American Psychologist, 43*(6), 455–464.

Hareven, T. K. (1982). American families in transition: Historical perspectives on change. In F. Walsh (Ed.), *Normal family processes* (pp. 446–465). New York: Guilford Press.

Harvey, D. M., & Bray, J. H. (1991). An evaluation of an intergenerational theory of personal development: Family process determinants of psychological and health distress. *Journal of Family Psychology, 4,* 42–69.

Harvey, D. M., Curry, C. J., & Bray, J. H. (1991). Individuation/intimacy in intergenerational relationships and health: Patterns across two generations. *Journal of Family Psychology, 5*(2), 204–236.

Hawking, S. W. (1988). *A brief history of time.* New York: Bantam Books.

Hoffman, L. (1990). Constructing realities: An art of lenses. *Family Process, 29*(1), 1–12.

Holloway, R. L., & Rogers, J. C. (in press). Physician adaptation to patients' locus of control and congruence with health recommendations. *Health Communication, 4*(1).

Jourard, S. M. (1971). *The transparent self.* New York: Van Nostrand Reinhold.

Jung, C. G. (1985). *The collected works of C. G. Jung, No. 4. Freud and psychoanalysis.* In G. Adler (Ed.), *Bollingen Series No. 20.* Princeton, NJ: Princeton University Press.

Justice, B. (1988). *Who gets sick.* New York: St. Martin's Press.

Karpel, M. (1976). Individuation: From fusion to dialogue. *Family Process, 15,* 65–82.

Keeney, B. P. (1983). *Aesthetics of change.* New York: Guilford Press.

Keith, D., & Whitaker, C. (1980). Add craziness and stir: Psychotherapy with a psychoticogenic family. In M. Andolfi & I. Zwerling (Eds.), *Dimensions of family therapy* (pp. 139–160). New York: Guilford Press.

Kerr, M. E. (1981). Family systems theory and therapy. In A. S. Gurman & D. P. Kniskern (Eds.), *Handbook of family therapy* (pp. 226–266). New York: Brunner/Mazel.

Kerr, M. E., & Bowen, M. (1988). *Family evaluation: An approach based on Bowen Theory.* New York: Norton.

Kiecolt-Glaser, J. K., Fisher, L. D., Ogrocki, P., Stout, J. C., Speicher, C. E. & Glaser, R. (1987). Marital quality, marital disruption, and immune function. *Psychosomatic Medicine, 49*(1), 13–33.

Kiecolt-Glaser, J. K., Kennedy, S., Malkoff, S., Fisher, L., Speicher, C.E. & Glaser, R. (1988). Marital discord and immunity in males. *Psychosomatic Medicine, 50*(3), 213–229.

Kinnier, R. T., Brigman, S. L., & Noble, F. C. (1990). Career indecision and family enmeshment. *Journal of Counseling and Development, 68,* 309–312.

Konner, M. (1982). *The tangled wing: Biological constraints on the human spirit.* New York: Harper Colophon Books.

Kuhn, T. S. (1962). *The structure of scientific revolutions.* Chicago: University of Chicago Press.

Laing, R. D. (1970). *Knots.* New York: Pantheon Books.

Laing, R. D. (1979, October). Comment made in his presentation at "Politics of the Family" workshop, Houston, TX.

Larzelere, R. E., & Huston, T. L. (1980). The Dyadic Trust Scale: Toward understanding interpersonal trust in close relationships. *Journal of Marriage and the Family, 42,* 595–604.

Lask, B. (1979). Emotional considerations in wheezy children. *Journal of the Royal Society of Medicine, 72,* 56–59.

Lask, B., & Matthew, D. (1979). Childhood asthma. A controlled trial of family psychotherapy. *Archives of Diseases in Childhood, 54,* 116–119.

Lerner, H. G. (1985). Dianna and Lillie: Can a feminist still like Murray Bowen? *Networker, 9*(6), 36–39.

Levinson, D. J., Darrow, C. N., Klein, E. B., Levinson, M. H., & McKee, B. (1978). *The seasons of a man's life.* New York: Ballantine.

Lewis, C. S. (1955). *Surprised by Joy: The shape of my early life.* New York: Harcourt.

Lewis, J. M., Beavers, W. R., Gossett, J. T., & Phillips, V. A. (1975). *No single thread: Psychological health in family systems.* New York: Brunner/Mazel.

Lowenstein, S. F. (1980). Mother and daughter: An epitaph. *Family Process, 20*(1), 3–10.

Luepnitz, D. A. (1988). *The family interpreted.* New York: Basic Books.

Madanes, C. (1981). *Strategic family therapy.* San Francisco: Jossey-Bass.

Maturana, H. R. (1978). Biology of language: The epistemology of reality. In G. A. Miller & E. Lenneberg (Eds.), *Psychology and biology of language and thought.* New York: Academic Press.

Maturana, H. R., & Varela, F. J. (1980). *Autopoiesis and cognition: The realization of living.* Boston: Reidel.

May, R. (1958). The origins and the significance of the existential movement in psychology. In R. May (Ed.), *Existence: A new dimension in psychiatry and psychology* (pp. 3–36). New York: Basic Books.

McCollum, E. E., Schumm, W. R., & Russell, C. S. (1988). Reliability and validity of the Kansas family life satisfaction scale in a predominantly middle-aged sample. *Psychological Reports, 62,* 95–98.

McCreanor, D. P. (1988). *The relationship between differentiation of self and perception of health in the family of origin and fusion and intimacy in the family of procreation.* Unpublished doctoral dissertation, Florida State University, Tallahassee, FL.

McGoldrick, M. (1989). Women and the family life cycle. In E. A. Carter & M. McGoldrick (Eds.), *The changing family life cycle: A framework for family therapy* (pp. 29–68). Boston: Allyn & Bacon.

McGoldrick, M., Anderson, C. M., & Walsh, F. (Eds.). (1989). *Women in families: A framework for family therapy.* New York: Norton.

McGoldrick, M., Pearce, J. K., Giordano, J. (Eds.). (1982). *Ethnicity and family therapy.* New York: Guilford Press.

Meinecke, C. E. (1981). Socialized to die younger? Hypermasculinity and men's health. *Personnel and Guidance Journal, 60,* 241–245.

Menninger, K. (1938). *Man against himself.* New York: Harcourt.

Menninger, K., Mayman, M., & Pruyser, P. W. (1963). *The vital balance.* New York: Viking Press.

Meth, R. L., & Pasick, R. S. (1990). *Men in therapy: The challenge of change.* New York: Guilford Press.

Miller, J. B. (1976). *Toward a new psychology of women.* Boston: Beacon Press.

Miller, J. B. (1986). *Toward a new psychology of women* (2nd ed.). Boston: Beacon Press.

Miller, J. B. (1983). *The construction of anger in women and men.* Wellelsey, MA: Stone Center, Work in Progress Series.

Minuchin, S. (no date). *Percepts: The personal aspects of therapy. The therapist and his therapy: Salvador Minuchin, M.D. Anorexia is a Greek word* (Perception Series, No. A 16; Audio-video tape). Boston, MA: Boston Family Institute.

Minuchin, S. (1974). *Families and family therapy.* Cambridge, MA: Harvard University Press.

Minuchin, S. (1978). *Psychosomatic families.* Cambridge, MA: Harvard University Press.

Napier, A. Y., & Whitaker, C. A. (1978). *The family crucible.* New York: Harper & Row.

National Institute of Mental Health. (1987). Series DN No. 6, *Family's impact on health: A critical review and annotated bibliography* by T. L. Campbell (DHHS Publication No. ADM 87–1461). Washington, DC: U.S. Government Printing Office.

Neill, J. R., & Kniskern, D. P. (1982). *From psyche to system: The evolving therapy of Carl Whitaker.* New York: Guilford Press.

Nhat Hanh, T. (1975, 1976). *The miracle of mindfulness.* Boston: Beacon Press.

Nhat Hanh, T. (1990). *Transformation and healing: The sutra on the four establishments of mindfulness.* Berkeley, CA: Parallax Press.

Nichols, W. C., & Everett, C. A. (1986). *Systemic family therapy: An integrative approach.* New York: Guilford Press.

Norbeck, J. S., & Tilden, V. P. (1983). Life stress, social support and emotional disequilibrium in complications in pregnancy: A prospective, multivariate study. *Journal of Health and Social Behavior, 24,* 30–46.

Olson, D. H., Bell, R., & Portner, J. (1978). *FACES-I: Family Adaptability and Cohesion Evaluation Scales.* St. Paul, MN: Family Social Science, University of Minnesota.

Olson, D. H., Portner J., & Bell, R. (1982). *FACES-II: Family Adaptability and Cohesion Evaluation Scales.* St. Paul, MN: Family Social Science, University of Minnesota.

Papp, P. (1980). The Greek chorus and other techniques of paradoxical therapy. *Family Process, 19,* 45–57.

Parsons, T., & Bales, R. F. (1955). *Family, socialization and interaction process.* Glencoe, IL: The Free Press.

Pasick, R. S., Gordon, S., & Meth, R. L. (1990). Helping men understand themselves. In R. L. Meth & R. S. Pasick, *Men in therapy: The challenge of change* (pp. 152–180). New York: Guilford Press.

Paul, N. (1967). The role of mourning and empathy in conjoint marital therapy. In G. Zuk & I. Boszormenyi-Nagy (Eds.), *Family therapy and disturbed families.* Palo Alto, CA: Science & Behavior Books.

Paul, N., & Grosser, G. (1965). Operational mourning and its role in conjoint family therapy. *Community Mental Health Journal, 1,* 339–345.

Paul, N. L., & Paul, B. B. (1975). *A marital puzzle: Transgenerational analysis in marriage counseling.* New York: Norton.

Peplau, L. A. (1982). Interpersonal attraction. In D. Sherrod (Ed.), *Social psychology.* New York: Random House.

Quick, J. F. (1987). *Relational health in psychotherapists' nuclear families and families of origin.* Unpublished master's thesis, University of Missouri, Kansas City, MO.

Reeve, R. B. (1988). *The effects of individuation/differentiation on marital intimacy and longevity.* Unpublished master's thesis, California Family Study Center, Covina, CA.

Rix, S. E. (1990). *The American woman 1990–91: A status report.* New York: Norton, for the Women's Research & Education Institute.

Rogers, C. (1951). *Client-centered therapy: Its current practice, implications and theory.* Boston: Houghton Mifflin.

Rogers, C. (1961). *On becoming a person.* Boston: Houghton Mifflin.

Rogers, J. C. (1990). The self-administered genogram. In R. E. Rakel (Ed.), *Textbook of family practice* (4th ed., pp. 1732–1739). Philadelphia: Saunders.

Rogers, V. V. (1985). *Perceptions of family relationships as predictors of diabetes treatment success.* Unpublished master's thesis, Texas Woman's University, Denton, TX.

Rorty, R. (1979). *Philosophy and the mirror of nature.* Princeton, NJ: Princeton University Press.

Sagan, L. A. (1987). *The health of nations.* New York: Basic Books.

St. Clair, S. A. (1984). *The relationship between differentiation of self, personal authority, and mate selection in the family system.* Unpublished doctoral dissertation, Texas Woman's University, Denton, TX.

Sarason, I. G., Sarason, B. R., Potter, E. H., & Antoni, M. H. (1985). Life events, social support, and illness. *Psychosomatic Medicine, 47*(2), 156–163.

Selvini-Palazzoli, M., Boscolo, L., Cecchin, G., & Prata, G. (1978). *Paradox and counter-paradox: A new model in the therapy of the family in schizophrenic transaction* (E. V. Burt, Trans.). New York: Jason Aronson.

Shah, I. (1980). *The way of the sufi.* London, UK: Octagon Press.

Shapiro, L. (1990, May 28). Guns and dolls: Scientists explore the differences between girls and boys. *Newsweek,* pp. 56–65.

Sheehy, G. (1974). *Passages.* New York: Dutton.

Sheely, C. N. (1982). *The Symptom Index.* Springfield, MO: Author.

Siegel, B. (1989, August). Author's notes from unpublished speech: *The psychology of illness and the art of healing,* Institute given at "Creativity and Consciousness: Meeting the Challenge of the 90's," 27th annual conference of the Association for Humanistic Psychology, Stanford University, CA.

Simon, F. B., Stierlin, H., & Wynne, L. C. (Eds.). (1985). *The language of family theraply: A systemic vocabulary and sourcebook.* New York: Family Process Press.

Skynner, A. C. R. (1981). An open-systems, group-analytic approach to family therapy. In A. S. Gurman & D. P. Kniskern (Eds.), *Handbook of family therapy* (pp. 39–84). New York: Brunner/Mazel.

Solomon, G. F. (1987). Psychoneuroimmunology: Interactions between central nervous system and immune system. *Journal of Neuroscience Research, 18,* 1–9.

Sosa, R., Kennell, J., Klaus, M., Robertson, S. & Urrutia, J. (1980). The effect of a supportive companion on perinatal problems, length of labor, and mother–infant interaction. *New England Journal of Medicine, 303*(11), 597–600.

Spanier, G. B. (1976). Measuring dyadic adjustment: New scales for assessing the quality of marriage and similar dyads. *Journal of Marriage and the Family, 38,* 15–28.

Spark, G. M., & Brody, E. M. (1970). The aged are family members. *Family Process, 9,* 195–210.

Speer, A. (1970). *Inside the Third Reich.* New York: Macmillan.

Srensen, L. V., Mors, O., & Skovlund, O. (1987). A prospective study of the importance of psychological and social factors for the outcome after surgery in patients with slipped lumbar disk operated upon for the first time. *Acta Neurochirurgica, 88*(3–4), 119–125.

Stanton, M. D. (1981). Strategic approaches to family therapy. In A. S. Gurman & D. P. Kniskern (Eds.), *Handbook of family therapy* (pp. 361–402). New York: Brunner/Mazel.

Stiver, I. P. (1984). *The meanings of "dependency" in female–male relationships.* Wellesley, MA: Stone Center, Work in Progress Series.

Surrey, J. L. (1983). The relational self in women: Clinical implications. In *Colloquium: Women and empathy.* Wellesley, MA: Stone Center, Work in Progress Series.

Taggart, M. (1985). The feminist critique in epistemological perspective: Questions of context in family therapy. *Journal of Marital and Family Therapy, 11,* 113–126.

Tannen, D. (1990). *You just don't understand.* New York: Morrow.

Tillich, P. (1952). *The courage to be.* New Haven, CT: Yale University Press.

Vaillant, G. E. (1977). *An adaptation to life.* Boston: Little, Brown.

Walker, L. E. (1980). Battered women. In A. M. Brodsky & R. T. Hare-Mustin (Eds.), *Women and psychotherapy: An assessment of research and practice* (pp. 339–364). New York: Guilford Press.

Walpole, H. (1769). [Found in letters to Horace Mann.]

Walsh, F. (1989). Reconsidering gender in the marital quid pro quo. In M. McGoldrick, C. M. Anderson, & F. Walsh (Eds.), *Women in families: A framework for family therapy* (pp. 267–285). New York: Norton.

Walsh, F., & Scheinkman, M. (1989). (Fe)male: The hidden gender dimension in models of family therapy. In M. McGoldrick, C. M. Anderson, & F. Walsh (Eds.), *Women in families: A framework for family therapy.* (pp. 16–41). New York: Norton.

Walters, M., Carter, B., Papp, P., & Silverstein, O. (1988). *The invisible web: Gender patterns in family relationships.* New York: Guilford Press.

Watzlawick, P. (1978). *The language of change: Elements of therapeutic communication.* New York: Basic Books.

Watzlawick, P. (Ed.). (1984). *The invented reality: Contributions to constructivism.* New York: Norton.

Watzlawick, P., Beavin, J. H., & Jackson, D. D. (1967). *Pragmatics of human communication: A study of interactional patterns, pathologies and paradoxes.* New York: Norton.

Watzlawick, P., Weakland, J., & Fisch, R. (1974). *Change: Principles of problem formation and problem resolution.* New York: Norton.

Weber, R. (1984, October). Inner Science Conference with the Dalai Lama, Amherst College, Amherst, MA.

Weiner, E. L. (1990). *Bowen's concept of emotional connectedness to former spouse and family of origin as a moderator of health in a divorced population: A partial test of Bowen theory.* Unpublished doctoral dissertation, College of Human Ecology, Kansas State University, Manhattan, KS.

Weissman, M. M. (1980). Depression. In A. M. Brodsky & R. T. Hare-Mustin (Eds.), *Women and psychotherapy: An assessment of research and practice* (pp. 97–112). New York: Guilford Press.

Whitaker, C. A. (1973). [Story told by Carl Whitaker at a family therapy conference in Boston.]

Whitaker, C. A. (1975). Psychotherapy of the absurd: With a special emphasis on psychotherapy of aggression. *Family Process, 14,* 1–16.

Whitaker, C. A. (1976). The hindrance of theory in clinical work. In P. J. Guerin (Ed.), *Family therapy: Theory and practice* (pp. 154–164). New York: Gardner Press.

Whitaker, C. A. (1980, Spring). *Three generational family therapy.* Paper presented at "Three Generational Family Therapy" workshop, Houston Family Institute, Houston, TX.

Whitaker, C. A., & Keith, D. V. (1980). Family therapy as symbolic experience. *International Journal of Family Psychiatry, 1,* 197–208.

Whitaker, C. A., & Keith, D. V. (1981). Symbolic–experiential family therapy. In A. S. Gurman & D. P. Kniskern (Eds.), *Handbook of family therapy* (pp. 187–225). New York: Brunner/Mazel.

Whitaker, C. A., & Malone, T. P. (1953). *The roots of psychotherapy.* New York: Blakiston.

White, B. B. (1989). Gender differences in marital communication patterns. *Family Process, 28*(3), 89–106.

White, K., Kolman, M. L., Wexler, P., Polin, G., & Winter, R. J. (1984).

Unstable diabetes and unstable families: A psychosocial evaluation of diabetic children with recurrent ketoacidosis. *Pediatrics, 73*(6), 749–755.

White, M. (1988, October). *Externalizing the problem.* Opening plenary address at annual conference of the American Association for Marriage and Family Therapy, New Orleans, LA.

Williamson, D. S. (1978, January). New life at the graveyard: A method of therapy for individuation from a dead "former parent." *Journal of Marriage and Family Counseling,* 93–101.

Williamson, D. S. (1981). Personal authority via termination of the intergenerational hierarchical boundary: A "new" stage in the family life cycle. *Journal of Marital and Family Therapy, 7,* 441–452.

Williamson, D. S. (1982a). Personal authority via the termination of the intergenerational hierarchical boundary: Part II. The consultation process and the therapeutic method. *Journal of Marital and Family Therapy, 8,* 23–37.

Williamson, D. S. (1982b). Personal authority in family experience via the termination of the intergenerational hierarchical boundary: Part III. Personal authority defined and the power of play in the change process. *Journal of Marital and Family Therapy, 8,* 309–323.

Williamson, D. S. (1983, May). The family's bloodless (r)evolution: Personal authority and personal reality in the family of origin. *Family Therapy Networker.*

Williamson, D. S. (1983). Coming of age in the fourth decade. In J. C. Hanson (Ed.), *Clinical implications of the family* (pp. 66–76). Rockville, MD: Aspen Systems Corporation.

Williamson, D. S., & Bray, J. H. (1985). The intergenerational view. In S. Henao & N. Grose (Eds.), *Principles of family systems in family medicine* (pp. 90–110). New York: Brunner/Mazel.

Williamson, D. S., & Bray, J. H. (1988). Family development and change across the generations: An intergenerational perspective. In C. J. Falicov (Ed.), *Family transitions* (pp. 357–384). New York: Guilford Press.

Williamson, D. S., & Malone, P. E. (1983, Winter). Systems-oriented, small group, family-of-origin family therapy: A comparison with traditional group psychotherapy. *Journal of Group Psychotherapy, Psychodrama and Sociometry,* 165–177.

Williamson, D. S., & Noel, M. L. (1990). Systemic family medicine: An evolving concept. In R. E. Rakel (Ed.), *Textbook of family practice* (4th ed., pp. 61–79). Philadelphia: Saunders.

Winnicott, D. W. (1986). *Home is where we start from.* New York: Norton.

Wynne, L. C., Ryckoff, I. M., Day, J., & Hirsch, S. I. (1958). Pseudomutuality in the family relations of schizophrenics. *Psychiatry, 21,* 205–220.

Index